THE MUSIC GUIDE TO AUSTRIA AND GERMANY

THE MUSIC GUIDE TO AUSTRIA AND GERMANY

Elaine Brody
Claire Brook

Dodd, Mead & Company New York

Printed in the United States of America

Library of Congress Cataloging in Publication Data

Brody, Elaine.
The music guide to Austria and Germany.

1. Music—Austria—Directories. 2. Music—Germany—Directories. I. Brook, Claire, joint author. II. Title.
ML21.B77 780′.2543 75-30822
ISBN 0-396-07217-8

Preface

This book was born of our frustrations and has continued to present us with problems. Originally conceived as a mammoth volume designed to include material covering eighteen countries, it has, like so many other projects, fallen victim to our current economic recession. As a result, the decision was taken to publish separate volumes, each to treat specific countries or regions.

How did this all start?

We both travel as much as our professional responsibilities will allow. We are both trained musicians married to men whose work requires them to spend some part of each year in Europe and we try to accompany them whenever possible. Too often, however, we have found ourselves in the right city at the wrong time or—worse still—in the right city at the right time without being aware of it until it was too late.

Often when faced with the delightful prospect of a few weeks abroad, we have been astonished at how difficult it is to acquire sufficient information to make these visits as fruitful as possible. The musical traveler has no central source of data on a multitude of questions practical, historical, or theoretical. There are those who want to be sure that if they are in Bayreuth on a Tuesday, they can visit the theater even though there is no performance; others may try for weeks to isolate the moment when the Musée d'Instruments of the Paris Conservatory receives visitors and allows them to play the instruments on display; the curious amateur may wish to locate the Brahms House in Baden-

Baden, while others may have heard that there is an interesting music festival in Fishguard without being able to guess exactly where it is and when it is held. Graduate students seeking to avail themselves of the resources of the Gesellschaft der Musikfreunde in Vienna will be grateful for precise information concerning the visiting hours and credentials requirements; the opera lover enjoying a performance at La Scala would have to be aware of the proximity of La Scala Theater Museum in order to explore it during an intermission. The young scholar arriving in Rome on a two weeks summer leave, only to find that all the libraries are closed and there is no one within miles to provide a bit of assistance, could have been forewarned had schedules been available to him. And so on and so on and so on.

The idea for *The Music Guide* came to us in recognition of the need for a handbook which could provide to the widest range of people —from the musical dilettante to the highly motivated specialist—a compendium of information of a practical nature. The idea seemed so straightforward and obvious that we could not understand why such a guide did not already exist. Once we had embarked on the project, we understood only too well; it had not already been done because it was utterly impossible!!!

But we are getting a bit ahead of ourselves. The *Guide,* once we began to classify and organize the areas for investigation, began to shape itself. Certain editorial decisions concerning the geographical limitations of this volume had to be made arbitrarily. In addition, we would not know just how to treat individual cities until enough information had been gathered to determine the extent of the musical activity and resources in each place. Questionnaires were prepared in five languages for five categories. With the invaluable cooperation of the official cultural offices in each of the eighteen countries we had decided to discuss, we amassed lists of places and people that formed the basis of a large initial mailing. So the process of information-gathering began. As the responses came in, most of our questions concerning inclusion, exclusion, format, and style were answered. The results are to be found in the volumes that follow.

Within each country, the physical, political, and musical organizations indigenous to that nation determined the ordering of the material. In some instances, a chapter consists of a series of short essays on individual cities; in others where there is only one important urban center, additional information applying to cities outside that center is provided by categories: i.e., miscellaneous opera houses and concert halls, libraries, conservatories, etc. We have taken it upon ourselves to enter the lists editorially by making evaluative judgments.

In addition to decisions of qualitative merit, we have had to take cognizance of length and usefulness. We have tried to maintain a reasonable level of consistency in approach and depth of information. Although we sent the same questionnaires to each country, the responses were incredibly uneven. In some cases information was unavailable because we received no replies and it was impossible to pursue the matter personally. In other instances one of us did the necessary legwork to ferret out answers when the official sources were uncooperative. Very often, however, we received invaluable help from many of the Music Information Centers (CeBeDeM in Brussels, Donemus in Amsterdam, the Music Information Centers of Finland and Sweden, to mention but a few) as well as from individuals whose professional affiliations enabled them to provide us with precise details in addition to general information.

Subject to geographical variations, the information we have prepared is organized under the following general headings: Opera Houses and Concert Halls; Libraries and Museums; Conservatories and Schools; Musical Landmarks; Musical Organizations; Miscellaneous; Business of Music. At the conclusion, there is a section devoted to Festivals, Competitions, and Periodicals.

Opera Houses and Concert Halls: we have tried to include the information necessary for the reader's use in determining season, program, and hours of performances. Although we mention some churches in which concerts usually take place, we have not attempted to be overly comprehensive, since almost every church will house the odd public concert from time to time and this does not automatically qualify it as a site for musical entertainment. There has been an increasingly prevalent tendency to present concerts, opera, and chamber music in castles, courtyards, parks, and gardens. The reader is therefore advised to consult a local newspaper or concert guide, which will be indicated at the beginning of most city segments, for details of the unusual events taking place in the unexpected places.

Libraries and Museums: to facilitate practical reference to specific collections, we have attempted to give library and museum names in their original languages. We wish to acknowledge here and now our gratitude for the scholarship and generosity of Rita Benton, whose

Directory of Music Research Libraries constituted the basic foundation of our investigations in this category. (Hence Ben. 1, 2, etc. found in our volumes refer to Dr. Benton's numbering system.) We are particularly grateful to Dr. Benton for permission to see the third volume of this important work while it was still in manuscript. For more detailed information about the institutions mentioned in this present volume, please consult her book. Where our questionnaires contained information at odds with hers, we assumed that we had the more recent data.

For the most recent and most comprehensive coverage of archives, collections, libraries and museums, consult the cumulative index (vols. I–V, 1967–1971) of *RILM* (acronym for the *International Repertory of Music Literature*), an absolutely essential reference work available at most libraries.

Established in 1966 by the International Musicological Society and the International Association of Music Libraries to attempt to deal with the explosion in musicological documentation by international cooperation and modern technology, *RILM,* a quarterly publication of abstracts of books, articles, essays, reviews, dissertations, catalogues, iconographies, etc. is available in the USA through the International RILM Center, City University of New York, 33 West 42 Street, New York 10036. European subscriptions are available from RILM Distributor for Europe, Bärenreiter Verlag, Heinrich-Schütz-Allee 31–37, D-3500 Kassel-Wilhelmshöhe, West Germany.

Institutes of Musicology are to be found under different rubrics according to their function within the host country. In France, for example, the Institute is part of the university and is found under Schools and Conservatories. In Spain, it is a library and publishing organization and will appear under Libraries.

Schools and Conservatories: we have had to eliminate ruthlessly all but the major musical institutions in the interest of keeping this book portable. Because course offerings and degree requirements differ from country to country, we have eschewed program descriptions and instead supplied an address from which the interested reader may obtain further information. Summer courses are included in this section, except where they are clearly allied with a festival, in which case they can be located through a cross reference. A cautionary word: those planning to attend seminars or master classes in European universities should bear in mind that no housing arrangements are made by the university. The administration will supply the names of private persons who take in boarders, but these arrangements should be made well in advance of arrival. A list of organizations with special services for the English-speaking student abroad can be found in the Appendix.

Musical Landmarks: after an enthusiastic beginning, it became apparent that it would not be possible to include every commemorative plaque and graveyard that concerned a musician or musical event without rivaling the telephone directory in size. Therefore, we have usually restricted ourselves to establishments which are open to the public but do not qualify as museums. Occasionally the address of such a place seems to differ in alternate descriptions of the same place. This is invariably due to the fact that building compounds may have entrances on several streets. Where a mailing address is at variance with the public entrance, we have indicated both.

Musical organizations of international significance have been mentioned and, in some exceptional instances, described in detail. The same criteria were applied to commercial musical establishments.

The concluding section, that devoted to Festivals, Competitions, and Periodicals, brings together a body of material never before found between the covers of a single volume. Because we did not wish to build immediate obsolescence into the book, we have not supplied exact dates or typical programs for Festivals and Competitions. Instead, we have sought to give an accurate name and address to which the reader might address himself for that information. We did attempt, wherever possible, to provide descriptive as well as factual material on the more colorful festivals.

The problems inherent in this kind of compendium are legion. Having to depend on the cooperation of hundreds of functionaries from secretaries to cultural ministers—disinterested at one extreme and overly zealous at the other—as well as on our own researching techniques and efforts, has resulted in somewhat uneven coverage with a somewhat variable accuracy quotient. Although we have visited almost every one of the cities discussed in depth and many of those covered more cursorily, we have not attended all the festivals nor have we physically investigated all the libraries, institutes, and museums. It has been utterly impossible to check all of our sources personally. We have tried to circumvent this lapse from scholarly grace by choosing our sources as carefully as we could.

Three years after we began this Herculean task, we halted the gathering, collating, checking, writing. It would not be accurate to say that we "finished," for we are both only too aware of the fact that we have barely skimmed the surface of the material. But our manuscript had already become five times the length contracted for, and other duties called. In those three years we had the good fortune to work with a group of exceptional people—exceptional not only because of their extraordinary sense of responsibility and selfless dedication to their nation's music, but also for the care and precision with which they answered our questions. We would like to thank the following people —and to apologize to those whom we have inevitably and inadvertently overlooked: John Amis (London), Dr. R. Angermüller (Salzburg), the Comtesse de Chambure (Paris), Ulla Christiansen (New York), Hans Conradin (Zurich), Adrienne Doignies-Musters (Brussels), Ady Egleston (New York), Dr. Georg Feder (Cologne), Marna Feldt (New York), Jean and Mimi Ferrard (Brussels), Prof. Kurt von Fischer (Zurich), Claire Van Gelder (Paris and Brussels), Dr. Jörn Göres (Dusseldorf), Marlene Haag (Salzburg), Prof. Edmund Haines (New York), Ernesto Halffter (Madrid), Dr. Hilde Hellmann (Vienna), Per-Anders Hellquist (Stockholm), Maurice Huisman (Brussels), Antonio Iglesias (Madrid), Dr. Erwin Jacobi (Zurich), Jean Jenkins (London), Newell Jenkins (Giglio and New York), Prof. Rudolf Klein (Vienna), Kare Kolberg (Oslo), Dr. Johanna Kral (Vienna), Dr. Gunnar Larsson (Stockholm), Albert Vander Linden (Brussels), Anders Lönn (Stockholm), Per Olaf Lundahl (Stockholm), René de Maeyer (Brussels), Matilde Medina y Crespe (Madrid), Per Onsum (Oslo), Dr. Alfons Ott (Munich), Pierluigi Petrobelli (Parma), Henry Pleasants (London), Andrew Porter (New York and London), Sheila Porter (New York and London), Anders Ramsay (Stockholm), Albi Rosenthal (London), Dag Schjelderup-Ebbe (Oslo), Torben Schousboe (Copenhagen), Jarmo Sermilä (Helsinki), Sheila Solomon (London), Anna van Steenbergen (Brussels), Jean Touzelet (Paris), Edmund Tracey (London), Tatu Tuohikorpi (New York and Helsinki), Renaat Verbruggen (Antwerp), Linde Vogel (New York), William Weaver (Monte San Savino), Henry Weinberg (Florence and New York).

We would also like to acknowledge the invaluable help we received from the team of graduate students and research assistants who have supplied so much of the energy and muscle for this project. They include: Louise Basbas, Asya Berger, Lisa Mann Burke, Pamela Curzon, Hinda Keller Farber, Anne Gross, Peter Kazaras, Debbie Moskowitz, and Barbara Petersen.

And, finally, we two very liberated women would like to thank our husbands for their encouragement, patience, and touching faith that sooner or later we would emerge from behind the mountains of colored questionnaires—better people for having written *The Music Guide.*

Elaine Brody
Claire Brook

Austria

Contents

Introduction

The history of music in Austria is closely associated with the development of music in Germany. Cultural ties such as a common language, and mutual claim to such composers as Haydn, Mozart, and Schubert, as well as Beethoven and Brahms, who were born in Germany but worked the better part of their lives in Vienna, make such an attitude understandable. Early Austrian composers included the minnesingers Walther von der Vogelweide (c. 1170–1230) and Neidhart von Reuenthal (fl. 12th–13th centuries) in the Middle Ages, Heinrich Finck (1445–1527) and Paul Hofhaimer (1459–1537) in the Renaissance, and J. J. Fux (1660–1741) and J. J. Froberger (1616–1667) in the Baroque. Italian was the language of the court during the seventeenth and eighteenth centuries, and many of Italy's most prominent Baroque opera composers saw their works staged first in Vienna. The House of Hapsburg, which ruled Austria in the seventeenth century, produced three emperors who, besides being patrons and lovers of music, were themselves active composers.

These royal musicians were Ferdinand III, Leopold I, the most prolific of the three, and Joseph I. Although no succeeding members of the family were active composers, all had some training in music, drama, and ballet. The Empress Maria Theresa, for example, appeared as a singer at court entertainments, and her son Joseph II was a pupil of the kapellmeister, Florian Leopold Gassmann (1729–74). It was Joseph II who founded the National Theater for which Mozart wrote *Die Entführung aus dem Serail,* his first work for the Viennese stage. Later,

Beethoven's pupil and patron Archduke Rudolf, also a Hapsburg, became Archbishop of Olmütz.

Besides court music, sacred music in the monasteries and seminaries of Austria was produced in considerable quantities. Over the centuries, Kremsmünster, St. Peter's in Salzburg, Gottweig, Heiligenkreuz, St. Lambrecht and St. Florian—this last very often associated with Bruckner—accumulated priceless musical treasures in their libraries and archives, making them a natural attraction for musicologists from other countries to do research there.

In addition to fostering the growth of opera and orchestral music (both sacred and secular), Vienna introduced the waltz to European composers. Derived from the popular Viennese *Ländler,* the waltz became the most important new dance form to enter the domain of art music. To the Viennese, the family of Johann Strauss, father and son, were better known than Mahler (1860–1911), Wolf (1860–1903), and the "other" Strauss, Richard, another German who worked in Vienna.

Finally, the shape of music in the twentieth century owes much to Schoenberg (1874–1951) and his two pupils, Berg (1885–1935) and Webern (1883–1945), who, together, constitute the Viennese School. The works of the more conservative musicians of the first part of this century, among them Franz Schreker (1878–1934), Joseph Marx (1882–1964), and Erich Korngold (1897–1957), have not achieved any hold on the public outside Austria.

It is indeed sad that music in Austria today cannot in any way be compared to music in Germany. Concerts, festivals, monuments, conservatories, even a few university departments of musicology exist, but there is no guiding light, no burning zeal to restore music to her proper place in the cultural firmament as has already been accomplished in Germany. Austria, and particularly the Viennese, are resting on their past laurels. The Austrians are musical conservatives. The Festival at Salzburg rarely programs contemporary works; many young Austrian composers feel it is nothing more than a museum. "Salzburg is a going concern. Why rock the boat?" seems to be the sentiment of the concert committee.

Many of the most famous twentieth-century composers left Austria after the Anschluss in 1938. Few returned. Of the third generation after Schoenberg, Michael Gielen, son of the well-known Joseph Gielen, former director of the Burgtheater, became director of the Stockholm Opera for a while before coming to the States. Another member of this generation, Friedrich Cerha, a talented violinist, remained in Austria and formed the ensemble known as Die Reihe, one of the few groups whose aim is to bring to the public the latest experiments in serial music. This group performs on occasion at the Museum of the 20th Century, and the Konzerthaus, both in Vienna. Johann Nepomuk David (b. 1895), one of the foremost Austrian composers of traditional music, has elected to live in Germany. The best known Austrian musician on the international scene is Gottfried von Einem, whose operas *Dantons Tod* and *Der Prozess* have received frequent performances throughout Europe. Ernst Krenek (b. 1900), another Viennese, shows the influence of both Mahler and Schoenberg in his work. His popular *Jonny spielt auf* (1923) brought him immediate fame, but he, too, left Vienna during the Hitler era and has been an American citizen for more than three decades.

Unlike the Germans, the Austrians have not given sufficient support to the creative arts, and the results are obvious to anyone who compares the approaches to music of each country. Before 1970, for example, there were very few attempts made to publish brochures in English in order to assist the numerous traveling music lovers from England and America who sought in vain to locate the dwelling places associated with their favorite composers. The municipal authorities of Vienna have begun to correct this situation. All such monuments are now decorated with flags, and literature in English has become available on request from the Fremdenverkehrsamt (Tourist Office) of the city of Vienna.

Other private institutions and individuals have been working more or less behind the scenes to collate and organize the enormous amount of musical material that exists on Vienna. The Oesterreichische Musikgesellschaft (the Austrian Music Society), dedicated to the promotion of music in the country, is located in lovely quarters in the center of Vienna, but efforts to support and publicize it are not at all comparable to those exerted by the Dutch, the Belgians, or the Germans. One of the few people who has singlehandedly done more than anyone else to promote the music of Austria is Rudolf Klein. His books on the Vienna Opera, the Salzburg musical tradition, and Beethoven's homes in Austria should be staples in any music library. His latest collaboration, *Österreichisches Musikhandbuch* (Vienna 1971), edited by Harald Goertz, has been the source of much of our information.

We must not forget that Vienna today is not the city it once was. No longer the capital of the Austro-Hungarian empire, an empire that included among its subjects over fifty million people in the so-called

Dual Monarchy, Vienna today is a small city living in the past, and loath to shake itself out of the comfortable lethargy that has enveloped it for close to sixty years. And yet, hundreds of thousands of visitors still believe her to be the musical city of Europe! Historically, she is, without question. Among the great and near great who spent time in the city during the last century alone are Cherubini, Reichardt, Spohr, Mendelssohn, Meyerbeer, Marschner, Zelter, Konradin Kreutzer, Rossini, Weber, Chopin, Nicolai, Schumann, Donizetti, Loewe, Berlioz, Lortzing, and von Flotow, besides the host of composers already mentioned. Under the circumstances it is easy to see why she has become complacent. The musical treasures of Vienna alone surely make Austria one of the foremost repositories of irreplaceable musical manuscripts. In addition to the great holdings of the Hapsburgs, countless abbeys, monasteries, and baroque churches number among their most prized possessions, valuable manuscripts, many of them still unclassified.

Considerable musicmaking takes place in Vienna, particularly within the confines of the many internationally known musical landmarks of the city, which include the Gesellschaft der Musikfreunde, the Konzerthaus, the Palais Augarten, the churches like St. Stephen's, the Votivkirche, the Franziskaner Kirche, the Dreifaltigkeit Kirche, where Beethoven's funeral took place, the Palais Kinsky, and the Schönbrunn palace.

The Vienna Philharmonic, the Vienna Symphony Orchestra, the Vienna Opera, and the Vienna Boys' Choir are among the most important performing organizations. They are also often recorded, and opera records with the Vienna Philharmonic are available on many labels. Enormous numbers of music publishers and music dealers make a good living in Vienna. They also cater to the needs of those who love "pop music," here called *Schlag* (whipped cream). Operetta and *Schrammel* (based on the works of the Schrammel brothers, popular nineteenth-century folksingers) are still significant features of contemporary musical life in Vienna. What with the National Library, the city library, the instrument collection in the Kunsthistorisches Museum, the memorials and monuments to composers, the casual visitor cannot help but feel he is surrounded by music. Yet summer musicmaking, too, is not as distinguished here as in Germany. In the summer, concerts are limited to outdoor orchestral concerts in the City Hall arcade, promenade concerts in the Belvedere Gardens, palace concerts, recitals in composers' homes, and outdoor park concerts. The Opera and the Gesellschaft der

Musikfreunde are usually closed. Several festivals bring summer visitors to Austria; among the best known are those at Salzburg and Bregenz, as well as the June festival in Vienna.

In time we are sure that the municipal authorities in Vienna as well as in other cities of Austria—Linz, Graz, Innsbruck, and even Salzburg—will recognize the need to do more to help the English-speaking visitor.

Austria

Austria

Guides and Services

Coming Events (Selected Highlights)

In English. Distributed by the Austrian National Tourist Office, 545 Fifth Avenue, New York 10017. Available gratis. Tel: (212) 697 0651.

Appears once a year, but often revised. Lists events taking place in Austria throughout the year. Covers the following events: festivals, opera, theater, concerts, art exhibitions, trade fairs and expositions, conferences and conventions, social events, folklore, and sports.

The above office also issues in advance, monthly programs for the Vienna State Opera, and in January the schedule of the Salzburg Festival (usually held from the end of July to the end of August).

For information about Austria in Great Britain, contact the Austrian National Tourist Office:

London: 16 Conduit Street, London WIR. Tel: 01 629 0461.

Manchester: 19 Mosley Arcade, Piccadilly Plaza, Manchester M 1 4AF. Tel: 061 236 2900.

NATIONAL HOLIDAYS

January	1 New Year's Day
	6 Epiphany
April	* Easter Monday

May	1 Labor Day
	* Ascension Day
	* Whit Saturday
	* Whit Monday
June	* Corpus Christi
August	15 Assumption Day
October	26 National Holiday
November	1 All Saints' Day
December	8 Immaculate Conception
	25 Christmas
	26 St. Stephen's Day

* = movable

SALZBURG

Tel. prefix: (06222)

Salzburg is the capital of the province of Salzburg, seat of the provincial government and residence of an archbishop who still bears the title, *"Primus Germaniae,"* first among Germans. The foremost holder of that office was the Archbishop-Prince Wolf Dietrich, whose designs for its future left an indelible imprint on the city.

Incredibly picturesque Salzburg is the junction of the main north-south and east-west roads and rail lines and offers direct communications with all the capitals of Europe. Historically, it has been a meeting place for people of many different nationalities. Today, however, Salzburg is synonymous with Festival, not even with all three festivals on which the city prides itself, but with the one festival for which Salzburg is internationally famous. To those in the know, however, Salzburg is much more: a delightful city, pleasing to the eyes as well as to the ears.

Situated in a spectacular natural setting, Salzburg offers its visitors a choice of eras. From the early Christian period of the catacombs in the cliff overlooking St. Peter's, to the medieval Hohensalzburg Fortress, down through the gothic, Romanesque, baroque and rococo churches and palaces that color her landscape, Salzburg displays tangible evidence of her history.

For music lovers, this is the city of Mozart, although Salzburg was a latecomer in giving him his due. The house in which he was born and another in which he lived are visited today by tourists from all over the world. Scholars and performers come to Salzburg to work in the Mozarteum, a complex in the center of town which houses both the International Mozart Foundation and the Academy of Music (see below). Curiously enough, recently Salzburg has also become a convention city. Because of its new and convenient facilities—a Congress Hall, conference rooms, etc.—many businessmen come here for work instead of for pleasure.

The 120,000 natives have acquired the grace and warmth of perpetual hosts, for that is what they are almost ten months of the year. During the summer alone, 150,000 tourists descend on Salzburg, and the streets, shops, and hotels of both the old city and the new are always crowded. (Mozartiana, incidentally, extends through both sections.) Among the annual celebrations, the principal Festival, presented in what was once the Archbishop's stables, takes place in late July and lasts through August; the week-long Easter festival from Palm Sunday through Easter Monday, Salzburg Musical Spring (May—June) and the Schlosskonzerte in summer, and the Mozart Festival at the end of January all figure prominently among the cultural contributions of the city. Don't overlook the museums: one, the Carolinus Augusteum, is an extremely modern structure. The art galleries, the libraries, the cathedral, the Residenz, the old churches and monasteries all make it extremely worth your while to leave plenty of time for your visit.

Guides and Services

For any information about musical activities in Salzburg, go to the Stadtverkehrsbüro Salzburg, (Municipal Tourist Office), Auersperstrasse 7. Tel: 71511, 73866, 74620. In addition, the information kiosks of the Verkehrsbüro at Mozartplatz 5, Tel: 71511/249 or 349, and at the main station, Tel. 71712, will be most helpful. These two are open all year.

Note: information and aid for foreign students studying in Austria are available from the Österreichischer Auslandsstudentendienst (ÖAD) whose branch office in Salzburg is at Kaigasse-Nonnbergstiege. Tel: 85251. The main office is, of course, in Vienna. Other branch offices are in Graz, Innsbruck, and Linz.

Opera Houses and Concert Halls

Kleines Festspielhaus (*Old Festival Theater, called the Small House*)
Hofstallgasse. Tel: (06222) 87441

Season: all year, particularly during the Festival periods in January, at Easter, and during the summer, in late July through August; opera (chamber or small-scaled) and concerts.
Box Office: for tickets, see information above.
Seating capacity: 1267 (1379 on their public announcements!)

The Festspielhaus adjoins the Grosses Festspielhaus. The Kleines Haus was opened in 1928, but today is the least impressive structure in the three-building complex.

The Felsenreitschule (Rocky Riding School)

Hofstallgasse. Tel: (06222) 87441
Seating capacity: 1560

Formerly the Archbishop's winter riding school, this theater contains ninety-six loggias in three tiers. Once a horse-training rink, this indoor-outdoor auditorium has been converted into a theater through the addition of bleachers and a sliding roof. The Stadtsaal, with large ceiling frescoes (1690) by Rottmayr and Lederwasch, also formerly part of the stables, is now a refreshment room and promenade for intermissions. Renovations were completed in 1970.

The Grosses Festspielhaus (New Festival Theater, the Large House)

Hofstallgasse. Tel: (06222) 87441

Built between 1956 and 1960 by Clemens Holzmeister, this theater, another part of the stables, is today Austria's most modern theater. The house represents an amalgam of new and old. The west door (1694), for example, is by Fischer von Erlach.

Tours of the house are conducted during the winter, Monday to Friday at 3:00 PM, and Saturday at 11:00 AM. During the summer, tours at 11:00 AM and 3:00 PM except on Saturday afternoons, Sundays and holidays. Only occasional tours are offered while the Festival is in progress.

Basically, the center for the Festival consists of a string of seventeenth-century buildings standing between the cliff known as the Mönchsberg and a broad street called the Hofstallgasse. Over the years, these structures, Wolf Dietrich's Court Stables (1607), have been converted into three theaters: the Grosses Festspielhaus, the Kleines Festspielhaus, and the Felsenreitschule. Acclaimed for its remarkable acoustics, the Large House offers opera on a grand scale, the Small House has the more intimate operas, and the Rocky Riding School offers concerts and dramatic spectacles, often incorporating the natural settings as part of the theatrical backdrop. Only a few blocks away from the Festspielhaus (the entire complex is called the Festspielhaus) on the Domplatz (the square in front of the cathedral), a stage set on the front steps of this cathedral is the site of the annual performances of *Everyman,* the medieval morality play, in a translation by Hugo von Hofmannsthal, playwright and librettist for several of Richard Strauss's operas. Hofmannsthal and the actor-director Max Reinhardt were the leaders behind the organization of this festival back in 1920.

It is almost impossible to get to hear the major performances in this city without having purchased your tickets in advance. Apply to the Austrian National Tourist Office, 545 Fifth Avenue, New York 10017 or write to the Ticket Bureau, Salzburg Music Festival, A-5010 Salzburg, for advance orders. The annual Easter Festival program is announced in August; ticket applications can be made at that time. The summer program, announced in late December, should be subscribed for early in January. The only chance of obtaining tickets on the spot, should you arrive without having purchased them in advance, is in the lobby of the Large or Small House itself. Somebody just *may* have to dispose of some tickets at the last minute. The chances, however, are indeed slim!

Grosser Saal und Wiener Saal des Mozarteums

Schwarzstrasse 26–28. Tel: 73154
Mailing Address: Postfach 34, A-5024 Salzburg.
Season: October to June. From the end of July to the end of August the Grosser Saal is made available to the Salzburg Festival for concerts.
Box Office: Schwarztrasse 26. *Mailing address:* same as above.
Hours: Monday to Friday 9:00 AM to noon and 2:00 PM to 6:00 PM.
Seating capacity: Grosser Saal 806
Wiener Saal 277

Landestheater

Makartplatz (corner Schwarzstrasse 22). Tel: (06222) 74086, 74087

Built in 1893, this theater was modernized in 1938.

Seating capacity: 784

Residenz

Residenzplatz.

The Residenz was the seat of the prince-archbishops from the twelfth century until the secularization of the princedom in 1803. In the Residenz you can find the conference room where Mozart frequently performed.

Operas and serenade concerts are performed in the courtyard during the Festival on a specially constructed stage (see *Everyman* and Hofmannsthal). The serenade concerts are given around the forty-foot-high Residenz fountain in the square. Across the square from the palace stands the glockenspiel tower containing a thirty-five bell carillon. Carillon concerts are heard regularly at 7:00 AM, 11:00 AM, and 6:00 PM offering tunes from the works of Haydn, Mozart, and Weber. (The bells were cast in Antwerp, and the glockenspiel chimes were installed in 1702.). These performances are followed by music played on the

"Salzburger Stier" (1502), the only completely preserved open-air organ in Austria, located in the Hohensalzburg Fortress. Both Paul Hofhaimer and Leopold Mozart wrote chorales to be played on this organ. You can listen to the organ from the square in town, although at the peak tourist season, traffic noise nearly drowns it out.

Marionette Theaters

Salzburger Marionettentheater
Neues Theater Mirabell, Schwarzstrasse 24
(formerly Kapitelplatz 6) Tel: 72406
Season: April to September; performances start at 8:15 PM from April to August and at 8:00 PM in September. In addition, in July, August, and September there are performances at 4:00 PM.

In this theater, home of the world-famous Salzburg Marionettes, Professor Aicher carries on a centuries-old tradition of his family. For two hundred years the Aicher family has made, exhibited, and presented marionettes in productions ranging from Mozart's *The Magic Flute, The Abduction from the Seraglio,* and *Don Giovanni,* through Rossini's *Barber of Seville,* and Tschaikovsky's *Nutcracker Suite.* The music today is recorded from the Festival performances.

Halls Where Concerts are Given

Marmorsaal in the Mirabell Palace (*see Salzburger Schlosskonzerte, following*).

Steinernes Theater in Hellbrunn Palace (*see Musical Landmarks; used only for the summer festival*).

Rittersaal der Residenz (*see Salzburger Schlosskonzerte, following*).

Concert Series

Hausmusik in Mozarts Wohnhaus (*Chamber Music in Mozart's Residence*)
Makartplatz 8.
Season: From July 1 to September 11, except for Sundays and holidays, chamber concerts are presented at 5:00 PM in the Tanzmeistersaal.

Salzburger Schlosskonzerte (*Salzburg Palace Concerts*)
Makartplatz 9. Tel: 74363
Season: throughout the year (see following).

Subscriptions including accommodations at selected hotels and pensions are available.

A series of concerts is given throughout the year under the patronage of the Mayor of Salzburg; in 1971, 160 concerts were given. Concerts are held in the Marmorsaal of the Mirabell Palace (see above) and in the Rittersaal of the Salzburg Residenz (see above). This series includes special "weeks" or mini-festivals such as the Salzburg Musical Spring (last ten days in May), Beethoven Week (about the last week in June), European Chamber Music Week in Salzburg (about the second week in July) and others. From June through August 21, concerts start at 9:00 PM; the rest of the year they begin at 8:00 PM. Seats are unnumbered, but seating accommodations are limited. Therefore, early application for tickets is advisable. For further information and booking, write Austrian National Tourist Office, 545 Fifth Avenue, New York 10017.

Should you be in Salzburg without having purchased your tickets in advance, you might be able to get last-minute tickets at the box office before the performance.

Outdoor Concerts in the Mirabell Gardens

There is a Promenade Concert every Sunday morning at 10:30 AM (April to September, weather permitting) by a wind band, and night concerts, when the fountains are illuminated, at 8:00 PM on Tuesdays and Thursdays from May to August. Tickets may be purchased at the box office before the performance.

Mozart and his sister Nannerl performed at Schloss Mirabell when they were youngsters.

Cathedral Concerts

From July 1 to September 1, there are daily thirty-minute organ recitals in the cathedral at 11:15 AM.

Folk Music and Band Concerts

From May to September, folk music, folksongs and folklore evenings are offered by the Alpinia group in the Stieglkeller, by the Salzburger Stierwascher group at the Hohensalzburg Fortress, by the Folklore group of the Salzburger Volkshochschule in the Gasthof Sternbräu, and local brass band concerts are presented every Saturday afternoon on the Alter-Markt.

Libraries and Museums

Mozarteum; Internationale Stiftung Mozarteum und Hochschule für Musik und Darstellende Kunst (International Mozart Foundation and

School of Music and the Performing Arts),
Bibliotheca Mozartiana [Ben. 34]
Schwarzstrasse 26. Tel: (06222) 73154
Hours: Monday to Friday 10:00 AM to noon and 3:00 PM to 5:00 PM. Closed September.

You will find about 1,000 Mozart autographs here. The summer school, although seemingly a part of the Hochschule, is not really affiliated with it. Courses, however, are given in the building under separate auspices (see Schools).

Musikwissenschaftliches Institut der Universität Salzburg Bibliothek [Ben. 35]
Getreidegasse 9/IV. Tel: (06222) 86111, ext. 251
Mailing Address: Postfach 505.
Hours: Monday to Friday 9:00 AM to noon and 3:00 PM to 6:00 PM.

The Institute, founded in 1966 and established on the fourth floor of the house in which Mozart was born, cooperates with the Mozarteum in Mozart research, especially on the new Mozart edition. The staff participates in cataloging other nearby collections like St. Peter's (see following). Bequests to the Institute include the libraries of Otto Erich Deutsch, Alfred Orel, and others.

Salzburger Museum Carolinus Augusteum Bibliothek [Ben. 37]
Museumplatz 6. Tel: (06222) 81137 or 85785
Mailing Address: Postfach 525.
Hours: Monday to Friday 9:00 AM to noon. Closed holidays.

Although the Museum is principally an art museum, now housed in a beautiful modern building, it also includes among its treasures a small instrument collection and many early music prints of Viennese publishers of the first half of the nineteenth century.

Der Dom Musikarchiv [Ben. 32]
Domplatz.

Sacred music formerly belonging to the Dommusikverein und Mozarteum is located here. Since 1880, when the Mozarteum and the Musikarchiv of the Dom separated, secular music has been held by the Mozarteum.

St. Peter Musikarchiv [Ben. 38]
St. Peter Bezirk 1. Tel: (06222) 85007

This library is rich in manuscripts by Mozart and Haydn.

Nonnberg Bibliothek [Ben. 36]
Nonnberggasse 2. Tel: (06222) 81607

In this oldest Austrian nunnery, founded about 700, there is considerable material on Salzburg's musical history.

Stadtbücherei Salzburg, Musikalienabteilung
Schloss Mirabell. Tel: 71511 and 72531/72591
Hours: Monday and Friday 10:00 AM to noon and 4:00 PM to 7:30 PM; Tuesday and Thursday 10:00 AM to noon and 4:00 PM to 6:00 PM; Wednesday 4:00 PM to 6:00 PM. Closed last two weeks in August, legal holidays, afternoon of Good Friday, September 24, November 2, December 24 and December 31.

Keltenmuseum Hallein (in the province of Salzburg, northeast of city)
Pflegerplatz 323. Tel: (06245) 2515
Hours: daily 9:00 AM to 6:00 PM from May 1 to September 30. Closed October 1 to April 30; open by arrangement in advance.

This library has the largest collection of F. X. Gruber, the composer of *Stille Nacht (Silent Night)*. The origin of this Christmas song is celebrated at Christmas in Oberndorf near Salzburg where the song was born, in Hallein where its composer Franz Gruber lies buried, and in Wagrain where its author, Father Mohr, is buried.

Bibliothek der Hochschule für Musik und darstellende Kunst in the Mozarteum in Salzburg
Schwarzstrasse 24. Tel: (06222) 74492/93
Hours: Monday to Friday 10:00 AM to noon and 3:00 PM to 5:00 PM.

Universitätsbibliothek Salzburg
Universitätsplatz 1. Tel: (06222) 81829, 84710
Hours: October 1 to June 30, Monday to Friday 9:00 AM to 4:00 PM; Saturday 9:00 AM to noon; special collections, Monday to Friday 9:00 AM to 4:00 PM; July and September, Monday to Friday 9:00 AM to 4:00 PM; August, Monday to Friday 8:00 AM to 10:00 AM.

Volksliedarchiv
Frohnburgweg 55 (Orff Institute). Tel: (06222) 87541
Hours: by prior appointment.

In addition to manuscripts and early prints, the Library has a tape archive.

Conservatories and Schools

Mozarteum (Hochschule für Musik und darstellende Kunst)

Schwarzstrasse 26. Tel: 74492

This renowned musical academy opened in 1880. Since 1914 it has also been the headquarters of the International Mozart Foundation or Mozarteum. The Mozarteum contains two concert halls, the Grosser Saal and the smaller Wiener Saal, so called because it was donated by the Vienna Mozart Society (see **Concert Halls**). The building also houses the Bibliotheca Mozartiana (see **Libraries**), a Mozart archive that includes 186 original letters and 65 musical autographs of W. A. Mozart and 360 letters from Leopold Mozart. These manuscripts are displayed every summer for the benefit of visitors on the conducted tours around the building.

In the Bastein Garden behind the Mozarteum stands the legendary "Magic Flute Summer-House" (*Zauberflötehäuschen*) where Mozart composed *The Magic Flute.* This house stood at that time in Vienna opposite the Freihaus Theater in a small garden in Der Wieden. In 1873, Prince Starhemberg intended to re-erect the summer house (which was his property) in the park of his manor in Eferding, Upper Austria, but at their request he presented it to the Foundation. The building was dismantled and brought to Salzburg where it was first set up in 1877 in that part of the Mirabell Gardens called the Zwergl Garten. Later it was removed to the slopes of the Kapuzinerberg overlooking the town, where it remained until 1948. It suffered from neglect during the war years so that once again it had to be dismantled and restored. It finally found its most appropriate home close to the Mozarteum, where the Foundation is able to arrange candlelight concerts in the summer months, conducted against the background of Mozart's summer-house.

Conducted tours of the Mozarteum on weekdays only from July to the end of August at 11:30 AM.

Visiting hours at the *Zauberflötehäuschen* are weekdays 9:00 AM to noon; 3:00 PM to 6:00 PM from May to October.

Universität Salzburg

Residenzplatz 1. Tel: 86111

(See **Libraries** for more information.) In the auditorium of the University, the 13-year-old Mozart's *La Finta Semplice* was given its first performance.

Summer Courses

Internationale Sommer Akademie Mozarteum Salzburg

Schwarzstrasse 26. Tel: 74492

Course of Study: about six weeks from mid-July to end of August.

This summer school functions as an educational counterpart to the Salzburg Festival (see **Festivals**).

Orff-Institut
Frohnburgweg 55.

Offers summer seminars; for information, write to the above address.

Musical Landmarks

Mozart-Museum in Mozarts Geburtshaus (house where Mozart was born)
Getreidegasse 9.
Hours: October 1 to May 15, daily 9:00 AM to 6:00 PM; May 15 to June 30, 9:00 AM to 7:00 PM; July 1 to August 31, 8:00 AM to 8:00 PM; September 1 to 30, 9:00 AM to 7:00 PM. Closed Christmas and New Year's. Because these hours occasionally change, it is advisable to verify them on arrival in Salzburg.

This building is first mentioned in documents in 1408. Since 1703 it has been in the possession of the family of Hagenauer, a merchant with whose grandson Leopold Mozart carried on an extensive correspondence. The Mozart family lived on the third floor from 1747 to 1773. Since 1880 the house has been a museum, and since 1917 it has belonged to the Internationale Stiftung Mozarteum. The most valuable exhibits, among a fine collection of pictures, autographs, and other mementos, are undoubtedly Mozart's clavichord and his grand piano made in 1780 by Anton Walter in Vienna. This piano was presented to the Mozarteum by the composer's son in 1856 on the occasion of the centenary of his father's birth. It is the instrument which Mozart preferred over all others for his concerts during the last ten years of his life.

"Mozart in the Theater," a special exhibit assembled in 1931, is also housed here. It shows the history of Mozart's operas as demonstrated by changing scenery and costumes through the centuries with *The Magic Flute* as its center. A collection of nearly a hundred miniature stage models, movable and illuminated, gives an idea of the varying interpretations of his works by succeeding generations. Included are examples from Mozart's own day, from the Biedermeier period and from the late nineteenth century, and the exhibit continues through the present day.

Mozarts Wohnhaus (house where Mozart lived)
Makartplatz 8 (formerly Hannibal Platz). Tel: 748973
Hours: from the end of June until the beginning of September in conjunction

with concerts given there on weekdays at 5:00 PM. Closed from the middle of September to the end of June.

Built at the beginning of the seventeenth century, in 1711 the house came into the possession of Anna Eva Speckner, wife of the court dancing master. It is therefore also known as the "Tanzmeisterhaus." In the fall of 1773, its new tenants were the Mozart family. Leopold lived here until his death in 1787. Since 1955 it has belonged to the Internationale Stiftung Mozarteum. It is now a museum and concert hall. Mozart spent his youthful years here, from 1773 to 1781, although during this period he was often away traveling.

On October 16, 1944, two-thirds of the Tanzmeisterhaus was destroyed in an air raid. Of the Mozart rooms, only the music room remained. In 1955 the Foundation bought that portion of the house still standing, with the express intention of restoring the remains of the house and its Music Room (Tanzmeister-Saal) to their original appearance and to use them for cultural events. Since 1956 many ceremonies and concerts have taken place here.

Now there is an instrument display in the Tanzmeister-Saal. It is also known that Michael Haydn held his wedding breakfast in this same room!

Mozart Monument

Mozartplatz.

In the Mozartplatz, not far from the cathedral where Mozart was organist from 1779 to 1781, stands the bronze statue designed by the Munich sculptor Ludwig von Schwanthaler and cast in Munich on May 22, 1841 by Johann Stiglmaier. At the beginning of September 1842, it was brought to Salzburg by wagon to be unveiled on September 4 on the occasion of the first music festival, in the presence of Mozart's two sons. Wolfgang, Jr., conducted a festival cantata he had composed in honor of his father. Mozart's widow, Constanze, died just a few months before the monument was unveiled. There is a memorial plaque to her at Mozartplatz 8, where she lived for a time.

Nannerl, Mozart's sister, lived and died at Sigmund-Haffner-Gasse 12. This house is now called the Barisani Haus.

At Robing-Hof, Schallmoos, Robingstrasse 1, you can see the home of the Robing family with whom Mozart was closely associated.

Steinernes Theater in Hellbrunn Palace

In 1617 in the Steinernes Theater, one of the earliest performances of opera in the German-speaking world occurred with the production of Monteverdi's *Orfeo,* ten years after its world premiere in Mantua.

The Organ in the Salzburg Cathedral

This organ, mainly the work of the Salzburg court organ-builder J. Christopher Egedacher, was built in 1702—1703. Frequently rebuilt, it was furnished with an electric mechanism when the cathedral was restored after World War II. Mozart played this organ regularly when he was organist here for three years. The composer was baptized in the baptismal font in the cathedral in the first chapel to the left of the entrance.

Abbey Church of St. Peter

Several of Mozart's works were heard here for the first time, the most important being the C-minor Mass (K. 427) performed on October 26, 1783, when Constanze sang the soprano solo with Mozart conducting.

Opposite St. Rupert's tomb, behind the St. Rupert altar, there is a monument to Michael Haydn with an urn containing his skull (!). In this aisle there is also a plaque in memory of Mozart's sister Nannerl (Marianne, Baroness Berchtold von Sonnenberg).

There is a Mozart Fountain in the main square of St. Gilgen on Lake Wolfgangsee. Mozart's mother was born in this little village a short distance from Salzburg, and Nannerl, his sister, also lived here.

Monuments

Paul Hofhaimer (1459–1537) was born at Radstadt 7, lived at Pfeifergasse 18, and is buried in the Petersfriedhof.

Festungsgasse 4, site of the house where **Michael Haydn** (1737–1806) lived, is now the lower station of the funicular railroad to Hohensalzburg.

Peter Cornelius (1824–1874), the opera composer and friend of Liszt and Wagner, stayed at the Gasthaus *Goldne Traube,* now Linzergasse 4, and at the *Nonnthaler Wirt,* Nonnthaler Hauptstrasse 20.

Joseph Mohr (1792–1848), who wrote the words of *Stille Nacht* (*Silent Night*), was born at Steingasse 9, in Hintersee, lived in Schulweg 77, Oberndorf, and lies buried in the graveyard of the Marktkirche von Wagrain—all near Salzburg.

Anton Diabelli (1781–1858), music publisher and composer, lived at Stiftsplatz 13. A plaque is affixed to the front of the house.

Hugo Wolf (1860–1903) lived at Bergstrasse 8. At twenty-two, Wolf had his first job in Salzburg as second (deputy-assistant) kapellmeister at the Municipal Theater. He stayed there from November 1881 to January 1882, directing and rehearsing the chorus and hating every minute of it.

Franz Schubert stayed at the Gasthaus *Zum Mohren,* Judengasse 9, in August 1825.

Hans Pfitzner (1869–1949), composer, teacher and conductor, lived at Haunspergstrasse 33.

Anton Webern (1883–1945) was killed in front of the house of his son-in-law, Mattl, at Mittersill Markt 100. He is buried in the Mittersill cemetery.

Ignaz Franz Heinrich Biber (1644–1704), well-known violin virtuoso and composer, lived at Judengasse 13. His grave and a memorial plaque may be found at Petersfriedhof.

Richard Strauss conducted the first performance of an opera, Mozart's *Don Giovanni,* at the Salzburg Festival in 1922. Strauss was also the first composer to have his work performed at the Festival during his own lifetime (1926, *Ariadne auf Naxos*). While in Salzburg, he stayed at the Österreichisches Hof. The city of Salzburg named a street for him in Parsch.

Gravesites

Sebastianskirche on Linzergasse was built between 1505 and 1512. Its cemetery contains some famous tombs, including those of the Mozart and Weber families. Leopold Mozart and Constanze, W. A. Mozart's wife, are buried here.

Petersfriedhof. At the entrance to the catacombs, in the first communal vault on the right, lie Nannerl Mozart and Michael Haydn (sister of W. A. Mozart and brother of Joseph Haydn, respectively). Paul Hofhaimer is also buried in this cemetery (see above).

Musical Organizations

Herbert von Karajan Stiftung (*Research Institute for Experiments in Psychology of Music at the Psychological Institute of the University of Salzburg*)

Akademiestrasse 20. Tel: (06222) 86111, Ext. 355

Historical and anthropological research on the development of music proceeds here; also research into neurophysiology and psychology as they relate to music.

Internationale Stiftung Mozarteum Salzburg (*International Mozart Foundation*) (*see Libraries*)

Schwarzstrasse 26. Tel: (06222) 73155

The Business of Music

Dealers

Alpenverlag GmbH
Rudolfskai 2.

H. Banzauner
Goldgasse 5.

Columbia
Sigmundplatz 2.
Records

E. Sigmund Höllringl
Haffnergasse 10.

F. König
Linzer Bundesstrasse 6.

Makart-Radio
Makartplatz 4.
Records

Mayerische Buchhandlung
Theatergasse.

M. Mora
Residenzplatz 2.
Music

Publishers

Alpenverlag GmbH
Rudolfskai 2.

Buchzentrale Oesterreichisches Burromauswerk
Kapitelplatz 6.

A. Hofer
Keyersstrasse 13.

Instrument Makers

H. Banzauner
Goldgasse 5.

Dreher & Reinisch
Fürbergstrasse 50.

F. Krieg
Getreidegasse 13.

K. Lang
Harrerstrasse 64.

H. Mauracher
Kaigasse 24.

J. Mertel
Neuhauserstrasse 32.

K. Pünringer
Getreidegasse 13.

VIENNA

Tel prefix: (0222)

Vienna, capital of the Republic of Austria, as well as one of its nine federal provinces, has a population of about 1,700,000 and is divided into twenty-three administrative districts known as *Bezirks.* This city of music, as she is regarded by most of the culture-conscious visitors from Europe and the States, can look back upon nearly two thousand years of history. As a result, she shows an unbounded confidence in herself and a recognition of her own value that nothing can destroy. It is indeed sometimes difficult for some of its inhabitants to remember that these are no longer the days of Franz Joseph and that Vienna is not still the seat of the Empire.

Founded about AD 50 as a Roman colony, she was ruled by the tenacious family of the Hapsburgs from 1276 to 1918. Fortunately for posterity, many members of this family, although afflicted with acquisitive instincts for lands and treasures, also collected books, manuscripts, and even musicians for their households. In addition, they supported cultural enterprises to an unprecedented extent. Despite the misfortunes of the Plague and the Great Fire in the fourteenth century, the University of Vienna was founded in 1365. By the fifteenth century, the Hapsburg emperor had established the magnificent Nationalbibliothek. In the seventeenth century, suffering again from the loss of nearly half her population as victims of the Plague, and threatened from the East with the capture of those of her citizens still alive, Vienna survived once more, as her generals turned the tables on the advancing Turks.

In the post-war years, the emperor appointed Fischer von Erlach court architect and Ludovico Burnacini court theater designer. Together they built over two hundred churches and palaces in the ornate baroque style. Schönbrunn and Belvedere are monuments to Vienna's two great architects of the Baroque, Fischer von Erlach and Lucas von Hildebrandt. Schönbrunn, where Mozart played for Maria Theresa, is still used for musical functions today. Badly damaged during the Second World War, it has since been restored. The fantasy world of the Austrians is clearly reflected in von Erlach's plans for Schönbrunn. One wonders how many rooms his original plans called for, but the economy version finally built consists of twelve hundred—forty-five of which are open to the public.

Vienna experienced her first Golden Age under Maria Theresa, an era to which Richard Strauss and Hugo von Hofmannsthal returned for their opera *Der Rosenkavalier.* During the second half of the eighteenth century, Gluck, Haydn, Mozart, and later, Beethoven and Schubert called this city home. For a short while, when the French occupied Vienna (during which time *Fidelio* received its first performance), Napoleon was in residence. Certainly in 1815, Metternich's city held center stage. Again in the limelight, Vienna returned to glory under Franz Joseph, who reigned from 1848 to 1916. Then it was Brahms, Bruckner, Mahler, Hugo Wolf, Schoenberg, and Berg among musicians; Arthur Schnitzler, Hugo von Hofmannsthal, Peter Altenberg, and Stefan Zweig among writers; Gustav Klimt, Egon Schiele, and Oscar Kokoschka among the painters who brought fame and renown to the city.

In 1938, after the Anschluss, the Jews, who represented about eleven percent of the population of Vienna at that time, left the city, most forever. Since the loss of this considerable number of musicians, artists, and intellectuals, Vienna has not been the same. Recently, however, there have been some changes. For the first time, Freud has been recognized by his home town. His office has been restored and is now a national landmark, as are the homes of many of Austria's prominent writers and musicians. The Staatsoper, rebuilt after the war with assistance from the United States, celebrated its hundredth anniversary in 1969 and remains one of the best companies in the world today. The Gesellschaft der Musikfreunde, known unofficially as the Musikverein, offers some of the best concert series in any city. The three halls of the Konzerthaus supply the Viennese with a wide variety of concerts and recitals. Instead of the six houses that presented operettas in the 1880s, the Volksoper is one of only two Viennese theaters that specialize in that genre today. The vast collections and libraries that once belonged exclusively to the Hapsburgs are now open to the public. Of course, the huge number of composers' homes makes it unlikely that anyone ever sees everything here even on repeated visits.

One word of caution: Vienna is not a summer city. Inasmuch as she offers so much from the first of September through the thirtieth of June, it is best to plan your visits accordingly. In the summer, the level of musicmaking is not very high; many of the libraries and conservatories are either closed or on limited schedules, and, just as in New York, concert life is in low gear. You may acquire an overview of the city through the many tours that are offered and through the castle concerts and outdoor spectacles that continue through July and August, but Vienna really becomes herself during the other ten months of the year.

Guides and Services

This Week in Vienna

A free weekly program of Vienna's cultural events is available at the information booth in the Opernpassage, the pedestrian underpass near the Opera House. It is also available at major hotels, newsstands and tourist offices throughout the city.

Wien

A handy monthly calendar of events is published by the Fremdenverkehrsverband für Wien, Stadiongasse 6–8.

Die Presse

Lists fully each Saturday exhibits, lectures, poetry readings, and theater and concert schedules.

During the summer months, the Kulturamt der Stadt Wien issues a *Musikalisches Sommerprogramm* for July through September. This booklet, too, is available at the Tourist Offices.

It is perhaps advisable to state here that the Tourist Office cannot serve as a ticket bureau. It will not make reservations for you. Do, however, make use of the various authorized ticket agencies available and listed below.

Vienna Tourist Board
Stadiongasse 6–8. Tel: 431608

This tourist bureau can be extremely helpful. Particularly knowledgeable is the talented director, Dr. Johanna Kral, who, if given sufficient notice, will go out of her way to provide you with personal assistance on your visit.

Opera Houses and Concert Halls

Wiener Staatsoper

Opernring 2. Tel: 527636

Season: September 1 to June 30; performances given every night except Christmas Eve and Good Friday. Opera and ballet are the staples, with about fifty operas in the repertoire.

Box Office Mailing Address: Kassenleitung Vienna I, Staatsoper.

Authorized Ticket Agencies: Österreichisches Verkehrsbüro, Friedrichstrasse 7; Tel: 572315 & 579657. Another Verkehrsbüro is at Stephansplatz 10; Tel: 630820 & 630800. Also the Wienerhausgesellschaft, Lothringerstrasse 20; Tel: 721211.

Seating capacity: 1642 seats; standing room for 567!

Operas and better concerts are usually sold out in Vienna, so your best bet is to buy your tickets long in advance. On weekdays during business hours, you can get tickets on the ground floor of the Opera entrance from the Operngasse. Each of the major state theaters (see entries for: Volksoper, Akademietheater, Burgtheater, as well as the Opera) has its own ticket counter in this office. An interpreter is available next to the opera counter. Tickets are placed on sale at the box office four days before a given performance. Hardly any tickets are available at this time. Standing room tickets go on sale about an hour and a quarter before the performance, but the line forms, depending on the opera and the cast, from two hours to half a day before the performance. One reviewer suggests that, once having gotten your standing room ticket, you claim your position by tying a handkerchief or scarf to the lower rung of the railing in front of you so that you can leave for dinner or a walk before the performance and still have your place when you return.

A large percentage of the audience for these operas is subscription. During the last six weeks of the season, for the June Festwochen, all seats are non-subscription, but still hard to get. A cardinal rule here is to write ahead for tickets. Schedules for about a month in advance are available from the Austrian National Tourist Office, 545 Fifth Avenue in New York. A minimum of two weeks is required for mail orders, but a month is better. You should be informed as to which tickets are available and your options for picking them up and paying for them. Some tickets may be available from a broker or hotel porter with additional commission, of course. On those rare occasions when tickets are not all sold in advance, remaining ones can be purchased within one hour before the beginning of a performance at the evening ticket office of the theater.

One final suggestion is in order, provided that you know exactly which performances you would like to see: write in advance to Vienna State Opera, c/o Bundestheaterverwaltung, Goethegasse 1, A-1010 Vienna I, Austria. You may follow this procedure for all three of the national theaters: the Burgtheater, the Volksoper, and the Akademietheater.

The Vienna Opera opened its doors for the first time on May 25, 1869. Since then, the Opera has been directed by Hans Richter, Gustav Mahler, Felix Weingartner, Richard Strauss, and Bruno Walter, among others. Owing to the war, the Opera House closed finally on June 30, 1944 after a performance, appropriately enough, of *Götterdämmerung*. On March 12, 1945, after two days of fires from Allied air attacks, the Opera House was completely destroyed except for the facade facing the Ring, part of the foyer, and, of course, the foundations.

For the next ten years, performances were given at the Theater an der Wien. The Opera House, first on the city's priority list for reconstruction after the war, reopened on November 5, 1955 with *Fidelio* under Böhm. He resigned shortly afterward, and the best known conductor since then has been von Karajan.

Guided tours of this building are given daily at 2:00 PM (in German) and at 3:00 PM (in English). Among the busts you will see in the theater are those of Wagner, Schubert, Marschner, Richard Strauss, Gluck, Boieldieu, Mozart, Cherubini, Rossini, Haydn, Beethoven, Weber, Dittersdorf, Meyerbeer, Mahler, Donizetti, and Karl Böhm. Notice Moritz von Schwind's magnificent drawings on the ceiling of the lobby and, on the walls of one of the two grand salons that flank the auditorium, look at the floor-to-ceiling tapestries depicting scenes from *The Magic Flute*. Remember, too, that evening dress is not out of place here for performances in this house where *Die Meistersinger* was premiered in 1870 and where Verdi himself conducted his *Requiem*.

Theater an der Wien

Linke Wienzeile 6. Tel: 579632

Mailing Address: Lehárgasse 5, A-1060 Vienna.

Season: entire year; closed from about May 10 to 23, June 24 to July 14, September 1 to 15. Theater presents concerts, ballets, operettas, etc. Except for opening nights, no evening dress is required.

Box Office: address same as above. Tel: 577151

Hours: daily from 10:00 AM to 8:00 PM.

Authorized Ticket Agencies: all agencies in Vienna.

Seating capacity: 1100

Standing Room: seventy tickets, sold one hour before performance.

The third oldest theater in Vienna, the Theater an der Wien opened in

1801. The first performances of Beethoven's Fifth and Sixth Symphonies were given here as were those of the Violin Concerto and *Fidelio.* Schubert's *Rosamunde,* Johann Strauss's *Fledermaus,* and Franz Lehár's *Merry Widow* all received their premieres here. One of the earliest directors of the theater was Schikaneder, the librettist for Mozart's *Magic Flute.* Lehár, Joseph Lanner, and Johann Strauss the elder conducted performances of their waltzes here. The theater was a center for elegant operetta performances in the late nineteenth century. It was renovated in 1962.

Volksoper Wien

Währingerstrasse 78. Tel: 343627

Season: September 1 to June 30 for operetta, opera, musical comedy, and ballet.

Box Office: same address as above. Tel: 343693

Hours: daily from 9:00 AM to 5:00 PM; Sundays and holidays from 9:00 AM to noon.

Seating capacity: 1620 seats and standing room for 136

The Volksoper theater was opened for plays in 1898. The first opera given there was in 1904. The premise behind the operation of this theater is the philosophy of "opera for the people."

Wiener Kammeroper (*Vienna Chamber Opera*)

Drachengasse 1 (public entrance).

Fleischmarkt 24 (theater address). Tel: 526943

Mailing Address: Bäckerstrasse 7, A-1010 Vienna.

Summer Productions: Schönbrunner Schlosstheater, A-1130 Vienna XIII.

Season: November to mid-June, performances Wednesday and Saturday only; Schönbrunn, July–August, performances daily, except Sunday.

Box Office: Fleischmarkt 24. Tel: 526943

Hours: daily except Sunday and holidays noon to 6:30 PM. Schönbrunner Schlosstheater, Tel: 823136/824206. Hours: daily from 10:00 AM to 8:00 PM.

Authorized Ticket Agencies: all those in Vienna.

Seating capacity: Wiener Kammeroper am Fleischmarkt: 306 (winter); Schönbrunner Schlosstheater: 440 (summer)

Operas, both early and chamber ones, as well as *Singspiele,* are offered.

Konzerthaus (*Wiener Konzerthausgesellschaft*)

Lothringerstrasse 20. Tel: 724686

1. Grosser Konzerthaus Saal
2. Mozartsaal
3. Schubertsaal

Season: October to May; Vienna Festival in May and June.

Box Office: in the Konzerthaus building at above address.

Hours: Monday to Friday 9:00 AM to 6:00 PM.
Seating capacity: Grosser Saal 1900; standing room 120. Mozartsaal 776; standing room 80. Schubertsaal 345.
Customary Dress: dressy clothes for these concerts.

Gesellschaft der Musikfreunde in Wien (also called the Musikverein)

1. Grosser Musikvereinsaal
2. Brahms Saal

Public Entrance: Dumbastrasse 3.
Mailing Address: Bösendorferstrasse 12. Tel: 658681
Season: September to June.
Box Office Mailing Address: Karlsplatz 6, 1010 Vienna. Theater Address: Bösendorferstrasse 12. Tel: 658690
Hours: Monday to Friday 9:00 AM to 1:00 PM and 3:00 PM to 6:00 PM; Saturday 9:00 AM to noon.
Seating capacity: Grosser Saal 1744
Brahms Saal 650
Standing Room: may be obtained in advance.
Customary Dress: evening clothes.

The Gesellschaft der Musikfreunde is Vienna's principal concert-giving organization. This building also includes offices of various musical societies, dealers, and publishers, as well as one of the most remarkable collections of books and manuscripts. The Vienna Philharmonic performs here in its traditional Sunday morning concert series (see Libraries).

Raimundtheater

Wallgasse 18–20. Tel: 576626 and 576627
Season: September 1 to August 31, although closed six weeks from mid-June to end of July.
Box Office: mail to above address. Box Office also in the Raimundtheater.
Hours: daily 9:00 AM to 6:00 PM.
Authorized Ticket Agencies: Wiener Kartenbüro.
Seating capacity: 1415
Customary Dress: Dress regulations are fairly liberal in this house that specializes in performances of operettas.

Redoutensaal (small concert hall of the Hofburg)

Josefsplatz 3.

Concerts are given occasionally, but not on a regular basis. In the summer months, catch some light opera here.

Schönbrunner Schlosstheater, Schönbrunn.

This theater in the castle is the oldest theater in Vienna. Mozart conducted here! The Wiener Kammeroper gives performances here during the summer (see Wiener Kammeroper for details about box office, etc.).

Recital Hall in the Graphische Sammlung Albertina
Augustinerstrasse 1. Tel: 524232 and 525769
Season: five concerts between October and April.
Box Office: in the Albertina.
Seating capacity: 235
Customary Dress: dark suits.

Österreich-Haus (Austrian Cultural Center)
Josefsplatz 6 (Palais Palffy). Tel: 525681
Season: all year, presenting chamber music and recitals.
Seating capacity: over 500 in different rooms

Konzertsaal of the Konservatorium der Stadt Wien
Johannesgasse 4a.

Sendesaal des Funkhauses (Radio Concert Hall)
Argentinierstrasse 30a.
Seating capacity: 250

Marmorsaal, in the old instrument collection of the Kunsthistorischesmuseum (Museum of Art History)
Neue Hofburg, Heldenplatz.

The instruments are used in chamber concerts here.

Marionette Theaters

Wiener Urania Puppentheater
Uraniastrasse 1.

Wiener Marionettentheater "der Regenbogen"
Avedikstrasse 27. Tel: 831472

"Arlequin" Marionettentheater im Café Mozart bei der Oper
Maysedergasse 5, Albertina Platz. Tel: 526471/526213

Palace Concerts

Although there are no regularly scheduled concerts in these palaces, concerts are given from time to time. Check with the Oesterreichisches Verkehrsbüro, Friedrichstrasse 7 (Tel: 572315) for dates and tickets.

Palais Auersperg (Palais des Rosenkavaliers)
Auerspergstrasse 1.

Gluck and Dittersdorf regularly conducted celebrated orchestral and operatic performances here in this eighteenth-century palace.

Palais Kinsky
Freyung 4.

Palais Lobkowitz
Lobkowitzplatz 2.

Prince Lobkowitz, one of Beethoven's patrons, had his own singers, actors, and private orchestra in residence. The first performance of the *Eroica* was given here.

Palais Pallavicini
Josefsplatz 5.

Palais Palffy (Figaro-Saal, Beethoven-Saal, Haydn-Salon)
Josefsplatz 6.

Palais Rasumofsky
Rasumofskygasse 23.

Prince Rasumofsky had regular quartet evenings in his palace. He himself played as a member of the quartet. Later he hired the Schuppanzigh Quartet. Many first performances of Beethoven's works were given here.

Palais Schwarzenberg
Rennweg 2.

First performances of Haydn's *Creation* and *The Seasons* were given here.

Esterhazy Palace
Wallnerstrasse 4.

Haydn often played in the tiny chapel here and led performances by the prince's celebrated orchestra and opera company.

Augarten Palace
Obere Augartenstrasse 1.

This building now houses the Vienna Boys' Choir. Mozart played in the summer house in the garden for Emperor Joseph II. In the nineteenth century, the Imperial family used the palace as a guest residence. Liszt and Wagner both played there.

Schloss Schönbrunn

Schönbrunner Schlossstrasse.

In 1762, Mozart, at the age of six, gave a celebrated recital here for Maria Theresa and her daughter, Marie Antoinette. Haydn, too, conducted concerts here.

The Viennese palace concerts take place between July and mid-September, usually Monday, Wednesday, and Thursday at 8:00 PM.

The Hofburg (Royal Palace)

Three generations of "Waltz-King" Strausses held the position of Director of Music for Court Balls from 1835 until well into the twentieth century. The Redoutensaal, the present concert hall (Josefsplatz 3), was created out of a court ballroom by Richard Strauss and Franz Schalk.

In the Hofburg, Haydn conducted a performance in 1795; Beethoven led a concert of his own works in 1815 for participants of the Congress of Vienna. The first concert by the Vienna Philharmonic was given here in 1842. The chapel was the private chapel of the Imperial family, dating from the fifteenth century. Heinrich Isaac, Ludwig Senfl, Antonio Draghi, Johann Joseph Fux, Georg von Reutter, Florian Gassmann, and Antonio Salieri were among those musicians employed here from the fifteenth through the eighteenth centuries.

The chapel carries on the musical tradition today with the Vienna Boys' Choir singing mass every Sunday morning.

Churches in Which Concerts Are Given

Stephansdom

Stephansplatz.

Haydn was a choirboy here. Mozart's wedding and funeral took place in this church. Many important musicians, among them Florian Gassmann and Georg Reutter, held the position of kapellmeister here. There are free organ recitals every Wednesday at 7:00 PM.

Basilika Maria Treu

Piaristengasse 43.

Franziskanerkirche

Franziskanerplatz 4.

Karlskirche

Karlsplatz.

George Matthias Monn was organist here during the first half of the eighteenth century.

Augustinerkirche
Augustinerstrasse 3.

Michaelerkirche
Michaelerplatz.

The Nikolaus Chapel was the center of the activities of the Nicolai Confraternity, a thirteenth-century musicians' guild, one of the earliest of its kind. The guild was active until the late eighteenth century.

Burgkapelle, Hofburg (see also Hofburg)
Schweizerhof.

From mid-September through June at 9:25 AM on Sundays and holidays, the Vienna Choirboys sing during mass. Tickets are available for advance sales on Friday at 5:00 PM (both here at the Burgkapelle and at Agency Lienerbrunner, Augustinerstrasse). Order tickets as early as possible. The chapel is so small that almost no one really sees the singers.

Summer Concerts

Outdoor concerts are given in the following parks: Puchsbaumplatz, Herderpark, Steinbauerpark, Märzpark, Kongresspark, Allerheiligenplatz, Wasserpark, Belvedere-Garten, Volksgarten, and Burggarten.

Concerts are also given in the arcade-flanked courtyard of the Rathaus (City Hall). Cancellations due to bad weather are announced over the radio. Tickets are available at the door, the ticket agencies, and booking offices.

Concerts of waltzes and operetta music are presented in the "Kursalon" in the Stadtpark daily in the summer.

From July to mid-September there are palace concerts (see above) in one or another of the palaces on Monday, Wednesday, and Thursday at 8:00 PM. Check the Verkehrsbüro, Friedrichstrasse 7 (Tel: 572315), for details.

Libraries and Museums

Österreichische Nationalbibliothek, Musiksammlung (Austrian National Library, Music Division) [Ben. 55]
Augustinerstrasse 1 (Albertina Museum Building) Tel: 521684
Hours: Monday, Wednesday, Friday noon to 3:30 PM; Tuesday, Thursday 9:00 AM to 1:00 PM; Saturday 9:00 AM to noon. Closed Sunday, holidays, first three weeks in September.

This incredible library has holdings of the Hofkapelle, the Theater an der Wien, Hofoper (court opera), Carltheater, Josefstädttheater, von Suppémuseum, R. G. Kiesewetter, Ambros, Modena collections, etc. It owns catalogs of most Austrian monastery libraries and it is also the home of the very important Hoboken Photogramme Archiv. The collection was founded in the late fifteenth century by Maximilian I. Today it includes manuscripts of medieval chantbooks; Monteverdi's autograph of *Il Ritorno d'Ulisse;* autographs by Froberger, Alessandro Scarlatti, Marc-Antonio Cesti, Telemann, Piccinni, Wagenseil, J. S. Bach, his sons C. P. E. Bach, W. F. Bach, and J. C. Bach; Gluck's *Telemacco;* Haydn's *Nelson* and *Theresien* Masses, sketches for the *Creation,* and the *Emperor* Quartet op. 76^3; Mozart's sketches for the *Requiem,* two Masses, the Flute Quartet; Beethoven's "Spring" Sonata, Violin Concerto, String Quartet (op. 95); and other autographs of Paganini, Liszt, Schubert, Schumann, Brahms, Bruckner, Mahler, Strauss and Berg. Autograph scores of Strauss's *Rosenkavalier* and Hindemith's Violin Concerto are also to be found here.

As we go to press, we have been informed by the Director of the Austrian National Library's Music Department that they have recently acquired the world-famous collection of Dr. Anthony van Hoboken, the internationally renowned Dutch specialist in Haydn research and author of the Haydn Catalogue. The collection comprises more than 10,000 titles: sets of first editions, early editions of the works of the Viennese Classical masters, as well as first editions of the compositions of other great composers. A special Hoboken Room in the Albertina is being prepared to receive this collection of material, and it should be open to the public by the summer of 1975.

A booklet entitled *The Music Collection of the Austrian National Library* is available free on request from

Cultural News from Austria
The Federal Chancellery, Information Department
2 Ballhausplatz, Vienna, A-1014

One word to scholars: requests for use of manuscripts are usually limited to three a day. (Only three call slips may be submitted.)

Wiener Stadtbibliothek, Musiksammlung (*Vienna Municipal Library, Music Division*) [Ben. 59]

Neues Rathaus. Tel: (0222) 42804

Hours: Monday to Friday 9:00 AM to 4:00 PM for music, until 6:30 PM for books.
Closed holidays, Saturday, Sunday, August 1 to 15.

This library contains prints and autographs of Austrian composers from pre-classical to contemporary periods; collections of Schubert, the publisher Artaria, and the Wiener Tonkünstler; early works of Hugo Wolf; manuscripts of Brahms, Bruckner, Johann Strauss, and others. Letters of musicians are in the manuscript department (Josefsplatz 1, closed September 1–20); music books and programs are with the general collection.

Beethoven letters and the autograph of his *Consecration of the House* Overture are also here.

Wiener Stadtbibliothek (Municipal Library)
Rathaus. Tel: (0222) 42804
Hours: Monday to Friday 9:00 AM to 6:30 PM; closed August 1 to 15; hours differ for various special collections.

The Handschriftensammlung (Manuscript Collection) of this library, like the Music Division (see above), is only open until 4:00 PM daily.

Musikwissenschaftliches Institut der Universität [Ben. 52]
Universitätsstrasse 7. Tel: (0222) 427611, ext. 627
Hours: Monday to Thursday 9:00 AM to 8:00 PM; Friday 9:00 AM to 6:00 PM. Closed August 1 to 31 and December 24 to January 6.

Universitätsbibliothek [Ben. 60]
Dr. Karl-Lueger-Ring 1. Tel: 427611
Hours: Monday to Friday 8:00 AM to 10:00 PM; Saturday 8:00 AM to 1:00 PM. Closed Christmas week and August. From July 15 to 31 and September 1 to 15, 9:00 AM to 4:00 PM.

Archiv und Bibliothek der Wiener Philharmoniker [Ben. 61]
Bösendorferstrasse 12. Tel: 6550972
Hours: open by appointment; write to Library in advance. Closed July to September.

This library has a card file of the orchestra's directors, soloists, concerts, and works performed; about 1,000 orchestral works, 1,000 books, 300 autographs, programs, photos, recordings, scrapbooks from its founding in 1842.

Archiv der Stadt Wien
Stiege IV, Rathaus. Tel: (0222) 42804
Hours: Monday to Friday 8:00 AM to 6:30 PM.

This archive contains documents relating to the history of the municipality, manuscripts associated with composers, wills of Haydn, Beethoven.

Österreichische Gesellschaft für Musik [Ben. 54]
Hanuschgasse 3. Tel: (0222) 524299
Hours: Monday to Friday 9:00 AM to 1:00 PM. Closed July and August.

This society, guided by the efforts of the Austrian musicologist Rudolf Klein (see Harald Goertz's *Österreichisches Musikhandbuch,* written in collaboration with Klein), disseminates information about Austria's musical resources.

Akademie (formerly Hochschule) für Musik und darstellende Kunst, Bibliothek [Ben. 47]
Lothringerstrasse 18. Tel: 561685
Hours: Monday to Friday 9:00 AM to 12:30 PM; 2:00 PM to 4:30 PM. Closed Christmas, Easter, summer, and semester vacations (see Hochschule under Conservatories).

Gesellschaft der Musikfreunde in Wien, Bibliothek [Ben. 48]
Bösendorferstrasse 12. Tel: 658681
Hours: Monday, Wednesday, Friday 9:00 AM to 1:00 PM. Closed July to September.

This rich collection includes autographs of Beethoven, Schubert, Mozart, Haydn, and contemporaries as well as early prints of these composers and *Kleinmeister* of the eighteenth and nineteenth centuries. Theoretical works of the seventeenth and eighteenth centuries, libretti, letters, iconography, programs of the Society and other theaters for 1830–1854 are also to be found here. In addition to collections of Brahms and Mahler material, the library has been enriched through personal bequests of Brahms, Köchel, and Gerber. Among the manuscripts to be found here are Schubert's *Unfinished* Symphony, Mozart's G Minor Symphony, the dedication copy of Beethoven's *Eroica* with Napoleon's name scratched out, a manuscript of the *Les Adieux* Sonata, and the autograph of Brahms' *Requiem.*

Bibliothek des Konservatoriums der Stadt Wien (Library of the Vienna Conservatory)
Johannesgasse 4a. Tel: 527747 and 527381
Hours: Monday to Friday 8:00 AM to noon; 1:00 PM to 5:30 PM. Closed July and August.

Graphische Sammlung Albertina (*see Concert Halls*)
Augustinerstrasse 1. Tel: 524232
Museum Hours: Monday to Friday 10:00 AM to 4:00 PM; Saturday and Sunday 10:00 AM to 1:00 PM, and Wednesday 10:00 AM to 6:00 PM. Closed Sunday in July and August.
Library Hours: Monday to Friday 1:00 PM to 4:00 PM. Closed July and August.

This is the largest collection of drawings, engravings, and prints in the world, with a famous section on Dürer.

Archiv der Wiener Konzerthausgesellschaft
Lothringerstrasse 20 (in the Konzerthaus building). Tel: 724686
Hours: no fixed hours; open by special arrangement. Closed July and August, all Catholic holidays, Saturday and Sunday.

Bibliothek und Archiv des Burgtheaters

Goethegasse 1.
Hours: weekdays from 9:00 AM to 4:00 PM and closed when the theaters are.

The collection here has manuscripts, books, periodicals, promptbooks, photographs, designs and technical plans, programs, playbills, press clippings, sketches of costumes, objects, portraits, and busts.

Archiv historischer Schallplatten und Schallplattenantiquariat Roland Teuchtler (Roland Teuchtler's Historical Archive of Records)

Schottengasse 3a. Tel: (0222) 632249

This archive contains phonograph records of singers, instrumentalists, conductors, and actresses. Many of the records are early pressings. Borrowing permitted for lecture and research purposes.

Several monasteries with important musical collections will be found in Niederösterreich, the area around Vienna. Arrangements for visits to these libraries must be made in advance. See *Benton Directory* for details.

Göttweig (Benedictine). Important music archives rich in eighteenth-century sacred and secular music.

Heiligenkreuz (Cistercian).

Lilienfeld (Cistercian).

Zwettl (Cistercian). Vocal and instrumental music of eighteenth and early nineteenth centuries.

Melk (Benedictine). Library includes thirteenth- and fourteenth-century liturgical manuscripts, sixteenth-century masses, Haydn collection.

Klosterneuburg (Augustinian). Twelfth- to sixteenth-century manuscripts; sixteenth-century printed music.

Herzogenburg. Mainly baroque church music; some eighteenth-century symphonies.

Sammlung alter Musikinstrumenten des Kunsthistorisches Museums (Music Instrument Collection of the Art History Museum)

Neue Hofburg, Heldenplatz (entrance on the Heldenplatz at the Prince Eugen monument, across the Ring from the Kunsthistorisches Museum).
Hours: Monday and Thursday 10:00 AM to 3:00 PM; Sunday 9:00 AM to 1:00 PM.

Founded in 1580, this is the oldest collection of its kind in existence. Instruments from the sixteenth to the nineteenth centuries are housed here. The collection derived first from the holdings of Archduke Ferdinand II of Tyrol and the extensive collection of the Obizzi family. Today the collection of the Gesellschaft der Musikfreunde is also a part of the Museum. Besides Beethoven's Erard piano and the square piano used at home by Schubert, you will find the piano made for Clara and Robert Schumann by Conrad Graf in 1840, given by them to Brahms, and later donated by him to the Gesellschaft.

The Museum restores its instruments to playing order and gives five concerts a year in its recital hall (see Concert Halls), using instruments from its collection.

Österreichisches Museum für Volkskunde (*Instrument Collection in the Museum of Austrian Folklore*)
Laudongasse 15–19 (in the Schönbrunn Palace).
Hours: Tuesday to Saturday 9:00 AM to noon; Sunday 9:00 AM to 1:00 PM. Closed Monday.

Historisches Museum der Stadt Wien
Karlsplatz.
Hours: Tuesday to Friday 9:00 AM to 4:00 PM; Saturday 2:00 PM to 6:00 PM; Sunday 9:00 AM to 1:00 PM. Closed Monday.

Classic, romantic, and Biedermeier periods in Vienna's history from 1800 to 1850 can be seen in this museum. Also on view are Mahler's bust by Rodin (a copy is in the Neue Gallerie), a Webern bust, and Schoenberg's portrait of Berg.

Goethe-Museum
Augustinerstrasse 1.
Hours: Monday, Tuesday, Thursday, Friday 1:00 PM to 4:00 PM; Wednesday 10:00 AM to 6:00 PM; Saturday and Sunday 10:00 AM to 1:00 PM. Closed Sunday in July and August.

Museum des 20. Jahrhunderts (*Museum of the 20th Century*)
Schweizergarten.
Hours: Monday, Thursday, Friday, Saturday 10:00 AM to 4:00 PM; Wednesday 2:00 PM to 9:00 PM; Sunday 10:00 AM to 1:00 PM. Closed Tuesday.

You will find some material here on Schoenberg, Berg, and Webern.

Österreichisches Circus- und Clown-Museum
Karmelitergasse 9. Tel: 4278495
Hours: Wednesday, 5:00 PM to 7:00 PM; Saturday, 2:30 PM to 5:00 PM; Sunday, 9:00 AM to noon.

Circus documents, photographs, programs, posters, costumes, etc., as well as material relating to clowns may be found in this museum.

Internationales Opernarchiv
Billrothstrasse 74. Tel: (0222) 3637334
Hours: By appointment.

Bibliothek des Museums für Völkerkunde
Neue Hofburg. Tel. (0222) 576211, 576233, Ext. 18
Hours: Monday to Friday 9:00 AM to noon.

This museum has on display folk instruments of Austria and neighboring countries.

Niederösterreichische Landesbibliothek
Teinfaltstrasse 8. Tel: (0222) 635711
Hours: Monday to Friday 8:00 AM to 4:30 PM.

Niederösterreichisches Landesarchiv
Herrengasse 11. Tel: (0222) 635711
Hours: Monday to Friday 8:00 AM to 4:30 PM.

Österreichisches Staatsarchiv
Minoritenplatz 1. Tel: (0222) 635631, Ext. 591
Hours: Monday to Friday 9:00 AM to 6:00 PM.

For people doing musicological research requiring sociological and historical background, this is an excellent library to consult.

Städtische Büchereien (Municipal Library)
Skodagasse 20. Tel: (0222) 426163, 426164
Hours: Monday, Thursday 10:00 AM to noon and 2:00 PM to 7:00 PM; Tuesday, Friday 2:00 PM to 7:00 PM.

Archiv der Universität Wien
Dr. Karl-Lueger-Ring 1. Tel: (0222) 427611
Hours: Monday to Friday 9:00 AM to 4:30 PM.

Archiv des Wiener Schubertbundes
Lothringerstrasse 20.
Hours: by appointment.

Heimatmuseum Alsergrund
Währinger Strasse 43. Tel: (0222) 423575
Hours: 10:00 AM to noon except holidays and school vacations.

Special exhibits as well as permanent items relating to Beethoven, Bruckner, Mozart, and Schubert are on display here.

Josefstädter Heimatmuseum
Zeltgasse 7.
Hours: Tuesday 6:00 PM to 8:00 PM, Sunday 10:00 AM to noon (closed July and August).

Autographs of Josef Matthias Hauer are available here.

Mariahilfer Heimatmuseum
Gumpendorferstrasse 4. Tel: (0222) 5799965
Hours: Sunday 9:30 AM to noon; otherwise by prior arrangement.

Material on the old Theater an der Wien, on Haydn, on Fanny Elssler, all are available here.

Niederösterreichisches Landesmuseum
Herrengasse 9. Tel: 635711
Hours: Tuesday to Saturday 9:00 AM to 5:00 PM; Sunday 9:00 AM to 1:00 PM.

Haydn material is available here.

Conservatories and Schools

Hochschule für Musik und darstellende Kunst
Lothringerstrasse 18. Tel: 561685 and 726756

The Conservatory is located next door to the Konzerthaus building. The school is descended from the Konservatorium of the Gesellschaft der Musikfreunde, whose faculty included Bruckner and students Hugo Wolf, Gustav Mahler, Alban Berg, Hans Richter, Fritz Kreisler, Guido Adler, and Elly Ney. The present faculty includes many teaching musicians from the Opera and the Vienna Philharmonic. (See Libraries)

Musikwissenschaftliches Institut der Universität Wien
Universitätsstrasse 7. Tel: 427611, Ext. 627

Musiklehranstalten der Stadt Wien (the parent institution is the Konservatorium der Stadt Wien)
Johannesgasse 4a. Tel: 527747 and 527381
This conservatory has fifteen branch schools in several districts of Vienna. (See Libraries, Concert Halls.)

Konservatorium für Musik und Dramatische Kunst
Mühlgasse 28–30.

In addition to classes in vocal and instrumental techniques, courses are also given here in music therapy.

Horak-Konservatorium für Musik und darstellende Kunst
Hegelgasse 3. Tel: (0222) 523485

Note for Students Intending to Study in Austria: A knowledge of German is required for admission to Austrian conservatory and university programs. The Österreichischer Auslandsstudentendienst (ÖAD, or Austrian Foreign Students'

Service), located at the University of Vienna, Dr. Karl-Lueger-Ring 1, A-1010 Vienna, publishes a brochure entitled "Information for Foreign Students at Austrian Universities." Write for this booklet that describes admission requirements, tuition fees, living costs, accommodations, and student organizations.

Branches of the Austrian Tourist Offices also distribute this booklet; other branches of the ÖAD are located at Graz, Linz, and Innsbruck.

Federal Ministry of Education
Minoritenplatz 5.

Five scholarships are available to university students from the States for study at Austrian universities and other institutions of higher learning; open only to unmarried candidates. For information write Institute of International Education, 809 United Nations Plaza, New York 10017.

For Americans in need of assistance in educational or cultural matters, the following two organizations should be helpful:

Amerika-Haus
Friedrich Schmidt-Platz 2. Tel: (0222) 347511, 346611

As part of the U.S. Information Service, this organization promotes concerts by American musicians as well as offers exhibitions and films to help foster a good exchange between the Americans and the Austrians.

Library Hours: Monday to Friday 10:00 AM to 6:00 PM. Tel: 346611, ext. 4620 and 4631

Austro-American Institute of Education (Amerika-Institut)
Operngasse 4.

This organization specializes in educational programs such as the development of music programs here that could be coordinated with programs of music schools in the States.

The Institute of European Studies, with main offices in Chicago, has a Vienna Program at Freyung 4, 1010 Vienna. Tel: (0222) 632778

Vienna International Music Center
Sponsored by the Council on Intercultural Relations, an Illinois non-profit corporation, the Vienna International Music Center is a new and unique foreign study program that combines classroom and lecture work with applied music study and active participation in Vienna's musical life.

Courses range from performance workshops and vocal training to music history courses on Schoenberg and the Vienna School, art song, opera, and nineteenth-century music in general. Further information may be obtained from Vienna International Music Center at 3 South Prospect Avenue, Suite 8, Park Ridge, Illinois 60068.

Council on Intercultural Relations
Musicological Research and Graduate Studies can be undertaken at the Vienna International Music Center. Introductory and group programs are directed to aid doctoral candidates doing research at the Vienna International Music Center. For further information write to Director of Council on Intercultural Relations, Bindergasse 5–9, 1090 Vienna, Austria.

The Austrian Culture Seminar in Vienna, under the auspices of the American Council for the Study of Austrian Literature in cooperation with the Austrian Institute in New York and the Austro-American Institute of Education in Vienna, is now conducting seminars in late June for about two weeks. These meetings deal with various aspects of Austrian culture such as art, music, theater, literature, history, education, etc. Write Austrian Institute at 11 East 52nd Street, New York, N.Y. 10022 for further information.

Musical Landmarks

Among streets named for composers, you will find:
Friedrich von Flotow: Flotowgasse.
Albert Lortzing: Lortzinggasse.
Gustav Mahler: Mahlerstrasse.
Heinrich Marschner: Marschnergasse.
Otto Nicolai: Nicolaigasse.
Robert Schumann: Schumanngasse.
Ludwig Spohr: Spohrstrasse.
Carl Maria von Weber: Webergasse.
Felix Mendelssohn-Bartholdy: Mendelssohngasse.
Franz Liszt: Lisztstrasse.

The following restaurants are associated with several Viennese musicians:

Zur Linde; Lindenkeller (two parts of the same restaurant; opened in 1435)
Rotenturmstrasse 12.
Brahms and Fanny Elssler both dined here regularly.

Schoner
Siebensterngasse 19.
This restaurant, long a favorite of the Imperial family, was also frequented by Lehár and the various Strausses.

Griechenbeisl

Fleischmarkt 11.

Augustin, the popular balladeer, sang here during the Great Plague of 1689.

Historical Associations of the Old University of Vienna

The structure on the Universitätsplatz, which formerly housed the University, is now headquarters of the Akademie der Wissenschaften (Academy of Sciences).

The University has been host to famous lecturers on music since the fourteenth century. Paul Hofhaimer (1459–1537), organist and composer, was a student here and Eduard Hanslick (1825–1904), eminent critic, lectured here in the nineteenth century.

As for the Library, it is the largest German-language university library in existence.

Haydn's greatest triumph occurred in the Festsaal, Dr. Ignaz-Seipel-Platz 2. As an old man, he attended his last performance in the hall, a performance of *The Seasons,* for which he sat with the Imperial family and received great adulation from the enthusiastic audience.

Gravesites

Since it is extremely difficult to locate in one source the various gravesites of the numerous composers buried in and around Vienna, we have included a partial list of those buried in Zentral Friedhof XI, 234 Simmeringer Hauptstrasse, Tor II (Gate 2):

Ludwig van Beethoven—32A, No. 29.
Theodor Billroth—Group 14A, No. 7.
Johannes Brahms—32A, No. 26.
Karl Czerny—Group O, No. 49.
C. W. von Gluck—32A, No. 48.
Eduard Hanslick—Group 18, Row 1, No. 19.
Ludwig Köchel—Group 16A, Row 7, No. 23.
Josef Lanner—32A, No. 16
Theodor Leschetizky—Group O, No. 94.
Eusebius Mandyczewski—Group O, No. 99.
Wolfgang Amadeus Mozart—32A, No. 54 (only a memorial; gravesite unknown, but in St. Marxer Friedhof).
Hans Pfitzner—Group 14C, No. 16.
Gustav Richter—Group 81, Row 19, No. 40.
Antonio Salieri—Group O, No. 54.
Franz Schmidt—32B, No. 16.
Franz Schubert—32A, No. 28.
Johann Strauss the Elder—32A, No. 15.
Johann Strauss the Younger—32A, No. 27.

Franz von Suppé—32B, No. 16.

Hugo Wolf—Group 32A, No. 10)

At Evangelischer Friedhof of the Zentralfriedhof is the grave of Karl Goldmark—52A, Row 1.

At Grinzinger Friedhof, An der langen Lössen 2, is the grave of Gustav Mahler.

In graves at Hietzinger Friedhof, Maxingstrasse 15, (next to Schönbrunn Park), Fanny Elssler, Grillparzer (see above), and Alban Berg are buried.

Homes of Composers

So many musicians and composers have at one time or another called Vienna home that it would be virtually impossible to document all the places in this city that have served such a purpose. Several attempts have been made, the most recent being Rudolf Klein's remarkable *Beethoven Stätten in Österreich* (Vienna, 1970 and translated as *Beethoven Places in Austria*). It certainly ranks among the best. Another, much earlier attempt to tackle all places of musical interest in Austria, *Die Musikstätten Österreichs* (edited by Dr. Alexander Fischer, Vienna 1928) is hopelessly out of date.

A selective list of homes and/or temporary dwelling places of many famous composers appears below:

Beethoven

Beethoven's Erinnerungsräume (Memorial Rooms)

Mölkerbastei 8, "the Pasqualatihaus."

Hours: Tuesday to Saturday 9:00 AM to 4:00 PM; Sunday 9:00 AM to 1:00 PM.

This house was the composer's home during several periods between 1804 and 1814 while he worked on *Fidelio,* the *Fourth, Fifth,* and *Seventh* Symphonies, *Leonore, Egmont,* and *Coriolanus* Overtures. Alma Goethe, the granddaughter of the great poet, died here. Adalbert Stifter, who both painted and wrote, lived here as well.

Beethoven Gedenkräume (Memorial Rooms)

Probusgasse 6.

Hours: Tuesday to Friday, Sunday, holidays, 9:00 AM to 1:00 PM; Saturday 2:00 PM to 6:00 PM.

Bought by the city for renovation during the 1970 Beethoven Bicentennial, this is the place where Beethoven wrote the Heiligenstadt Will on October 6, 1802.

Doblinger Hauptstrasse 92.

Hours: Tuesday, Friday, Sunday, holidays, 9:00 AM to 1:00 PM; Saturday 2:00 PM to 6:00 PM.

Beethoven finished his *Third* Symphony, the *Eroica,* here in 1803. The building is currently undergoing renovation.

The following places are not museums, but are marked by plaques:

Lobkowitz 2: an elegant Baroque townhouse built around 1700, with a main portal by the great architect Fischer von Erlach, this is the site of the first performance of the *Erocia* before a private, invited audience. (See *Palaces,* under *Concert Halls.*)

Seilerstätte 21: Beethoven took lessons here from Haydn.

Ungargasse 5: During the winter of 1823–24, Beethoven lived here and completed the *Ninth* Symphony and the *Galitzin* Quartets.

Trautsohngasse 2: Parts of the *Missa Solemnis* were composed here during Beethoven's period of residence from 1819 to 1820.

Alserstrasse 30: the former site of Prince Lichnowsky's Palace where Beethoven found his first home in Vienna.

Schwarzpanierstrasse 15: Beethoven died here. He was consecrated in 1827 at the Minoritenkirche der Alservorstadt.

Hetzendorferstrasse 75a, where parts of the *Ninth* Symphony were composed, has today been replaced by a new building.

Grinzingerstrasse 64: Beethoven finished his *Pastorale* Symphony here in 1808.

Pfarrplatz 2, around the corner from Probusgasse 6 (see above), is a house built in the seventeenth century. Beethoven lived here in 1808 while working on the *Pastorale,* and he returned here in the summer of 1817. Nowadays, summer concerts of Schrammelmusik (sentimental Viennese popular music) are a frequent occurrence on the Pfarrplatz (the village square). This is the most famous Beethoven house in Vienna.

A Beethoven monument, designed in 1880 by Kaspar Zumbusch, stands on the Beethovenplatz in the Stadtpark. The monument, a more-than-lifesized bronze Prometheus with bound feet, was donated by admirers, including Brahms and Liszt.

Robert Weigl's Heiligenstädter Park statue, showing Beethoven "fleeing" the city and withdrawing to solitude, was erected in 1910.

See *Palaces* (under *Concert Halls*) for the Lobkowitz Palace, at Lobkowitzplatz 2, which is now the Institut Français. Beethoven participated in numerous musical evenings at Prince Lobkowitz's palace as well as at Rasumofsky's. Prince Rasumofsky, the Russian ambassador to Vienna, lived at Rasumofskygasse 23 in the vicinity of the Belvedere.

Pfarrplatz 3, the Beethoven-Gesellschaft (Beethoven Society).

Berg

Trauttmansdorfgasse 27: behind Schloss Schönbrunn, the corner house in the suburb of Hietzing is still the residence of Helene Berg, Alban Berg's widow

(See *Gravesites,* above, for his final resting place at Hietzinger Friedhof, Group 49, No. 24F).

Brahms

Karlsgasse 4: Brahms composed the double concerto and his four symphonies here. It is also the site of his death. Unfortunately, the original house no longer exists. (See Baden-Baden in Germany, and also Brahms monument in Hamburg.) Brahms also lived at Landstrasser Hauptstrasse 96 and Wollzeile 32. A Brahms monument stands in Resselpark (See *Gravesites* in Zentral Friedhof for his grave). Finally, the Brahmssaal, one of three auditoria in the Gesellschaft der Musikfreunde building, was named in his honor.

Bruckner

Bruckner lived at Hessgasse 7 and at Schottenring 5 from 1877 to 1895. Because of ill health, he was forced to move from his fourth-floor apartment to the *Kustodentrakt* (Caretaker's cottage) in Upper Belvedere Gardens. The composer also lived for a while at Währingerstrasse 41. The Bruckner monument is in the Stadtpark; the Bruckner-Gesellschaft is located at Bösendorferstrasse 12.

Dvořák

Dvořák lived at Wiedner Hauptstrasse 7.

Gluck

Gluck died at Wiedner Hauptstrasse 32. His body was exhumed from the Catholic Matzleinsdorfer Friedhof and buried in the Zentral Friedhof (see *Gravesites*). An inscription at the grave (Group 32A, No. 48) reads, *Hier ruht ein rechtschaffener deutscher Mann, ein eifriger Christ, ein treuer Gatte, Christoph Ritter Gluck, der erhabene Tonkunst Meister* (Here rests a righteous German man, an enthusiastic Christian, a true mate, Christoph Knight Gluck, the exalted music master). A monument to Gluck is beside the Karlskirche.

Goldmark

Karl Goldmark lived at Neubaugasse 49.

Haydn

Haydn Museum

Haydngasse 19.
Hours: Tuesday to Saturday 9:00 AM to 4:00 PM; Sunday 9:00 AM to 1:00 PM.

In 1793, Haydn bought this house for his wife. He lived here from January

1797 until his death in 1809. Unfortunately, none of the original furnishings survives. On exhibit at the house (in original or photocopies) are the first editions of *The Creation* and *The Seasons,* both of which Haydn wrote here, as well as other memorabilia. A Haydn monument is at Mariahilferstrasse.

After his expulsion from St. Stephen's choirboys (his voice had begun to break), in about the year 1750, Haydn lived at Kohlmarkt 11.

Eisenstadt, the capital of Burgenland, lies about thirty-five miles from Vienna. A trip there takes an hour by car and a little longer by the bus that leaves from Schillerplatz in Vienna and goes there directly. Haydn stayed in Eisenstadt from 1761 to 1790 as Kapellmeister, and from 1766 to 1778 he lived at Haydngasse 21, just a few steps from the castle, in a small house that today has become the Haydn Museum. Haydn is buried in the church at Eisenstadt, where his late masses had their first performances.

(See *Palaces.* Haydn often performed in the tiny chapel of the Esterhazy Palace in Vienna at Wallnerstrasse 4.)

Lanner

Josef Lanner was born at Mechitaristengasse 6; his monument is in the Rathauspark.

Lehár

Franz Lehár, composer of *The Merry Widow,* lived at Leopoldgasse 16, and also at Schikaneder Schlossel, Hackhofergasse 18. Some of the Lehár family still occupy the Schlossel; it may be visited by telephoning 36 28 863 in advance. Lehár conducted at the Theater an der Wien (see *Concert Halls*).

Liszt

Liszt lived at Freyung 6, Weihburggasse 3, and Schottenhof (1869–86) while on visits to Vienna from Budapest.

Mahler

Mahler lived in Auenbruggersgasse 2 and is buried in the Grinzinger Friedhof (see above). The Mahler-Gesellschaft is at Bösendorfer 12. Rodin's statue of Mahler is in the foyer of the Wiener Staatsoper, where he was director from May 11, 1897 to October 15, 1907.

Mozart

Mozart Erinnerungsraum ("Figarohaus")

Domgasse 5/Schulerstrasse 8.

Hours: Tuesday to Saturday 9:00 AM to 4:00 PM; Sunday, holidays 9:00 AM to 1:00 PM.

Mozart lived at this address from September 1784 to April 1787 and was visited here by Haydn and Beethoven. It was also here that he composed three of the "Haydn" Quartets, *Das Veilchen,* and *Le Nozze di Figaro.* Items on display include engravings, miniatures, and medals of Mozart and his family, the first announcement of Nissin's biography of Mozart (1828), the first German libretto of *Figaro,* the first Viennese piano score of it, and many other mementos of Mozart's works and his associates. The rooms have been restored to the appearance they might have had when Mozart lived there.

Other houses associated with Mozart are:
Singerstrasse 7 ("Deutsches Haus," 1781);
Milchgasse 1 (*Entführung*);
Währingerstrasse 26 (*Così fan tutte* and the last three symphonies; this house was destroyed.);
Rauhensteingasse 8, where he died; this house, too, was destroyed;
Tuchlaben 6: house where Mozart rented a room from the Weber family.

Mozart's wedding and funeral took place in the Stephansdom.

Mozart's grave in the St. Marxer Friedhof is unmarked. (This cemetery, located at Leberstrasse 6–8, is only open during daylight hours in the summer months.) Nobody knows which is his grave. A monument to him, however, can be found in the musicians' section of the Zentral Friedhof (see above). Another Mozart Denkmal (monument) is in the Burggarten.

Nicolai

Otto Nicolai, 30 Seilerstätte. Although born in Germany, Nicolai (1810–1849) became Kapellmeister at the court in Vienna, and later in Berlin. Of his many operas, surely the most famous is his *Die lustigen Weiber von Windsor* (*The Merry Wives of Windsor*) of 1849, based on the same Shakespeare play which provided Verdi with part of his *Falstaff* libretto.

Schubert

Schubert-Museum in Franz Schuberts Geburtshaus

Nussdorferstrasse 54.

Hours: Tuesdays to Saturday 9:00 AM to 4:00 PM; Sunday, holidays 9:00 AM to 1:00 PM.

Schubert-Sterbezimmer (Room Where Schubert Died)

Kettenbrückengasse 6.

Hours: Tuesdays to Saturdays 9:00 AM to 4:00 PM; Sunday, holidays 9:00 AM to 1:00 PM.

In the Stadtpark near the Ringstrasse is a stone figure of Schubert sitting with music book and pencil. Donated by the Wiener Männergesang-Verein, it was unveiled in 1827.

At Alserbachstrasse-Liechtensteinstrasse is a Schubert fountain by F. Mathuschek with a stone sculpture by T. Stundl. It was erected in 1929.

The best-known portrait of Schubert is at the Historisches Museum der Stadt Wien (see *Libraries*). Original autographs of the symphonies (all except the Fifth) are at the archives of the Gesellschaft der Musikfreunde. Most of the preserved Schubert autographs and Schubert prints are at the Wiener Stadtbibliothek, first floor, staircase IV; other autographs are at the Österreichische Nationalbibliothek and the archives of the Wiener Männergesang-Verein. The Schubertbund is located at Lothringerstrasse 20 (Concert Hall).

Schubert's original burial place was close to that of Beethoven, near the eastern park wall of the Schubert-Park (opposite Währingerstrasse 140). A copy of the original Dialer bust at the tomb stands in the park today. The remains of both Schubert and Beethoven were exhumed in 1888 and moved to honorary tombs in the Zentral Friedhof (see above). The sculpture on Schubert's honorary grave is by C. Kundmann, and dates from 1888.

Other houses associated with Schubert include:
Dr. Ignaz-Seipel Platz 1 (1803–13 as a choirboy),
Grünentorgasse 9–11 (Schubert's schoolhouse, 1818–25),
Säulengasse 3 (where he wrote *Erlkönig*),
Spielgasse 9 (where he wrote the *Unfinished* Symphony),
Seidengasse 3.

Schumann

Robert Schumann lived at Schönlaterngasse 7a.

Strauss, J.

Johann Strauss, the Elder
Born at Flossgasse 7 (house no longer standing), Strauss died at Kumpfgasse 11. His body was exhumed on June 13, 1904 from the Döblinger Ortsfriedhof and moved to the Zentral Friedhof, Group 32A, No. 15 (see *Gravesites*).

Johann Strauss, the Younger
Born at Lerchenfelderstrasse 15 (house no longer standing), Strauss wrote the "Blue Danube" at Praterstrasse 54, and composed *Die Fledermaus* at Maxingstrasse 18. He died at Johann-Strauss-Gasse 4, a house that no longer survives, and he was buried at the Zentral Friedhof, Group 32A, No. 27.

Strauss conducted concerts at a casino at Döblinger Hauptstrasse 76. There is a Strauss-Denkmal in the Stadtpark.

Strauss, R.

Richard Strauss lived at Jacquinstrasse 10.

Manuscripts of *Die Aegyptische Helena* and *Der Rosenkavalier* are at the Österreichische Nationalbibliothek (see Libraries).

Wagner

Wagner composed *Die Meistersinger* at Hadikgasse 72 in Penzing. He also lived at the Imperial Hotel for two months.

Weber

Weber composed *Euryanthe* while living at Kärntnerstrasse 49 and at Walfischgasse 1. A portrait of Weber is in the Musikverein; a bust is at the "Mozarthof," Rauhensteingasse 8.

Wolf

Hugo Wolf wrote his *Spanisches Liederbuch* and other songs in Perchtoldsdorfer Landhaus, Brunnergasse 26 in Pertoldsdorf (or Petersdorf, as the Viennese prefer to call it). Admission on application to the Hugo-Wolf-Zimmer here. The room has changed very little since the time he lived there.

Other houses inhabited by the peripatetic Wolf included:

Neuer Markt 15,
Schwindgasse 3,
Piaristengasse 32,
Brunnergasse 26.
Kumpfgasse 9.

At Villa Köchert on Billrothstrasse 68, he wrote the *Italienisches Liederbuch* and the Goethe songs. Melanie Köchert, wife of the court jeweler, was Wolf's close friend.

Wolf is buried in the Zentral Friedhof, Group 32A, No. 10. The monument there is by Hellmer.

Miscellaneous Landmarks

Drei Mäderl Haus

Schreyvogelgasse 10

A major tourist attraction, billed as the house of the heroines in Romberg's operetta *Lilac Time,* based on the life of Schubert. Unfortunately the story is not true!

Although it would be virtually impossible to see all the above-mentioned items on any ten tours of Vienna, Tours for the Friends of Music are available through the City Tourist Office. From May 1 to September 30, daily at 9:30 AM, a bus leaves the Vienna Opera House on a tour that includes Mozart's "Figaro House," the Schubert Museum, Lehár-Schlossl, the original tombstones of Beethoven and Schubert, several concert halls and other monuments of great composers.

Daily, except Monday and Wednesday, from June 25 to September 11, a bus leaves from the Österreichisches Verkehrsbüro at 5:30 PM for Vienna Operetta Tour. You are taken through Mödling, Gumpoldskirchen, and Baden. Dinner at a Baden restaurant is followed by a performance at the Badener Stadttheater. Tour ends at 11:00 PM at the Staatsoper.

Theater in der Josefstadt

Josefstadterstrasse 26. Tel: 427631

This theater is the oldest in Vienna after the Schönbrunner Schlosstheater. Weber's *Oberon,* Lortzing's *Zar und Zimmerman,* Auber's *La Muette de Portici* (billed here as *Die Stumme von Portici*), were all performed here. Konradin Kreutzer composed his *Nachtlage von Granada* for this theater.

In 1822 the building was completely redone, and Beethoven was commissioned to write the music for the consecration of the new house. On October 3, 1822, Beethoven conducted his overture *Weihe des Hauses* (op. 124).

No longer the scene of musical events, the Theater in der Josefstadt is now used only for plays. In addition to the Theater in der Josefstadt, several other buildings once used for musical events are either no longer in existence or function in different capacities. Among these are the Winterreitschule, the Landständische Saal (today the meeting hall of the Lower Austrian Provincial Government, at Herrengasse 13), the Jahn'sche Saal, the restaurant of Ignaz Jahn in which the Augarten concerts were held in the event of inclement weather (today a porcelain factory, at Obere Augartenstrasse 1), and the old Burgtheater, replaced by a new building in which only plays are given.

Musical Organizations

Arbeitsgemeinschaft der Musikerzieher Österreichs (AGMÖ) (Music Educators Society)

Lothringerstrasse 18.

Arbeitsgemeinschaft der Österreichischen Diözesankommissionen für Kirchenmusik (principal professional organization concerned with church music in various dioceses in Austria)

Stock im Eisen-Platz 3. Tel: 528749.

All questions relating to performance of church music can be directed here.

Various branches of the principal organization may be found in Eisenstadt,

Klagenfurt, St. Pölten, Linz, Salzburg, Graz, Innsbruck, and Vandans. Inquire at above address, Stock im Eisen-Platz 3, for details.

Arbeitsgemeinschaft Österreichisch-Ausländischer-Gesellschaften
Josefsplatz 6, Palais Palffy, 1010 Wien. Tel: (0222) 525681.

Austrian Society for Contemporary Music
Parkring 4.

BACH: Bachgemeinde Wien
Hadikgasse 56. Tel: (0222) 8210933

BEETHOVEN: Beethoven-Gesellschaft
Pfarrplatz 3.

BRUCKNER: Internationale Bruckner-Gesellschaft
Bösendorferstrasse 12 (Musikvereinsgebäude).
Sekretariat: Bäckerstrasse 18.

Bundesministerium für Unterricht und Kunst
(Ministry of Education and Art)
Minoritenplatz 5.

Bundesministerium für Wissenschaft und Forschung
(The Ministry of Science and Research) is also located at the above address.

CHOPIN: Internationale Chopin Gesellschaft, Wien
Lothringerstrasse 18. Tel: 561685

Freie Typographia, Chorvereinigung
Zieglergasse 25.

Freunde der Kammermusik
Berggasse 6/15. Tel: (0222) 3467034.

Gesängverein Österreichischer Eisenbahnbeamten
Lothringerstrasse 20.

Gesellschaft der Autoren, Komponisten und Musikverleger (AKM)
Baumanngasse 8. Tel: 625666.

Gesellschaft der Musikfreunde
Dumbagasse.

Gesellschaft für Musiktheater
Albertgasse 4/9. Tel: (0222) 431419

Gesellschaft zur Herausgabe von Denkmälern der Tonkunst in Österreich
Universitätsstrasse 7. Tel: 427611

HAUER: Josef Matthais Hauer-Kreis (first society for the promotion of 12-tone music)
Lichtenfelsgasse 7/2.

HAYDN: Joseph Haydn Gesellschaft Wien
Friesenplatz 7/2/15. Tel: 6296222

Institut für Wissenschaft und Kunst
Museumstrasse 5. Tel: (0222) 932256.

International Institute for Music, Dance, and Theater in the Audio-Visual Media (IMDT)
Metternichgasse 12. Tel: (0222) 725344.

International Music Center (Internationales Musikzentrum)
Vienna Academy of Music, Lothringerstrasse 18.

IGNM (Int'l Society for Contemporary Music) Austrian Section
Hanuschgasse 3/III. Tel: 524299.

International Society for Contemporary Music Universal Edition
Karlsplatz 6.

Internationale Gesellschaft für Neue Musik (IGNM)
Obere Bahngasse 6. Tel: 7259084

Internationales Kulturzentrum
Annagasse 20. Tel: (0222) 526951.

Kulturamt der Stadt Wien (Summer concerts)
Schmidtplatz 5. Tel: (0222) 42800/2730

LEHÁR: Franz-Lehár-Gesellschaft
Seilerstatte 13.

MAHLER: Internationale Mahler-Gesellschaft
Bösendorferstrasse 12.
Sekretariat: Obere Bahngasse 6. Tel: 7259084

MOZART: Mozart Boys Choir
Buchengasse 30.

MOZART: Mozart-Gemeinde
Metternichgasse 8.

MOZART: Mozart Society of Vienna
Bösendorferstrasse 12.

Musikalische Jugend Österreichs
Bösendorferstrasse 12. Tel: 656357.

Niederösterreichisches Tonkünstler-Orchester
Kolingasse 19.
Presents popular Sunday afternoon concerts in Vienna.

Österreichisch-Amerikanische Gesellschaft
Stallburggasse 2. Tel: (0222) 523982, 524784.

Österreichische Gesellschaft für Musik
Hanuschgasse 3. Tel: 524999.
Open Monday–Friday 9:00 AM–1:00 PM.
The country's music information center.

Österreichische Gesellschaft für Zeitgenössische Musik (ÖGZM)
Strassergasse 43–47. Tel: (0222) 3237372.

Österreichische Phonothek
Webgasse 2 A. Tel: 573669.

Österreichischer Gewerkschaftsbund (ÖGB) (Musicians' Union, similar to our 802)
Hohenstaufengasse 10–12.

Österreichischer Komponistenbund (ÖKB) (Austrian Composers Society)
Baumannstrasse 10.

Österreichischer Musikrat (Austrian Music Council)
Lothringerstrasse 18.

Österreichischer Rundfunk
Argentinierstrasse 30a. Tel: (0222) 65950.

Orchester des Österreichischen Rundfunks (Radio Orchestra)
Argentinierstrasse 30a.

Österreichischer Sängerbund
Kärntnerstrasse 51.

Österreichischer Volksliedwerk
Fuhrmanngasse 18/5.
This organization sponsors collections and assists in the formation of archives of Austrian folksongs.

Österreichisches Kulturzentrum
Josefsplatz 6, Palais Palffy. Tel: (0222) 525681/83.

Sängerbund für Wien und Niederösterreich
Kärntnerstrasse 51.

SCHMIDT: Franz-Schmidt-Gemeinde
Schliessfach 9. Tel: 7338323.

SCHUBERT: Wiener Schubertbund
Lothringerstrasse 20.

SCHÜTZ: Internationale Heinrich-Schütz-Gesellschaft, Austrian Section
Dorotheergasse 10. Tel: 523504.

Staatlich genehmigte Gesellschaft der Autoren, Komponisten und Musikverleger für Österreich (AKM)
Baumannstrasse 8–10. Tel: (0222) 731555.
A member of the Confédération Internationale des Sociétés d'Auteurs et Compositeurs (CISAC), this organization protects the rights of authors, composers, and publishers of Austria.

Staatsoper (*See Concert Halls*)

STRAUSS: Johann Strauss-Gesellschaft Wien
Rathaus. Tel: (0222) 42800.

STRAUSS: Internationale Richard Strauss Gesellschaft, c/o Staatsoper
Opernring 2. Tel: 527636.

Studio Burgenland
Argentinierstrasse 29. Tel: (0222) 6595.

Studio Niederösterreich
Argentinierstrasse 29. Tel: (0222) 6595

Studio Wien
Argentinierstrasse 30a. Tel: (0222) 6595.

Verband der Arbeiter-Musikvereine Österreichs (VAMO)
Fischerstiege 4. Tel: (0222) 639165

This organization promotes musical activities of amateurs.

Verband der Bühnenverleger Österreichs
Kiningergasse 6.

Vienna Chamber Opera
Argentinierstrasse 30a.

Vienna Musica Antigua Ensemble
Minoritenplatz 2, Arkadentrakt. Tel. 635531.

Vienna Octet

Vienna Philharmonic
Bösendorferstrasse 12.

Vienna Symphony Orchestra
Lothringestrasse 20.

Deutschmeister Kapelle

Brass band founded in 1741 as the band for the Emperor's house infantry regiment.

Volksoper (See Concert Halls)

WAGNER: Österreichischer Richard-Wagner-Verband
Schwindgasse 19/14. Tel: 657293.

WEBERN: International Webern Society
c/o Österreichische Gesellschaft für Musik
Hanuschgasse 3.

Wiener Konzerthausgesellschaft
Lothringerstrasse 20. Tel: (0222) 724686.

Wiener Konzerthausgesellschaft Chamber Orchestra
(same address as Vienna Symphony)

The society provides much of the new music heard in Vienna.

Wiener Kulturkreis
Prinz Eugen-Strasse 3. Tel: (0222) 736115.

Wiener Männergesangverein
Bösendorferstrasse 12.

Wiener Sängerknaben

Founded by Maximilian I in the late fifteenth century. Schubert was a member.

WOLF: International Hugo Wolf Society
Bäckerstrasse 18.

Miscellaneous

Pietro Metastasio (1698–1782), court poet and librettist, lived in the Michaelers Stiftungshaus, adjoining St. Michael's Kirche, at the corner of Kohlmarkt 11. His tomb is in the Minoritenkirche.

The poet and playwright **Hugo von Hofmannsthal** (1874–1929), a prominent citizen of Vienna, who was also largely responsible for the success of the Salzburg Festival, lived in Vienna many years. His father had been president of one of the foremost synagogues there. He first lived at Rennweg 12; later he moved to Himmelpfortgasse 17, an old house full of the traditional Viennese atmosphere. Then he moved to the old Fuchs Villa, now known as the Hofmannsthal Villa, in the Rodaun section of Vienna at Johann Stelzer Gasse 5.

In his student days **Stefan Zweig** (1881–1942) lived at Kochstrasse 8. Both Zweig and Hofmannsthal are familiar to musicians as librettists for Richard Strauss.

The dramatist **Franz Grillparzer** (1791–1872) lived much of his life in Vienna, where he was once a neighbor of Beethoven and a close friend of Schubert. He was born in the *Haus zum goldenen Wagen* at Bauernmarkt 10 (it has since been rebuilt). In 1808 he lived at Grinzingerstrasse 64 at the same time as Beethoven, and the house is now called the Beethoven-Grillparzer Haus. He was also a resident of the Schottenhof, Freyung 6, of which only the walls remain. In the Municipal Museum, you will find a Grillparzer room with his own furniture.

AUSTRIA, GENERAL

Opera Houses and Concert Halls

Besides Graz and Linz (see below), the following cities have concert halls or opera houses of significance: Baden bei Wien, Innsbruck, Klagenfurt, and St. Pölten.

Graz

Vereinigte Bühnen Stadt Graz Opernhaus (*Opera house and theater*)
Kaiser Josef-Platz 10.
Mailing Address: Vereinigte Bühnen, A-8010 Graz. Tel: 76451
Season: September 26 to June 30; closed July 1 to August 17, December 24, Good Friday, and May 1.
Box Office: Landhaus, Herrengasse 11. Tel: 87289
Hours: Monday to Saturday 9:00 AM to 2:00 PM and half an hour before performance.
Seating capacity: Opera house: 1400; Theatre: 600
Standing Room: sold half an hour before performance.
Customary Dress: for premiere, formal evening clothes, otherwise dark suit and cocktail dress.
Opera, operettas, plays, musicals.

Linz

Landestheater Linz
Promenade 39. Tel: (07222) 23254, 24305
Mailing Address: Postfach 271, A-4010 Linz.
Season: end of September to beginning of July; closed July to September, December 24, and Good Friday.
Box office: addresses same as above. Tel: Grosses Haus: 24242; Tel: Kammerspiele: 24493
Hours: Tuesday to Saturday 9:00 AM to 12:30 PM and 4:00 PM to 8:00 PM; Sunday and holidays 4:00 PM to 7:30 PM.
Seating capacity: Grosses Haus: about 700; Kammerspiele: About 400
Opera, operettas, musicals, ballet, plays.

Libraries and Museums

Like Germany, Austria possesses a vast treasury of musical material. In addition to *Benton,* a far more comprehensive source of information (on Austrian libraries and museums with extensive collections of music, music manuscripts, and instruments) is Harald Goertz's *Österreichisches Musikhandbuch,* published by Jugend und Volk Verlagsgesellschaft, Wien-München 1971.

For example, collections of sacred and early musical manuscripts as well as some early prints will be found at monasteries or churches in the following cities: Bregenz, Breitenau, Enns, Fiecht, Gmund, Gmunden, Göttweig, Graz, Güssing, Heiligenkreuz, Herzogenburg, Klagenfurt, Klosterneuberg, Krems, Kremsmunster, Lilienfeld, Maria Taferl, Mariazell, Melk, Michaelbeuern, Neuberg, Reichersberg, Rein, St. Florian, St. Lambrecht, St. Paul im Lavanttal, Schlägl, Schlierbach, Seckau, Seitenstetten, Solbad Hall, Sonntagberg, Stams, Tulln, Vorau, Wilhering, and Zwettl.

Extensive folksong archives (Volksliedarchiv) are located in the following cities: Bregenz, Eisenstadt, Graz, Innsbruck, Klagenfurt, and Linz.

Collections of interest to visitors include the following:

Arnsdorf

Franz Xaver Gruber-Museum

5112 Arnsdorf 9.
Hours: advance appointment with Director, Sepp Aigner.

Baden

Beethoven Gedenkstätte (*see Musical Landmarks*)

Rathausgasse 10, 2500 Baden.
Hours: daily except Thursday 9:00 AM to 11:00 AM, 3:00 PM to 5:00 PM.

Beethoven stayed here during the summers of 1821–23.

Bad Ischl

Haenel-Pancera-Familien-Museum

Concordiastrasse 3, 4820 Bad Ischl-Kaltenbach.
Hours: May 1 to Sept. 30, daily 9:00 AM to 5:00 PM.

Scores of Brahms, Liszt, Grieg, Richard Strauss, and others on display.

Heimatmuseum

Franz Lehár Kai 8, 4820 Bad Ischl. Tel: (06132) 2292
Hours: May 15 to September 30, daily 9:00 AM to noon, and 2:00 PM to 5:00 PM.

Lehár-Villa (see Musical Landmarks)
Franz Lehár-Kai 8, 4820 Bad Ischl. Tel: (06132) 2992
Hours: May 15 to September 15, daily 9:00 AM to noon and 2:00 PM to 5:00 PM.

Gmunden

Museum der Stadt Gmunden
Kammerhofgasse A-4810 Gmunden. Tel: (07612) 3381 ext. 76

Brahms Collection: autographs (letters), contemporary photograph and portrait collection, concert programs, personal objects.

Graz

Museum für Kulturgeschichte und Kunstgewerbe
Neutorgasse 45, 8010 Graz. Tel: (03122) 75541 ext. 458, 808
Hours: by appointment, Monday to Saturday 9:00 AM to noon.

An excellent display of early musical instruments, mostly of the nineteenth century, is on view here.

Stadtmuseum
Eggenberger Allee 90, Schloss Eggenberg, 8020 Graz.

This museum has various memorial rooms dedicated to the works of composers like Hugo Wolf and Joseph Marx as well as numerous minor Austrian composers. It also has a collection of early instruments.

Hallein

Keltenmuseum (formerly Stadtmuseum)
Hallein 5400.
Hours: May 1 to September 30, daily 9:00 AM to noon and 1:00 PM to 6:00 PM.

In the Franz Xaver Gruber memorial room, you will find the manuscript of his "Silent Night, Holy Night."

Innsbruck

Innsbruck has a rich musical past, largely due to the city's position as an imperial center in the Renaissance. Emperor Maximilian I held court there. (His palace was damaged by earthquake and fire; it was rebuilt under Empress Maria Theresa in the eighteenth century.) Among the musicians in residence in Maximilian's famous musical establishment, around 1500, were the celebrated organist Paul Hofhaimer (1459–1537) and composer Heinrich Isaac (c. 1450–1517). Maximilian's tomb is in the Court Church. (The wooden organ in this church, still in use, dates from about 1600.)

Musikwissenschaftliches Institut der Universität Innsbruck [Ben. 15]
Innrain 52, A-6020 Innsbruck. Tel: (05222) 22701. ext. 472 02 473
Hours: Monday to Friday, 9:00 AM to noon, 3:00 PM to 6:00 PM; Saturday, 9:00 AM to noon.

Linz

Oberösterreichisches Landesmuseum [Ben. 25]
Museumstrasse 14, 4020 Linz. Tel: (07222) 23455
Hours: for the display, go to Linzer Schloss, Tummelplatz 10, Tuesday to Saturday mornings and afternoons; Sunday mornings only. Selected instruments are on exhibit. The displays change regularly.

The museum contains a rich collection of historical musical instruments of the seventeenth and eighteenth centuries.

Mödling

Beethoven Gedenkstätte (*see Landmarks*)
Hauptstrasse 79, 2340 Mödling.
Hours: apply in advance at the municipal museum (Stadtmuseum), Mödling.

Missionsmuseum St. Gabriel
Gabrielerstrasse 171, 2340 Mödling, St. Gabriel. Tel: (02236) 2117
Hours: daily 9:00 AM to 6:00 PM; tours by prior arrangement from October 1 to May 31 from 9:00 AM to 4:00 PM.

The museum owns a collection of non-Western musical instruments.

Museum der Stadt Mödling
Museumsplatz 2, 2340 Mödling. Tel: (02236) 4159
Hours: Saturday 3:00 PM to 6:00 PM; Sunday and holidays 10:00 AM to noon and 3:00 PM to 6:00 PM. Closed during the winter.

Early instruments and a Wagner manuscript on display here.

Raiding

Franz Liszt Museum
Lisztstrasse 42, 7321 Raiding. Tel: (02619) 2059/92
Hours: daily from March 1 to October 31; at other times, by prior arrangement.

Photos of the composer, letters, documents, newspaper clippings, and records of his music are available here.

Rohrau

Haydn Gedenkstätte (*see Landmarks*)
2471 Rohrau.
Hours: March 15 to November 15, Tuesday to Saturday 9:00 AM to 5:00 PM.

St. Florian

Bruckner Gedenkräume
4490 St. Florian, Stift.
Hours: by prior arrangement
Memorabilia from Bruckner's estate is available here.

Conservatories and Schools

Graz

Hochschule für Musik und darstellende Kunst
Nicolaigasse 2, A-8010 Graz. Tel: (03122) 97244

Musikwissenschaftliches Institut der Universität Graz
Mozartgasse 3, A-8010 Graz. Tel: 31581, ext. 383
Catalog or brochure available from: Dekanat der philosophischen Fakultät.

Innsbruck

Konservatorium der Stadt Innsbruck
Museumstrasse 17a. Tel: (05222) 23447

Musikwissenschaftliches Institut der Universität Innsbruck
Innrain 52, Third floor; A-6020 Innsbruck. Tel: 26741, ext. 473
Catalog available from: Rektorat der Universität Innsbruck.

Linz

Musikschule der Stadt Linz
Lederergasse 7.

Bruckner-Konservatorium des Landes Oberösterreich
Wildbergstrasse 18, 4020 Linz. Tel: (07222) 31306/08

Every year at the end of the school semester, public concerts are given by the chamber orchestra of the school. These concerts are given in both St. Florian and Linz.

Klagenfurt

Kärntner Landeskonservatorium
Miesstalerstrasse 8, 9020 Klagenfurt. Tel: (04222) 83197

Note: music education, applied music, and musicology are considered separate branches of musical instruction. Although numerous teacher training schools and adult education courses are listed in that most informative book, *Österreichisches Musikhandbuch,* we have chosen not to list them.

Summer Courses

Graz

Graz American Institute of Musical Studies
Mailing Address: Richard Owens, 3000 Amherst, Dallas, Texas 75225.

Eight-week intensive course for singers and pianists. Includes a chance to attend the Salzburg Festival.

Innsbruck

Internationale Sommerakademie für alte Musik
Blasius-Buber-Strasse 12, 6020 Innsbruck.

Ossiach

Internationales Musikforum Ossiachersee
A-957 Ossiach/See. Tel: (04243) 4975

Late June to early July. Seminars, lectures, and concerts.

Musical Landmarks

Altmünster

Many musicians have been attracted to Altmünster, the oldest settlement on the Traunsee. Of those musicians who have lived here at one time or another, the most notable are Brahms and Wagner. Wagner composed *Tristan und Isolde* in Otto Wesendonk's villa here.

Baden bei Wien

Hours: May 1 to October 31, daily (except Thursday), 9:00 AM to 11:00 AM and 3:00 PM to 5:00 PM; November 1 to April 30, Tuesday 3:00 PM to 5:00 PM, Thursday 9:00 AM to 11:00 AM and Saturday 3:00 PM to 5:00 PM. PLEASE RING DOORBELL.

Transportation from Vienna: bus from the Südbahn.

Ludwig van Beethoven lived in the house at 10 Rathausgasse in the summer months of 1821, 1822, and 1823. In the last year there (1823), he sketched the greater portion of the Ninth Symphony. The *Missa Solemnis* was completed there. The two rooms on the first floor are maintained as a memorial to the composer.

Badgastein

Franz Schubert stayed here at the Gasthaus Straubinger.

Bad Ischl

Lehár-Villa

Hours: May 15 to September 30, 9:00 AM to noon and 2:00 PM to 5:00 PM.

Note: Bad Ischl was the setting for Eisenstein's summer house in Johann Strauss' *Die Fledermaus.*

Lehár-Villa is now maintained as a Lehár museum. Franz Lehár wrote the majority of his works here and died here in 1948. The rooms remain as they were in his lifetime.

Oscar Straus (composer of such operettas as *The Chocolate Soldier*) died in Bad Ischl in 1954.

Eisenstadt

Kirche ("Haydnkirche") mit Kalvarienberg und Haydnmausoleum

Early in the eighteenth century, Prince Paul Esterhazy had a church and a Kalvarienberg built in Eisenstadt. The six late Haydn Masses, written one-a-year for the Esterhazy Princess's name-day in September, were given their first performances in this church. The body of Joseph Haydn lies in an elaborate white marble tomb in the crypt of the church. He was originally buried in the Hundsthurm Churchyard in Vienna, but was later reburied in Eisenstadt on June 5, 1954, attended by official ceremony.

Schloss Esterhazy (Esterhazy Palace)

The Esterhazy Palace was the home of the famous Hungarian aristocratic family whom Haydn served as kapellmeister and composer for a good portion of his life. The Palace has an Esterhazy archive (see Libraries) and is open to the public.

Haydns Wohnhaus

Josef Haydngasse 21, A-7000 Eisenstadt.

Hours: daily, 9:00 AM to noon and 1:00 PM to 5:00 PM. Easter Sunday to October 31; closed annually November 1 to Saturday before Easter.

This was Haydn's home from 1766 to 1788. It is now open to the public as a Haydn museum. It contains iconography, early prints, manuscripts, letters of Haydn and contemporaries. It also contains relics and mementos of Franz Liszt and the ballerina Fanny Elssler.

Liszt-Geburtshaus

Lisztstrasse 42, Raiding (near Eisenstadt).

Transportation from Vienna to Eisenstadt: trains from south station in Süd Tiroler Platz. Buses from Schiller Platz 4.

Contained here are souvenirs of Liszt in the house in which he was born. Admission is granted upon application to the above address.

There is a Liszt monument at Esterhazy Platz.

Linz

Abbey of St. Florian (south of Linz)

Anton Bruckner was the organist in this abbey. He is now buried in a grave under the organ of the abbey church.

Bruckner was also organist at the Old Cathedral (also called St. Ignatius Church or Jesuit Church) in Linz from 1856 to 1868.

Rohrau

Haydn-Gedenkstätte Rohrau (The Haydn Memorial House in Rohrau)

Hours: March 15 to November 15, Tuesday to Sunday, 9:00 AM to 5:00 PM.

The small thatched farmhouse in Rohrau, which the wheelwright Matthias Haydn is supposed to have built himself about 1728, is one of Austria's important memorials. Here Franz Joseph Haydn was born on March 31, 1732; his brother Michael was born in this same house on September 14, 1737. The sign with the inscription "To Haydn" made this house a popular monument. In 1877, the male choir, Arion, of which Johann Strauss was a member, unveiled the first memorial plaque. In 1899, the roof was destroyed by fire; in 1909, the house, of which the larger room remained intact, was outwardly restored. It was only after the government of Lower Austria had acquired the property in 1958 that a renovation in the original style could begin. A dignified memorial was erected finally in 1959.

Steyr

Anton Bruckner composed his Sixth Symphony in the Parish House in Steyr. There is a Bruckner room in the Mesnerhaus.

Historical Organs

For those who should like to know the location of historical organs (from the sixteenth to the nineteenth centuries) in the numerous towns and villages of Austria, the following selective list may prove helpful.

Absam
Adriach
Alpbach
Altenburg
Arnoldstein
Bartholomäberg
Baumgartenberg
Bergheim
Birkfeld
Bludesch
Bruck an der Mur
Brückl
Brunnental
Churburg
Edlitz
Ehrenhausen
Eisenstadt
Frauenberg/Admont
Frauenberg/Leibnitz
Frauenberg Ma. Rehkogel
Gleink
Göss (Loeben)
Götzis
Gurk
Hafnerberg
Herzogenburg
Höchst
Hollabrunn
Innsbruck
Kaisers/Lechtal
Klasdorf
Kappl/Paznaun
Karnabrunn
Kefermarkt
Klosterneuburg
Lambach
Lilienfeld
Linz
Maria Dreieichen
Maria Saal
Matrei in Osttirol
Mauern bei Steinach
Melk
Mondsee
Münsteuer
Münzbach
Neumarkt im Mühlkreis
Oberalm
Obernberg am Brenner
Obervellach
Ossiach
Pöllau
Pöllauberg
Reichersberg
Ried im Oberinntal
Röschitz
Rohrbach im Mühlviertel
Salzburg
St. Florian
St. Leonhard/Kundl
St. Pölten
St. Veit am Vogau
St. Wolfgang
Schlägl
Schlierbach
Schwaz
Seckau
Sibratsgfäll

Solbad Hall
Sonntagberg
Spiss/Samnaun
Stadl-Paura
Stadt Schlaining
Stams
Strassburg in Kärnten
Traun
Tulln
Udersn/Zillertal
Unterretzbach
Unterweissenbach
Viktring
Vill
Vinaders
Waldhausen
Wels
Wien
Wilhering
Wolfurt
Wörgl
Zwettl

Festivals

Bad Ischl

Operetta Festival
Dates: mid-July to mid-September.
Box Office: Kurhaus, Bad Ischl. Tel: (06132) 3766
Advance Sales: Operettenbüro, Pfarrgasse 2, A-4820 Bad Ischl.
Operettas.
Performances begin at 8:00 PM.

Baden bei Wien

Operetta Festival
Dates: July and August.
Summer Arena.

Bregenz

Festspielgemeinde Bregenz (Bregenz Festival)
Kornmarktstrasse 6, 6900 Bregenz. Tel: 23005
Dates: held from the end of July to the end of August.
Box Office: address above.
Customary Dress: evening clothes.
Seating capacity: Seebühne (floating stage), 6400. Theater, 690.
Opera, concerts, operettas, plays, chamber music, ballet.
For tickets in the United States apply to your travel agent or the Austrian National Tourist Office, 545 Fifth Avenue, New York 10017. Tel: 212 697 0651.

For housing accommodations, write to Verkehrsverein Bregenz, 3 Weiherstrasse, 6900 Bregenz. Correspondents are asked to indicate the exact number of people, exact number of nights, and whether hotel, pension, or private family accommodations are preferred. In addition, it is desirable to state whether you are traveling by train or car.

Advertised as the "world's largest open air theater," the main attraction at the Bregenz Festival seems to be the "floating stage" on Lake Constance.

Graz

Grazer Sommerfestspiele (Graz Summer Festival)
Steirischer Herbst, Landaus, 8010 Graz. Tel: 76311/224
Dates: mid-June to mid-July.

Opera, operetta, drama, orchestral concerts, ensembles, church music.

Styrian Autumn
Generalsekretariat des Steirischen Herbstes,
38 Mandellstrasse, A-8010 Graz. Tel: (03122) 77307, 77309, 77310.
Dates: three weeks in October.
Box Office: Zentralkartenbüro, 7 Herrengasse, A-8010 Graz. Tel: 81481

Contemporary music, theater, ballet, chamber music, organ recitals, choral concerts, multimedia programs.

For housing accommodations, write to Steiermärkisches Landesreisebüro, 14 Hauptplatz, A-8010 Graz. Tel: 76456

At the Styrian Autumn Festival, the emphasis is on avantgarde music, including many works by young composers.

Klagenfurt

Woche der Begegnung
Rathaus, Neuer Platz 1. Tel: (04222) 83681, ext. 432
9020 Klagenfurt.
Dates: mid-June.

The Festival consists of a series of symposia that deal with cultural problems. Each year the festival focuses on a different area; in 1971, for instance, the topic under discussion was "Musik und Zukunft." The meetings and concerts take place in the Festsaal des Rathauses Klagenfurt, in the Konzerthaus, and in the Studio Klagenfurt des ORF (Österreichischer Rundfunk Gesellschaft mbH).)

Mörbisch

Seespiele Mörbisch
Seebühne am Seeufer.

Mailing Address: Intendanz der Seespiele Mörbisch. Tel: 02685/8220
Dates: last Sunday in June to next-to-last Sunday in August.
Box Office: Österreichisches Verkehrsbüro, Österreich-Abteilung/IIIE, 7 Friedrichstrasse, 1043 Vienna. Tel: 572315
Hours: Monday to Friday, 8:00 AM to 6:00 PM; Saturday 8:00 AM to 1:00 PM.
Customary Dress: warm, with protection in case of rain.
Seating capacity: 2400

Operetta; occasionally comic opera.

For housing accommodations, write to the above box office address.

Ossiach

Internationales Musikforum Ossiachersee

A-9570 Ossiach/See, Kärnten. Tel: (04243) 497
Dates: end of June through beginning of July.

A series of seminars, lectures, and concerts built around a theme; for example, in 1969 the theme was: "Freedom and License, Order and Constraint—As Reflected in Music.

Carinthischer Sommer (Carinthian Summer Festival)

Carinthischer Sommer, A-9570 Ossiach.
Dates: mid-July to the end of August.

This festival includes the International Music Forum, a wide variety of concerts and recitals, and many master classes and seminars. There are also visiting orchestras, soloists, and conductors.

Salzburg

Mozart Week

International Mozarteum Foundation, Salzburg. Tel: (06222) 73155
Dates: one week at the end of January.

Symphony, opera, chamber music, recitals. Many prominent Austrian and foreign artists take part in this Festival.

Salzburger Festspiele (Salzburg Festival)

Grosses Festspielhaus,
Hofstallgasse 1. Tel: (06222) 87441
Dates: end of July to end of August.
Box Office: Festspielhaus.
Mailing Address: Kartenbüro der Salzburger Festspiele, Postfach 140, A-5010 Salzburg.

They will send detailed program in English. Ticket sales by mail begin mid-December. The few tickets left by summer are sold at the Festspielhaus box office. (There are decent acoustics in the Festspielhaus; most seats are good). Most performances begin at 8:00 PM or at 8:30 PM.

Hours: Monday to Friday, 9:00 AM to noon, 3:00 PM to 6:00 PM from April to the end of August.

Authorized ticket agencies in Salzburg:

American Express, 5 Mozartplatz.

Wagons-Lits/Cook, 1 Münzgasse.

Reisebüro Dr. Degener & Co., 4 Linzer Gasse.

Landesreisebüro, 16 Dreifaltigkeitsgasse.

Theaterkartenbüro Neubar, 14 Getreidegasse.

Theaterkartenbüro Polzer, 22 Bergstrasse.

These travel agencies charge twenty percent for their services.

Ticket agency in the United States: Austrian National Tourist Office, 545 Fifth Avenue, New York, 10017. Tel: 212 697 0651

There is no extra charge for the services of the Austrian National Tourist Office.

There is no standing room at the Festival.

Seating capacity: Grosses Festspielhaus 2170, Kleines Festspielhaus 1379, Felsenreitschule, 1560, Kollegienkirche 691, Domplatz 2414, Mozarteum (Grosser Saal) 867, Landestheater 784, Residenz 802.

Customary Dress: evening dress.

Note: A very special Festival Service exists by which you can

1. receive the preliminary program and the detailed program of the Salzburg Festival;
2. be informed about casts;
3. be informed about world premieres and first performances;
4. be notified promptly about important changes in casts, etc.;
5. receive any additional information about the Salzburg Festival.

For this service, send AS 30 to one of the following banks with a covering letter explaining your request (in English):

Landes-Hypothekenanstalt Salzburg, Kto. Nr. 13.035.

Salzburger Sparkasse, Kto. Nr. 280.

Bankhaus Carl Spängler & Co. Salzburg, Kto. Nr. 18.042.

Creditanstalt-Bankverein, Filiale Salzburg, Kto Nr. 95-24.059.

Länderbank, Filiale Salzburg, Kto. Nr. 8.443.713.

Be sure to mention the reference "Festival-Service."

For housing accommodations, write to Stadtverkehrsbüro, Salzburg.

One of the most famous festivals in Europe, the Salzburg Festival was started in 1920 by poet-playwright Hugo von Hofmannsthal, stage director Max Reinhardt, and composer-conductor Richard Strauss. Reinhardt created *Jedermann,* Hofmannsthal's adaptation of the *Everyman* story, on the lovely square in front of the Salzburg Cathedral (Domplatz), a production that still enthralls Festival audiences every Sunday at 5:00 PM.

The Salzburg Festival attracts a record number of visiting orchestras, famous soloists, and other performers to participate in its many offerings each summer.

Salzburger Schlosskonzerte (*The Salzburg Pre-Festival Summer Palace Concerts*)

Kartenbüro der Salzburger Schlosskonzerte, 9 Makartplatz, Salzburg. Tel: 74363

Dates: end of June to the end of July.

Box Office: above address. Performances usually start 9:00 PM during the summer.

Authorized Ticket Agencies:

Kartenbüro Neubaur, 14 Getreidegasse.

Kartenbüro Polzer, 22 Bergstrasse.

Reisebüro Hummer, 9 Makartplatz.

Reisebüro Dr. Degener & Co., 4 Linzer Gasse.

Landesreisebüro, 16 Dreifaltigkeitsgasse.

Reisebüro RUEFA, Kongresshaus.

American Express Co., Mozartplatz.

In the United States: Austrian National Tourist Office, 545 Fifth Avenue, New York, 10017. Tel: 212 697 0651

Chamber and orchestral concerts.

The Festival makes some arrangements with local hotels and pensions for a package, including a subscription to various concerts and accommodations. The prices include admission to the concerts, bed, breakfast, service, and taxes. Information concerning the package may be obtained by writing to the Festival's mailing address (above).

Osterfestspiel (*Easter Festival*)

1 Hofstallgasse. Tel: 87441

Dates: one week, from Palm Sunday to Easter Monday.

Box Office: Osterfestpiel Ges. m.b.H., Kartenbüro. Address and telephone number same as above.

Hours: Monday to Friday, 8:00 AM to noon; 3:00 PM to 6:00 PM. It is advisable to order tickets months in advance. They are also available through the Austrian National Tourist Office, 545 Fifth Avenue, New York, 10017.

Seating capacity: Grosses Festspielhaus, 2170

Customary Dress: evening dress.

Operas and concerts.

For housing information, write to Wohnungsbüro of the Salzburger Festspiele, at the above address.

This festival, although indirectly associated with the Salzburg Festival, does not stress Mozart (e.g., the opening performance of the 1972 Easter Festival was *Tristan;* in 1970 it was *Fidelio;* and in 1969 it was *Götterdämmerung*). There is a special package available for the Festival; tickets, however, very quickly become unobtainable.

Vienna

Wiener Festwochen

Direktion der Wiener Festwochen, Rathausstrasse 9,
1082 Vienna. Tel: 42804
Dates: From the end of May to the end of June.
Box Office: Österreichisches Verkehrsbüro, Wiener Festwochen, 7 Friedrichstrasse, A-1011 Vienna. Tel: 579657
Ticket reservations for guests from abroad may be made only through the following agencies: Österreichisches Verkehrsbüro, Friedrichstrasse 7, A-1011 Vienna; Tel: 572315, 579657. Verkehrsburo, Stephansplatz 10, A-1010 Vienna; Tel: 630820, 630800, Cable address: Austriaverkehr Vienna. Wiener Konzerthausgesellschaft, Lothringerstrasse 20, A-1030 Vienna; Tel: 721211
Hours: Monday to Friday, 8:00 AM to 6:00 PM; Saturday 8:00 AM to 1:00 PM.
Seating capacity: Staatsoper, c. 2400; Volksoper, c. 2000; Akademietheater, c. 600 (not primarily a musical theater); Burgtheater, c. 1000; Theater an der Wien, c. 1300; Musikverein, c. 1300.
Customary Dress: "Appropriate to the Festival character of the performances."

Orchestral works, chamber music, solo recitals, theater, puppet shows, opera, art exhibits.

For housing accommodations, write to Österreichisches Verkehrsbüro, Wiener Festwochen, 7 Friedrichstrasse, 1043 Vienna.

The Vienna Festival, one of Europe's most diverse and extensive festivals, offers a total of 1,000 performances throughout Vienna. In addition to the magnificent musical programs complete with international visiting artists and orchestras, the Festival includes a World Festival of Puppet Shows, avant-garde theater, and ballet from all over the world, art exhibitions in museums throughout Vienna, and many premieres of musical and theatrical events. The complete program of each festival is issued at the beginning of every April preceding the Festival. It may be obtained at the Friedrichstrasse address above.

Competitions

Graz

Hugo Wolf International Competition

Biennial competition for organ improvisation; in alternate years (though not regularly), a competition for lieder singers, ages 18 to 30.

Awards: total of approximately 45,000 Austrian schillings.

Apply to: Internationaler Hugo-Wolf-Wettbewerb (für Orgelimprovisation or für Liedersänger), Hochschule für Musik, Nikolaigasse 2, A-8023 Graz, Austria. Tel: (03122) 77244

Vienna

Schubert International Competition

Quadrennial competition for voice and piano.

Age limits: for men singers, 22 to 32; women singers, 20 to 30; pianists, 17 to 30.

Awards: three cash awards in each category; concerts.

Deadline: September.

Apply to: Preis des Schubert Wettbewerbes, Konservatorium der Stadt Wien, Johannesgasse 4a, A-1010 Vienna, Austria.

Vienna International Music Competition

Biennial competition; categories change (for example: violin and cello in 1967, piano works of Beethoven in 1969, lieder and Haydn string quartets in 1971).

Age limits: vary, but usually not over 32 years.

Awards: first prize, approximately 60,000 schillings; second prize, approximately 40,000 schillings; third prize, approximately 25,000 schillings.

Deadline: March.

Innsbruck

Paul Hofhaimer-Wettbewerb der Landeshauptstadt Innsbruck

Fallmerayerstrasse 6, 6010 Innsbruck.
(Kulturamt der Stadt Innsbruck) Tel: (05222) 27879

The competition is held for three days at the beginning of September. The "Paul Hofhaimer-Preis" is given for the interpretation of organ compositions. For further information write to the above address.

Leoben

"Jugend musiziert," Instrumentalwettbewerb für die Jugend Österreichs

Hauptplatz 16, 8700 Leoben. Tel: (03842) 2347

This competition, held every two years (odd-numbered years), is sponsored by the Musikalische Jugend Österreichs, Sektion Leoben. The categories change with every competition. For further information write to the address above or to: Generalsekretariat der Musikalischen Jugend Österreichs, Bösendorferstrasse 12, 1010 Vienna; Tel: (0222) 656356, 656357. The competition usually takes place in the middle of October.

Salzburg

TV-Opernpreis der Stadt Salzburg

Argentinierstrasse 22, 1041 Vienna. Tel: (0222) 6595, ext. 683
(ORF-Fernsehen—Austrian Radio-Television)
This competition is held every three years at the end of August. The next competition will take place in 1977. The prize is awarded for operas written specifically for television. (The competition is administered from Vienna.)
Apply to: Secrétariat du concours international de musique, Hochschule für Musik, Lothringerstrasse 18, A-1030 Vienna, Austria. Tel: (0222) 561685

Kompositions Wettbewerb zum Internationalen Welt-Musikfest der IGNM (Composition Contest of the International Festival for Contemporary Music)

Contest held at the Konzerthaus in October.
Deadline: November 20.
For information apply to: IGNM Sektion Oesterreich, Hanuschgasse 3, A-1010 Vienna.

Foundations

Theodor Körner-Stiftungsfonds zur Förderung von Wissenschaft und Kunst (Foundation for the Promotion of Science and Art)

Rennweg 1/III, 1030 Vienna.

The Foundation offers an annual prize to composers and musicologists. The decision on the bestowal of the prize rests with a committee.

Stiftungen der Ersten Österreichischen Spar-Casse (Foundation of First Austrian Savings Bank)

Graben 21, 1010 Vienna. Tel: (0222) 634761

Intending to foster the discovery of musical talent, this organization aids qualified Austrian candidates to enter musical competitions. The Foundation also helps to get them concerts afterward.

Stiftungen der Hochschule für Musik und darstellende Kunst
(Foundation sponsored by the music school. See Conservatories)
Lothringerstrasse 18, 1030 Vienna. Tel: (0222) 561685

Through funds available to it from several different foundations, this Hochschule Foundation provides scholarships to needy students at the school.

Wiener Kunstfonds der Zentralsparkasse der Gemeinde Wien
(Cultural Funds of the Central Savings Bank
of the Viennese Community)
Vordere Zollamtsstrasse 13, 1030 Vienna. Tel: (0222) 725128, ext 32, 33

Funds are made available to artists and composers to promote their works. In the case of composers, this means funds for first performances, copying of manuscripts, etc., as well as concerts of their contemporary works.

Periodicals

Anzeiger des Oesterreichischen Buch-, Kunst- und Musikalienhandels
(Newsletter of the principal association of Austrian book dealers)
Gruenangergasse 4, 1010 Vienna.
semi-monthly

Beiträge zur Jazzforschung—Studies in Jazz Research
Leonardstrasse 15, 8010 Graz. Tel: (03122) 32053/54.
three issues a year

Blues Notes (the only German-language blues magazine)
Bischofstrasse 9, A-4020 Linz.
bi-monthly

BRUCKNER: Mitteilungen des Bruckner-Bundes für Oberösterreich
Landhaus, 4010 Linz. Tel: (07222) 26821.
according to need

Chopin-Jahrbuch
Minoritenplatz 3/1, 1014 Wien. Tel: (0222) 635631, ext. 836
Published by: Internationale Chopin-Gesellschaft, Wien.

Der Chormeister
Fachorgan der Arbeitsgemeinschaft der Chormeister des Österreichischen Arbeiter-Sängerbundes
Gymnasiumstrasse 38, 1180 Wien. Tel: (0222) 342114.
irregular

Doblingers Verlagsnachrichten
Musikverlag Ludwig Doblinger (Bernhard Herzmansky) D.G.
Postfach 882, 1011 Vienna.
three to four issues a year

Die Harmonika
Harmonikaverband Oesterreichs, Gesellschaft zur Förderung der Harmonikamusik
Steingasse 3, 1030 Vienna.
bi-monthly

Haydn-Nachrichten
Mitteilungsblatt der Joseph-Haydn-Gesellschaft Wien
Friesenplatz 7/2/15, 1100 Wien. Tel: (0222) 6296222.
irregular

IMZ Bulletin (Bulletin of the International Music Centre Vienna)
International Music Centre
Lothringerstrasse 20, 1030 Vienna.
quarterly

Innsbrucker Theater-und Konzertspiegel
Rennweg 2, 6020 Innsbruck. Tel: (05222) 21771.
monthly, ten times a year

Internationale Stiftung Mozarteum Mitteilungen
Internationale Stiftung Mozarteum
Schwartzstr. 26, Salzburg.
semi-annual (membership)

Jahrbuch der Gesellschaft für Wiener Theaterforschung
Hofburg, Batthyanystiege, 1010 Wien. Tel: (0222) 522187.
Published by: Gesellschaft für Wiener Theaterforschung

Jahrbuch des Österreichischen Volksliedwerkes
Fuhrmanngasse 18, 1080 Wien. Tel: (0222) 420140.

Published by: Österreichisches Volksliederwerk beim Bundesministerium für Unterricht und Kunst.

Kommission für Musikforschung Mitteilungen
(*Austrian Academy of Sciences*)
Dr. Ignaz Seipel-Platz 2, 1010 Vienna.

Der Komponist
Fachblatt des Österreichischen Komponistenbundes
Baumannstrasse 8-10, 1031 Wien. Tel: (0222) 731555/35.
four times a year

Kulturring
Welser Kulturring
Alois Auerstr. 13, A 4600 Wels.
monthly; free

Linzer Theaterzeitung
Landestheater, 4010 Linz. Tel: (07222) 23254.
monthly

Mitteilungen der Internationalen Stiftung Mozarteum
Internationale Stiftung Mozarteum
Schwarzstrasse 26, Salzburg.
irregular

Mitteilungsblatt des Wiener Kulturkreises
Prinz-Eugen-Strasse 3, 1030 Wien. Tel: (0222) 736115.
irregular

***Mozartgemeinde Wien* (*Newsletter of the Mozart Group of Vienna*)**
Metternichgasse 8, 1030 Vienna.

Mozart-Jahrbuch
Schwarzstrasse 26, 5020 Salzburg. Tel: (06222) 73155.
Published by: Internationale Stiftung Mozarteum.

Music Austria-Vie Musicale Autrichienne
Hanuschgasse 3, 1010 Wien. Tel: (0222) 24999.
two to three times yearly

Musikblätter der Wiener Philharmoniker
Bösendorferstrasse 12, 1010 Wien. Tel: (0222) 656525.
at every concert

***Musikerziehung* (*Music Education*)**
Österreichischer Bundesverlag
Schwarzenbergstrasse 5, A-1015 Vienna.
five times yearly

Musikprotokoll
Oesterreichischer Rundfunk
Studio Steiermark, Graz.

Musikwissenschaftlicher Verlag
Musicological Publishers
Bäckerstr. 18/18, 1010 Vienna.

Musikzeitschrift Oesterreichischer Verlag
Wiedner Hauptstr. 15, 1040 Vienna.

***Der Opernfreund* (*the contemporary journal for music theater*)**
Dr. Anton Stiepka
Tigergasse 4, 1080 Vienna.
monthly

Österreichische Blasmusik
Brucknerstrasse 1, 6850 Dornbirn.
ten times a year

Österreichische Gesellschaft für Musik
Hanuschgasse 3, 1010 Vienna.

Österreichische Musikzeitschrift
Hegelgasse 13/22, 1010 Vienna.
monthly

Österreichischer Musikrat
Lothringerstrasse 18, 1030 Wien. Tel: (0222) 561685.
irregular

Phono
G. W. Hamilton
Konzerthaus
Lothringerstr. 20, 1030 Vienna.
bi-monthly

***Podium* (*Int'l. Bulletin of Music, Film, Radio and Television*)**
Metropol-Verlag
Postfach 28, 2340 Mödling.
monthly

Publikationen des Instituts für Musikwissenschaft der Universität Salzburg
Getreidegasse 9/IV, 5020 Salzburg. Tel: (06222) 86111, ext. 251.

Die Reihe
Universal Edition, A. G.,
Karlsplatz 6, 1010 Vienna.
irregular

SCHUBERT: Mitteilungen des Wiener Schubertbundes
Lothringerstrasse 20, 1030 Wien. Tel: (0222) 732429.
according to need

***Singende Kirche* (*Journal of Catholic Church Music*)**
Stock-im-Eisen-Platz 3, 1010 Vienna.
quarterly

Der Spielvogel
Merangasse 51, Graz.
quarterly

Studien zur Musikwissenschaft
Beihefte zu den Denkmälern der Tonkunst in Österreich
Universitätsstrasse 7, 1010 Wien. Tel: (0222) 427611, ext. 625.

Tabulae Musicae Austriacae
Kataloge Österreichischer Musiküberlieferung
Dr. Ignaz Seipel-Platz 2, 1010 Wien. Tel: (0222) 524721.
irregular

***Theaternachrichten* (*Theater, Concerts, Performances, Lectures*)**
Grazer Theatergemeinschaft, Burggasse 16, A-8010 Graz.
weekly

***Ventil* (*Austrian Cultural Bulletin*)**
Piaristengasse 33/2/10, A-1080 Vienna
quarterly

Wiener Beiträge zur Musikwissenschaft
Universitätsstrasse 7, 1010 Wien. Tel: (0222) 427611, ext. 625.

Wiener Figaro
Mitteilungsblatt der Mozartgemeinde Wien
Metternichgasse 8, 1030 Wien. Tel: (0222) 726848
irregular

Germany

Contents

Germany

Introduction

If we were to name a single country in which music is literally king, it would have to be Germany—even more than Austria or Italy. No other country has as much musicmaking (*Musizieren*), both amateur and professional; no other governments—federal, state, and municipal—are so completely committed to the support and encouragement of this art; and no people appear so heavily concerned with music as the Germans. Yet their involvement began relatively late.

Although their minnesingers and meistersingers played a significant role in the history of Western music, several of the most famous of these musicians, Walther von der Vogelweide (c. 1170–c. 1230), Neidhart von Reuenthal (c. 12th–13th centuries), and Oswald von Wolkenstein (1377–1445) were Austrian. During the Renaissance, other foreign musicians—Flemings and Italians—engaged in musicmaking in the various city-states that comprise present-day Germany. Of all the national groups, the Germans were the last to write in the polyphonic style. Opera and keyboard music developed in the seventeenth century, but within two hundred years their decided preference for instrumental music culminated, during the nineteenth century, in the complete musical domination of Europe by German music and musicians.

The science of musicology and the resulting establishment of libraries, collections, classification of instruments, and research into attributions and performance practice, officially began in Vienna in 1885 under Guido Adler. The Germans' natural affinity for this kind of discipline soon enabled them to assume the leadership in this field as well. The piano was invented in Italy in 1709, but by the nineteenth century it had been considerably improved and mass-produced in Germany by several companies. We need not dwell on the significance of German musicians of this epoch, men like Beethoven, Schumann, Brahms, and, of course, Wagner (who was also responsible for shaping the music of the early twentieth century). Their names are familiar even to the uninitiated, because their works comprise the bulk of today's concert repertory.

To understand why music means so much to the Germans, we must look into their past history. For decades Germany was divided into small principalities. Each sovereign had his own musical entourage to provide him and his court with opera performances and orchestral concerts. Furthermore, the Germans have always had considerable respect for hard work; musicians, like other craftsmen, sought to perfect their skills. Before the end of the nineteenth century, Germans could boast of music flourishing throughout the country. After the unification of Germany in 1870, the small principalities became municipalities or towns with built-in opera companies and symphony orchestras composed of skilled musicians. The municipal governments continued to support these groups, and for this reason it is a rare town in Germany today that does not have an active musical life. In those towns or cities with inadequate facilities, regular arrangements are made either to bus children and adults to special performances for them in the nearest large city or to bring an entire troupe in buses to their town. Detmold, for example, services seventeen surrounding villages!

The German penchant for organization and classification has led to the establishment of active associations of music publishers, musical societies, musical instrument makers and repairers, musical antiquarians, music teachers, music researchers, music wholesalers, music conservatories and *Hochschulen,* musical institutes and libraries, separate associations of opera, chamber, and choral singers, and societies for professionals and amateurs (*Kenner und Liebhaber*). Only in Germany does the Ministry of Information publish a brochure in which music, music education, and musicology are treated as distinct categories, each with appropriate and relevant comments.

During the Hitler period the situation was considerably different. Many of Germany's top artists, musicians, and writers were either fortunate enough to emigrate before the Holocaust or they suffered the same fate as millions of other victims of the Nazi terror. It is beyond comprehension how much talent was lost to Germany and to the world in the mass murders of Jews in the death camps of the 1930s and 1940s. Those who escaped remained abroad, enriching the cultural life of their host country. As a result, Germany, who used to export performers, today often has to entrust her orchestras to foreign conductors and regularly advertises for string players in the United States.

Leipzig (in East Germany), Berlin, and Munich are leading centers for training professional musicians. Torrents of music students from all over the world came here in the early twentieth century. Nowadays there are many smaller educational centers throughout the country, some of these developed from celebrated older institutes, and others newly founded.

Sacred music finds many devotees throughout Germany. The Catholic cathedral choirs of Aachen, Cologne, Bamberg, and Regensburg, the annual Bach and Schütz Festivals (see Festivals), and even some of Wolfgang Fortner's newly composed sacred music manage to inject new ideas into traditional church ceremonies. Choral music is a favorite in this country. Besides 15,000 (!) secular choirs, there are additional numbers of church choirs, numerous folk music groups, community-singing oratorio choirs, and glee clubs, all increasing yearly.

During the last five years, twenty-four theaters with seating capacities ranging from two hundred to thirteen hundred were built in the Federal Republic. Many of the theaters that were built or renovated after 1945 are multipurpose buildings, presenting opera, ballet, and other kinds of musical performances. In 1967, at the peak of the boom, about 200 million dollars were spent for the maintenance of operas, theaters, and orchestras, and of this sum, 165 million dollars came from public funds. Even the private theaters (there were seventy-six in 1968) require subsidies—and receive them. Hamburg usually leads in number of performances, with Munich and Berlin almost sharing second place. Hamburg also leads in the number of commissions awarded for compositions and, as a result, tends to program more contemporary works.

It just might be in order to indicate here that East Germany, too, has forty-eight state orchestras; the Gewandhaus Orchestra in Leipzig, the Dresden State Orchestra, and the Radio Symphony Orchestras of both Leipzig and East Berlin are probably the best. In addition, East Germany supports thirty opera houses, and there are ensembles in Berlin, Leipzig, Dresden, Schwerin, Weimar, Dessau, and Rostock. The star attraction is unquestionably Walter Felsenstein's Komische Oper of East Berlin. The Bach and Schütz Festivals in Leipzig and Dresden, the Handel Festival in Halle, the Boys' Choirs and the Thomas Church Choirs in Leipzig, as well as the Cross Choir in Dresden are all first-rate.

Four West German opera houses have experimental theaters today—in addition to Kassel, Kiel, and Cologne, the Munich National Theater, with its studio accommodating one hundred forty, is the most recent of the larger companies to establish this kind of operation. Here composers and multimedia teams have a chance to offer their latest productions for discussion; opera directors and musical experts can test the possibilities for change in the musical theater.

Because the new forms of music theater have difficulty blending with the standard repertories of the traditional opera houses, radio and television studios are primary outlets for such works. Similarly, whereas contemporary instrumental music tends to remain an alien element in the regular concert repertory, the Radio Symphony Orchestras of Germany believe it their obligation to present this material to the listening public. Several Radio Orchestras are among the finest performing bodies in Germany today. They include the orchestras of Baden-Baden, Berlin, Hamburg, and Cologne, and many of them are specialists in contemporary music, particularly those of Darmstadt, Donaueschingen, and Cologne.

In West Germany today, numerous universities and institutes have departments of musicology. In conservatories and music schools, amateurs as well as professionals are prodded to acquire a proficiency at their instruments that was undreamed of fifty years ago. Over eighty towns and cities have their own opera companies, and more than two dozen of these companies present more than one hundred opera performances a year. The importance of innovative staging and the need for an imaginative stage director are well recognized. There are presently more permanent opera stages here than in all the rest of the countries of the world put together. Although most houses have the same repertory, the young Wagner grandsons at Bayreuth, Felsenstein in East Berlin, Rennert, and Sellner, have tried new concepts and have seen their ideas influence musicians in many other countries.

Subscriptions and tickets for individual concerts are available well in advance of performances either by mail, from box offices on the premises of the theaters, or at various ticket offices strategically located throughout the larger cities. Performances begin at about the same time as those in the States. Students benefit from reduced prices, although less emphasis is placed on workers, possibly because a thriving economy permits most Germans to live reasonably well. (Menial work is generally performed by foreign labor resident in Germany for that specific purpose.)

Music publishing is a big business, and so is concert management. Reprints of musical monuments of the past are published with increasing frequency. Concerts, recitals, musical exhibits, and festivals attract a large percentage of the population and also bring in huge sums of tourist dollars. All events are well-publicized; many announcements are printed in English and French as well as German. Entire pamphlets introducing Munich or Stuttgart are printed in the visitors' languages to assure easy comprehension. An intensive effort is being made to eradicate the memory of the Germany of the thirties and forties and to replace it with that of a cultured, *gemütlich,* friendly nation eager to please its guests and make them feel at home. Unquestionably, music, always a means for breaking down national barriers, has here become a tool for promoting international understanding.

Germany (West)
Hamburg
Berlin
Hannover
Kassel
Düsseldorf
Köln
Bonn
Wiesbaden
Frankfurt
Bayreuth
Würzburg
Darmstadt
Nürnberg
Stuttgart
München

Germany

Guides and Services

Events

In English. Published by the Deutsche Zentrale für Tourismus—DZT (German National Tourist Association), Beethovenstrasse 69, D-6000 Frankfurt. Tel. 740531, 740536

Available gratis in the United States at the following locations:

Chicago: German National Tourist Office, 11 South La Salle Street, Chicago, Illinois 60603. Tel: (312) AN3-2958

New York: German National Tourist Office, 630 Fifth Avenue, New York 10020. Tel: (212) 757-8570/71/72

San Francisco: German National Tourist Office, 323 Geary Street, San Francisco, California 94102. Tel: (415) 986-0796

Appears twice a year (April–October, November–March). Diary of events taking place throughout Germany and throughout the year. Covers theater, music, religious events, exhibitions, fairs, folk festivals, conventions, congresses, and sports.

Deutsches Musikleben

In German. Published by Inter Nationes, Kennedyallee 91–103, D-5300 Bonn–Bad Godesberg.

Appears once a year. Provides a chronological listing of the most important music festivals, congresses, master courses, and competitions held in Germany throughout the year.

Bundesrepublik Deutschland

In German. Published by Inter Nationes, Kennedyallee 91–103. D-5300 Bonn–Bad Godesberg.

Appears once a year. Covers music festivals, art exhibits, book exhibits, symposia in a variety of areas, congresses, German language and culture courses, photography exhibits, and film festivals.

Both Inter Nationes booklets are available gratis at the German National Tourist Office, 630 Fifth Avenue, New York 10020.

Tel: (212) 757-8570/71/72.

For information about Germany in Great Britain:

German Institute
51 Princes Gate, London SW7.

German National Tourist Office
61 Conduit Street, London W1.

German Academic Exchange Service
11 Arlington Street, London SW1.

German Embassy
23 Belgrave Square, London SW1 X8PZ

Anglo-German Chamber of Commerce
11 Grosvenor Crescent, London SW1 X7EE

NATIONAL HOLIDAYS

January	1	New Year's Day
	6	Epiphany
February	*	Carnival
March	*	Good Friday
April	*	Easter Monday
May	1	Labor Day
	*	Ascension Day
	*	Whit Monday
June	*	Corpus Christi
	17	German Unity Day (Remembrance Day)
August	15	Assumption

* = movable

Self-dial long distance prefix numbers for the most important cities in Germany:

Bad Godesberg	0 22 29
Bonn	0 22 21
Cologne (Koln)	02 21
Darmstadt	0 61 51
Dortmund	02 31

Düsseldorf	02 11
Duisburg	0 21 31
Essen	0 21 41
Frankfurt	06 11
Freiburg-im-Breisgau	07 61
Hamburg	04 11
Hanover	05 11
Kassel	05 61
Kiel	04 31
Mainz	0 61 31
Mannheim	06 21
Munich	08 11
Nürnberg	09 11
Saarbrücken	06 81
Stuttgart	07 11
Wiesbaden	0 61 21

BAYREUTH

Tel. prefix: 0921

Opera Houses and Concert Halls

Richard Wagner Festspielhaus

9 Luitpoldplatz. Tel: 8921 5722
Director: Wolfgang Wagner.
Public Entrance: same as mailing address.
Season: open entire year except month of September; Festival in August.
Seating capacity: 1800
Box Office: same as above.

Although Wagner had already written idealistically about his plans for this theater in 1851, it was not until twenty-five years later that the Festspielhaus opened in Bayreuth with a production of the *Ring.* Originally, King Ludwig II of Bavaria, Wagner's patron, had agreed to subsidize the composer and build a festival theater in Munich. Persuaded by his constituents of the folly of this plan, he withdrew his support, and Wagner left Munich for Triebschen, where he remained for several years.

In 1871 the composer returned to Bayreuth and convinced the local authorities of the value of locating a festival house in the town. By 1872, on his fifty-ninth birthday, Wagner laid the foundation stone of the theater. On this occasion, too, he conducted a performance of Beethoven's Ninth Symphony with an orchestra composed of the most prominent German musicians of the time. Finally, with the help of funds raised by admirers and members of the Wagner Vereine, Wagner clubs with branches in major cities of Europe and America, the Festspielhaus at Bayreuth was built.

The theater is essentially a wooden and brick structure that was meant to be temporary. Its acoustics, however, were so fine that a more permanent theater was never constructed. The covered orchestra pit was only one of Wagner's innovations. The theater was built in the style of the ancient amphitheaters and seated eighteen hundred, a staggering number of persons for that time. The plans for the theater were carried out with the assistance of the theater architect, Karl Brandt of Darmstadt.

In 1874 Wagner moved into his new home, Villa Wahnfried at Bayreuth, a gift from Ludwig II. On August 13, 1876, the new Festspielhaus opened with *Das Rheingold,* starting the first complete *Ring* cycle, and an audience numbering among its members Liszt, Grieg, Tschaikovsky, Bruckner, Mahler, Saint-Saens, and the philosopher Nietzsche, among others. The conductor was Hans Richter. The performances were well received, but the composer, faced with financial problems, had to wait until 1882 to hold another festival. That year he concentrated on performances of *Parsifal.*

The success of the Festival dates from this time (see Festivals). After Wagner's death in 1883, his wife Cosima took over the direction of the project until 1908, when she handed the reins to her son Siegfried. Both Siegfried and Cosima died in 1930, and from 1930 to 1944, the Festival was conducted by Siegfried's widow, Winifred, who at the time was rumored engaged to Adolf Hitler. For seven years after the war, no festivals were held. Then, in 1951, Wagner's grandsons, Wolfgang and Wieland Wagner, became the directors at Bayreuth. They sought numerous scenic innovations, many of them controversial at the time. Since Wieland Wagner's death in 1966, Wolfgang has carried on alone.

Markgräfliches Opernhaus

Opernstrasse.

Seating Capacity: 500

Considered the oldest baroque theater in Germany, this ornate architectural gem contrasts sharply with the stark burnt-orange brick building that is the Festspielhaus. Seen from the outside, it, too, discloses little to prepare the visitor for the magnificence of the interior. Once inside, however, tourists can begin to appreciate the splendor surrounding eighteenth-century royalty. Built originally in 1748 for the Margrave, a sister of Frederick the Great, the theater remained for many years the province of royalty, later becoming a museum. It reopened after World War II—which fortunately left it undamaged—as an opera house, and it is now used also for concerts and recitals. Guided tours are offered daily between April and September.

Libraries and Museums

Richard Wagner-Gedenkstätte
Neues Schloss.
Glasenappweg 2. Tel: 96181 Ext. 351
Hours: Monday to Friday 9:00 AM to noon and 2:00 PM to 5:00 PM; Sunday 9:00 AM to 5:00 PM. Closed September.

The first floor of this Wagner museum houses letters, portraits, photographs, and biographical material about Wagner. The second floor is devoted to material on the Festival. Books in all languages, concerned with Wagner and his activities, records of historical performances, publications of the festivals themselves, plus a small study with three desks at which scholars can work may be found on this floor.

Behind Wahnfried (see ***Musical Landmarks***), Wagner's home, and at the side of this Wagner museum, is the cemetery where so many of the famous Wagnerians are buried.

Conservatories and Schools

Kirchenmusikschule der Evang. (Lutheran) Kirche in Bayern
Wilhelminenstrasse 9. Tel: (0921) 65048
Course of Study: three years.
Prerequisites: entrance examination required.
Areas of Instruction: church music training; seminar for private music teachers; summer courses.

Summer Courses

Internationales Jugendfestspieltreffen
(International Youth Festival Meeting)
Festspielhaus.
Course of study: three weeks in August, during Wagner Festival.
Prerequisites: students preferably between 18 and 25 (older students only exceptionally) are selected to participate in these courses.
Areas of instruction: orchestra, choir, chamber music, seminar for music and theater criticism, Wagner seminar. Boulez has taught here several times. Professor Kurt Blaukopf is another member of the faculty.

Musical Landmarks

Wahnfried

This residence, designed by Wagner himself, was his home from April 1874 until his death in 1883. His wife Cosima took charge of the estate until her death in 1930. In 1945 the house was bombed, but it has since been restored. Presently, Wahnfried contains the archives of the Wagner family. Members of the family still reside here. It is *not* open to the public.

Stadtfriedhof

Franz Liszt, the writer Jean Paul, the conductor Hans Richter, and Marianne Thekla Mozart (Mozart's cousin "Bäsle," who lived in Bayreuth from 1814 to her death in 1841) are all buried at the municipal cemetery. See also a memorial to "Bäsle" on the Postei, Jean-Paul-Platz in Bayreuth.

Two inns with musical associations are the *Eule* at Kirchgasse near the Stadtkirche and *Rollwenzelei* at Königsallee, in the direction of Lustschloss Eremitage. This latter was a favorite haunt of Jean Paul.

Franz Liszt's house is located near Wahnfried. He died there in 1886. Jean Paul (whose full name was Jean Paul Friedrich Richter) lived in the house at 5 Friedrichstrasse.

Musical Organizations

Richard-Wagner-Verband

Elsastrasse 5. Tel: 0921/23713

Membership in this Wagner Society will help you to get tickets to the Festival!

BERLIN

Tel. prefix: 0311

Berlin, an "island city," has an aura that is difficult to describe. It was—and still is—not only the largest city in Germany, not only the de facto capital, but also the intellectual and cultural center of the two Germanies. It is perhaps fitting that each side claims a portion. It is still the meeting place of East and West, a center for vital, stimulating theater, first-rate opera, magnificent concerts, splendid museums and galleries, superb shopping, and fantastically modern architecture. A sleek, progressive city, rebuilt from the ground after World War II, Berlin today is more cosmopolitan in her new life than she ever was before. The curious paradox of a youthful city with a centuries-old tradition makes a visit to Berlin a unique experience.

The Prussian Cultural Foundation (Preussischer Kulturbesitz, the name given to the state museums) in Dahlem, which is one of Berlin's newest and most attractive suburbs, offers a complex of museums of a variety and diversity not easily duplicated. One of the finest instrument museums in Europe is in the building opposite the Bundeshaus (Federal Building). The Ethnographical Museum (Museum für Völkerkunde) has a superb East Asia department with non-Western instruments on display there. A remarkable collection of Impressionist paintings awaits visitors in the Orangerie of Charlottenburg Palace. The Palace itself, erected in 1696 for Queen Charlotte, is well worth a visit.

The above-mentioned instrument collection, formerly housed at the Municipal Conservatory, started with two hundred forty pieces and now numbers over a thousand. Historically, the Conservatory ranks among the most celebrated in the world, if we take into consideration the names of some of its former students (see below).

The Free University in Dahlem and the Technical University in Charlottenburg have a combined enrollment of more than 24,000 students. Besides the Academy of Fine Arts, the College of Music, and the teaching colleges, there are numerous engineering schools and institutes in Berlin. Established in 1948, the Free University first occupied empty buildings and residences belonging to the Kaiser Wilhelm Institute. In 1950 the Ford Foundation financed new buildings, including a tower of books, a five-story annex completely filled with stacks of books.

The American Memorial Library (Gedenkbibliothek) near the old city gate (Hallesches Tor) was a gift from the United States in 1954. It houses a record library and more than 600,000 books, thus making it the largest public lending library in Germany.

The Kurfürstendamm, Berlin's Great White Way, is ablaze nightly with lights from over twelve hundred shops, one hundred cafes, seventeen theaters, and the nearby Deutsche Oper and Philharmonie. These two auditoriums, as well as Mies van der Rohe's Gallerie of the 20th Century (a square, glass pavilion), and the new Congress Hall in the Tiergarten (thought by some to be the most exciting building in the city) designed by Hugh Stubbins for conventions, are among the best examples of modern architecture here.

Back on the Kurfürstendamm, the windowless facade of the Deutsche Oper, designed by Berlin architect Bornemann, and Hans Scharoun's fantasy building, known as the Philharmonie, each compete for attention with the music produced there. Both of these were constructed to meet the deadlines of Berlin Festival Weeks, the Oper in 1961, the Philharmonie in 1963. To those who remember Berlin in the twenties, the city has changed and will probably never be the same. To newcomers as well as to the young, Berlin represents a refreshing change of pace from the rest of Germany.

Guides and Services

The Berlin Program

Appearing on the first, eleventh, and twenty-first of each month, lists details covering opera, theater, concerts, museums, art exhibitions and other points of interest in Berlin. It is available at the Tourist Information Office, 7–8 Fasanenstrasse (Tel: 240111) and at the following branches: Pavillon at Zoo (Tiergarten) Station, 20 Hardenbergstrasse (Tel: 31 70 94/95), and Pavillon at Tempelhof Airport. (Tel: 690 93 03)

Die Monatsvorschau (published by the Verkehrsamt Berlin)
1 Berlin 12. Tel: 24 01 11

This is another excellent guide that covers two months of presentations in Berlin. It is also available on sale at the Fasanenstrasse address (see above). Incredibly complete, this double-faced broadside (about three feet by one and a half feet) contains material on concerts, school concerts, cabarets, museums, operas, sports, exhibits, plays, children's theaters, etc., for East as well as West Berlin. Of course it is more complete for West Berlin.

Führer durch die Konzertsäle Berlins

Cunostrasse 69.
1 Berlin 33 (Grünewald). Tel: 8 23 55 55

At the offices of this publication recommended to us by the Verkehrsamt of Berlin, you may phone for concert information Monday to Friday from 10:00 AM to 4:00 PM.

Further information and tickets may be obtained at the following offices: Informationsbüro, Alexanderplatz; Tel: 51 53 03 and 51 59 04; Informationsbüro, 162 Friedrichstrasse Tel: 22 19 88; Anrechtszentrale, Oberwallstrasse 607 Tel: 20 05 71; Informationszentrum Berlin, 20 Hardenbergstrasse, second floor (special information not exclusively for tourists) Tel: 31 03 71; and a ticket agency—Theaterkasse Sasse, Kurfürstendamm 24 Tel: 881 42 09. Finally, a central phone number to call for theater and concert information in Berlin is 11-56.

In special cases, people wishing information to help further their research should write to: Senator für Wissenschaft und Kunst, Bredtschneiderstrasse 5–8, 1 Berlin 19. Tel: 30 32 551

Presse und Informationsamt des Landes Berlin
Europa Center
1 Berlin 30.

Opera Houses and Concert Halls

Deutsche Oper Berlin

Bismarckstrasse 34–37, Charlottenburg. Tel: 341 30 81
Season: middle of August to beginning of July; closed beginning of July to middle of August, and December 24.
Box Office: daily 10:00 AM to 2:00 PM and one hour before curtain. Tickets go on sale Sunday for the following Thursday to Sunday, and on Thursday for the following Monday to Wednesday.
Location: entrance hall at Bismarckstrasse (see above).
Mailing Address: 10 Richard-Wagnerstrasse, 1 Berlin 10.
Seating capacity: 1900

Rebuilt in 1961 on the site of the pre-War Opera House, this modern structure opened its doors with a performance of Mozart's *Don Giovanni,* followed immediately, the next night, by the premiere of Giselher Klebe's *Alkmene.* The stage was thus set for the roles that this house would play; traditional opera and contemporary pieces are cultivated side by side. An extremely large repertory includes the works of Beethoven, Bizet, Flotow, Humperdinck, Leoncavallo, Lortzing, Mascagni, Mozart, Puccini, Rossini, Schoenberg, Strauss, Wagner, Weber, and Verdi, as well as compositions by Berg, Blacher, Britten, Dallapiccola, Egk, von Einem, (Wolfgang) Fortner, Henze, Hindemith, Klebe, Krenek, Nono, Orff, Stravinsky, Sutermeister, (Winfried) Zillig, and others.

Producers and directors are concerned with creating a fresh interpretation of the inherited classics of the musical repertory. In addition, there is an attempt to restore original versions of works that had been tampered with often during the preceding century. Hans Uhlmann's abstract metal sculpture is effective against the severe facade of this building, whose spacious foyers are functional as well as attractive. In the interior, see the busts of Bruno Walter, Karl Böhm, and Ferenc Fricsay. There are also refreshments available on each level, and a cloakroom where check numbers match the numbers of the seats. Patrons are able to enjoy the end of a performance without having to worry about any line awaiting them when they try to retrieve their coats!

The managing director, Gustav Rudolf Sellner, who led the opera house for eleven years, recently handed over its direction to the Viennese-born Dr. Egon Seefehlner, who had been his deputy during the entire tenure of his office. A lawyer and industrialist, Seefehlner came to Berlin from the Vienna State Opera. His love for opera won over his interest in law and business. Seefehlner must handle twelve hundred people on his payroll (New York's Metropolitan has a thousand) including sixty singers, a ballet company of fifty, a chorus of one hundred twenty, and a one hundred forty-three-piece orchestra. His budget for 1972–73 amounted to forty million DM (about $12.5 million) of which only fifteen percent is covered by the box office and the Berlin taxpayers pay the balance.

The Deutsche Oper dates back to 1912. The old house on Bismarckstrasse was destroyed during the Second World War, but even before the house was rebuilt in September 1945, shortly after the end of the war, the company gave its first post-war performance, *Fidelio.* Its permanent ensemble today includes the internationally famous singers Dietrich Fischer-Dieskau, Christa Ludwig, and the Americans Evelyn Lear and James King, among others. Americans should feel at home—American operatic history was made in Berlin when Roger Session's *Montezuma* was given its premiere here.

Philharmonie

Kemperplatz, Tiergarten.

Season: late August through late June; closed beginning of July almost to end of August.

Box Office Hours: Monday to Friday 3:00 PM to 6:30 PM; Saturday and Sunday 11:00 AM to 2:00 PM. Tel: 261 43 83

Undoubtedly one of the most photographed buildings in Berlin, the new Philharmonic Hall, constructed between 1960 and 1963, was designed by Hans Scharoun. The orchestra plays surrounded on all sides by the audience. Scharoun describes his philosophy:

"A center of music from the very beginning . . . was the uppermost thought around which the contours of the Philharmonic's new auditorium took shape, an auditorium that reflects its character throughout the entire structure. The orchestra and conductor become the literal center of attention, for, although not located in the mathematical center of the room, they are surrounded on all sides by rows of guests. "Producer" and "consumer" so to speak, do not form two bodies situated directly opposite each other; the audience's seats have been arranged in groups, placed on different levels that encompass the orchestra. Man, space, music—these things are presented together here in a completely new light."

Guided tours of Philharmonic Hall, lasting thirty minutes, are given every half hour, Monday through Saturday from 1:30 PM to 3:00 PM, and on Sunday from 2:30 PM to 3:30 PM. If these times are inconvenient, arrangements for individual tours can be made by calling 25-92-51.

Saal der Akademie der Künste
Hanseatenweg 10. Tel. 39 32 81
Seating capacity: 750

The entire Hansa District, destroyed in the war, was rebuilt through an international architectural competition. It is a residential area whose cultural center is the Akademie der Künste. The building was designed by Werner Düttmann. Lectures, exhibitions, plays, and concerts are all offered here.

Theater des Westens
Kantstrasse 12 (Charlottenburg). Tel: 313 72 50
Box Office: daily advance sale from 11:00 AM to 7:00 PM.

Musical comedies or operettas such as Lehár's *The Merry Widow* are produced here.

Kongresshalle (Congress-Hall)
Tiergarten (and facing the John-Foster-Dulles-Allee) Tel: 39 2011
Seating capacity (theater): 380

America's architectural contribution to the International Building Exhibition held in 1957, this structure has been called the most exciting building in the city. It houses a theater, exhibition hall, restaurants, and a garden cafe. Conventions are held in the large conference room.

Guided tours daily 10:00 AM to 5:00 PM (except on days when there are performances. It is best to call ahead).

Internationales Institut für vergleichende Musikstudien und Dokumentation
Winklerstrasse 20. Tel: 89 28 53
Season: specific exhibits, such as "Woche asiatischer und afrikanischer Kunst," during the first week in June. Concerts, theater, dance, and exhibitions offered at this time.
Seating capacity (hall): 600

Konzertsaal der Staatlichen Hochschule für Musik und darstellende Kunst
Hardenbergstrasse 33. Tel: 31 03 31 Ext. 372
(Public entrance is at the corner of Fasanenstrasse and Hardenbergstrasse.)
Season: September 1 to June 30 for concerts and occasional operas in concert (unstaged) versions.

Box Office Hours: Monday to Friday 3:00 PM to 6:30 PM; Saturday, Sunday 11:00 AM to 2:00 PM. Tel: 31 63 83

Seating Capacity: 1340; no standing room

This hall is considered a significant one for concerts. Programs are carried in the principal city concert guides. The Philharmonic Orchestra played in this hall before their Philharmonie was completed.

Puppentheater Berlin
Berlinerstrasse 53–54 Tel: 48 49 46
110 Berlin-Pankow

Grosser Sendesaal (Music Hall in the radio station "Sender Freies Berlin")
Masurenallee 8–14, Haus des Rundfunks.
Berlin-Charlottenburg 9 Tel: 3 02 72 43

This hall with the Philharmonic and the Hochschule hall are the three principal concert halls in Berlin. Radio-Symphonie-Orchestra of Berlin performs here.

Summer Concerts

Summer concerts are often given in the Eosander chapel of the Schloss Charlottenburg. Usually chamber music is heard here. The organ in the chapel is a modern one incorporating parts of the original 1706 instrument that were salvaged from the bombings of 1943.

Saalbau Neukölln
Karl-Marx-Strasse 141

Konzertsaal am Steinplatz
(Steinplatz runs into Hardenbergstrasse)
Berlin-Charlottenburg

Ernst-Reuter-Saal
Wittenau, Eichborndamm 215–239 Tel: 49 70 12/Ext 534

Ernst-Reuter-Haus (Recital Hall)
Strasse des 17. Juni 112 Tel: 398 491

Festsaal
Onkel-Bräsig-Strasse 76–78
Transportation: U-Bhf. Blaschkoallee

Freie Volksbühne
Schaperstrasse 24 Tel: 881 37 42

Box Office: advance sale 10:00 AM to 2:00 PM and one hour before performances
Concerts are given here although the hall is primarily a theater for plays.

Caeciliensaal
Nikolsburger Platz 5, Wilmersdorf

Parkhaus im Englischen Garten
Tiergarten
Chamber concerts.

Serenade Concerts: check local papers for time

Jagdschloss Grünewald

Schloss Charlottenburg

Schloss Tegel

Additional Outdoor Concerts

vor der Villa Borsig

Halbinsel Reiherwerder

Open Air Theaters

Waldbühne, near Olympia Stadium

Volkspark Rehberge, in Wedding

Volkspark Hasenheide

Zitadelle Spandau

Other Theaters

Berliner Operettentheater
Schlossstrasse 5

Komödie
Kurfürstendamm 206
Box Office: open daily from 10:00 AM to 2:00 PM and from 6:00 PM until the beginning of the performance.
Musicals are presented here.

Kleine Oper Berlin
Kreuzbergstrasse 47
Light operas are performed here.

Cultural Centers

Amerika Haus
Hardenbergstrasse 22

British Center
Hardenbergstrasse 20

Maison de France
Kurfürstendamm 211

Urmuz
Kurfürstendamm 131
For jazz and rock, nightly from 8:00 PM.

Churches

Jesus-Christus-Kirche
Dahlem, Thielplatz

Paulus-Kirche in der Alten Dorfkirche am Rathaus Zehlendorf
Transportation: Bus 1, 3, 10, 18, 53, 60

St. Matthäus-Kirche an der Philharmonie
Kemperplatz

Libraries and Museums

Staatsbibliothek (Preussischer Kulturbesitz): Musikabteilung und Mendelssohn-Archiv [Ben. 33]

Musikabteilung
Archivstrasse 12–14. Tel: 76 50 91
Mailing Address: Postfach 59, 1 Berlin 30.
Hours: Monday, Tuesday, Thursday 9:00 AM to 4:30 PM; Wednesday, Friday 9:00 AM to 5:30 PM. Closed holidays.

The emphasis in this remarkable collection is on eighteenth- and nineteenth-century works, with extensive holdings of Mendelssohniana and others, including a Busoni bequest. Significant manuscripts held here are Mozart's *Die Entführung aus dem Serail, Figaro, Così fan Tutte, Zauberflöte,* as well as non-operatic autographs. In addition, special exhibits are also presented at various times.

The Mendelssohn-Archiv (*Forschungs- und Gedenkstätte*) is part of the Musikabteilung but is located in a different building and has different hours.
Archivstrasse 11. Tel: 832 70 91
Hours: Monday to Friday 10:00 AM to 4:00 PM.

Staatliches Institut für Musikforschung (*Stiftung Preussischer Kulturbesitz*), *Bibliothek* [Ben. 32]

Stauffenbergstrasse 14 (Tiergarten). Tel: 261 15 61
Hours: Monday to Friday 8:30 AM to 5:00 PM; Wednesday 8:30 AM to 4:00 PM. The Museum at 1–12 Bundesallee is closed on Monday (see **Musikinstrumenten-Museum** below).

Meyerbeer's letters and diaries and J. Joachim's letters are among other holdings here.

Staatliche Hochschule für Musik und darstellende Kunst, Bibliothek (*formerly known as Kgl. Akademische Hochschule für Musik*) [Ben. 30]

Fasanenstrasse 1. Tel: 314 26 44
Hours: daily except Saturday from 10:00 AM to 2:00 PM. Closed holidays (Easter and during the summer, or mid-March to end of April and mid-July to beginning of October).

Amerika-Gedenkbibliothek (*Berliner Zentralbibliothek*), *Musikabteilung* [Ben. 23]

Blücherplatz 2. Tel: (0311) 69 10 11
Hours: Monday 4:00 PM to 8:00 PM, Tuesday to Saturday 11:00 AM to 8:00 PM. Closed Good Friday, Easter, Ascension, Pentecost, Busstag (in November), December 24 to 26, and 31.

This library has depository copies of all UNESCO publications; documentation on music festivals, competitions, master courses; and a special collection of twentieth century, United States, and East European music. It is the largest public lending library in Germany.

Musikbücherei Charlottenburg [Ben. 26]

Platanenallee 16. Tel: (0311) 305 13 41
Hours: Monday, Wednesday, Friday 1:00 PM to 7:00 PM; Tuesday, Thursday 1:00 PM to 5:00 PM. Closed school vacations.
Note: Bücherei means "library."

This library is a separate department of the Stadtbücherei Charlottenburg, the municipal library. It is the reference library for the Berlin Volksmusikschule and contains considerable chamber music and teaching material.

Musikwissenschaftliches Institut der Freien Universität [Ben. 27]
Auf dem Grat 47. Tel: 76 90 627
Hours: Monday to Friday 9:00 AM to 7:00 PM; Saturday 10:00 AM to noon. Closed three to four weeks in summer.

Internationales Musikerbrief-Archiv (*Archive of Musicians' Letters*)
153 Kantstrasse.

For access to this private library, write directly to Siegfried Borris, c/o Deutscher Musikrat, Michaelstrasse 4a, Bonn-Bad Godesberg.

Staatliche Museen Preussischer Kulturbesitz, Kunstbibliothek [Ben. 31]
Jebenstrasse 2. Tel: 31 01 16
Hours: Monday to Friday 9:00 AM to 9:00 PM, Saturday 9:00 AM to 1:00 PM.

This is a reference library of a museum specializing in costume, graphics, posters, etc.

Musikinstrumenten-Museum des Staatlichen Instituts für Musikforschung Preussischer Kulturbesitz
Bundesallee 1–12 (formerly Joachimsthal Gymnasium, before that, housed in Schloss Charlottenburg). Tel: 881 78 35
Hours: Tuesday, Thursday, Friday, Saturday 9:00 AM to 5:00 PM; Wednesday 11:00 AM to 8:00 PM; Sunday 10:00 AM to 2:00 PM. Closed Monday. Guided tours every Saturday 11:00 AM to 1:00 PM and by arrangement.

The museum is primarily a collection of European instruments from the sixteenth to twentieth centuries. There are about 1,700 instruments in all. Of special interest are the wind instruments of the sixteenth and seventeenth centuries (particularly the instruments from the St. Wenzelskirche in Naumburg), the cembali and clavichord, and the viola da gamba. Almost all instruments are playable. A library and a collection of graphics, photographs, and records are also housed here.

Philip Spitta helped found the collection in 1888. Gifts from Paul de Wit of Leipzig and the families of Meyerbeer, Weber, and Mendelssohn can also be seen here. Further large bequests in 1902 and 1957 came from César Snock of Ghent, Belgium.

This instrument museum was formerly known as the Hochschule Museum.

Das Museum für Völkerkunde
Berlin-Dahlem.
Mailing Address: Arnim-Allee 23–27.

Public entrance: Lansstrasse 8. Tel: 76 00 11
Hours: Tuesday to Friday 9:00 AM to 5:00 PM; Sunday 10:00 AM to 5:00 PM.

This museum is also (like the one above) part of the Preussischer Kulturbesitz. It has a collection of about 1,400 non-European instruments, and Curt Sachs prepared the first catalog for the Museum, which is primarily a general anthropological institution.

Phonograph Archives

Deutsche Bibliothek, Abteilung Deutsches Musik Archiv
Rudesheimerstrasse 54–56.

Apparently this institution replaces the Deutsche Musik Phonothek of Blücherplatz, which is no longer in existence.

Phonogrammarchiv
c/o Museum für Völkerkunde
Arnim-Allee 23–27.

Although it is a part of the Museum für Völkerkunde, notice that the address for the entrance of this archive is different from that of the Museum.

Sender Freies Berlin (SFB) Schallarchiv (Record Archive)
Masurenallee 8–14. Tel: 308 27 24
Hours: not public; visited by arrangement only.

Deutsches Rundfunkmuseum
Messehallen am Funkturm, Messedamm. Tel: 302 21 86
Hours: daily except Monday from 10:00 AM to 5:00 PM; Sunday and holidays 10:00 AM to 4:00 PM.

Conservatories and Schools

Institut für Musikwissenschaft der Freien Universität
Garystrasse 35. Tel: (0311) 838 36 27

No housing provisions. Catalog or brochure available from Buchhandlung Elwer & Meurer, 101 Hauptstrasse. The Free University was founded in 1948 by a group of scholars who left East Berlin. It represented an attempt "to adapt the whole educational system to the demands of the new society," part of a widespread movement among German universities.

Staatliche Hochschule für Musik und darstellende Kunst
Fasanenstrasse 1.
1 Berlin 12 (Charlottenburg). Tel: (0311) 32 51 81

Founded in 1869, its first director was Joseph Joachim, who remained there until 1907. Their faculty has included Philip Spitta, Curt Sachs, E. Humperdinck, G. Schünemann, P. Hindemith, and Werner Egk. Egk and Schünemann were directors at one time. Recently, amid much pomp and ceremony, the school celebrated its hundredth anniversary. Four hundred students are taught by ninety-eight full-time and seventy part-time faculty. The concert hall here (see above), one of the three main halls in Berlin, was designed by Paul Baumgarten and opened in 1954.

Technische Universität
Hardenbergstrasse 34, Berlin-Charlottenburg 2. Tel: 32 51 81

Lectures on music are included in the general studies program. The late H. H. Stuckenschmidt, critic and writer on contemporary music, taught here.

Internationales Institut für vergleichende Musikstudien und Dokumentation
Winklerstrasse 20. Tel: 89 28 53

This institute for comparative musicology (ethnomusicology) sponsors an annual festival (see below) of non-European music, dance, etc., such as *"Woche äussereuropäischer Musik"* and *"Woche asiatischer und afrikanischer Kunst,"* from the end of May through the beginning of June.

Staatliches Institut für Musikforschung Preussischer Kulturbesitz
Stauffenbergstrasse 14. Tel: 13 15 61
1 Berlin 30 (Tiergarten).

This research center has a good music library (see above) and one of the largest European collections of Western musical instruments (Musikinstrumenten-Museum). Two relatively new departments organized there include the *Abteilung für musikalische Akustik* (department of musical acoustics) and the *Abteilung für musikalische Volkskunde* (the department of musical folklore).

Städtisches Konservatorium (formerly the Julius Stern Conservatory)
Bundesallee 1–12. Tel: 310 331 Ext. 323

The faculty here has at one time or another included Hans von Bülow, Hans Pfitzner, and H. J. Moser. The school, founded in 1850, was closed by Hitler in 1933.

Musikschule an der Volkshochschule Schöneberg
Mailing Address: John-F.-Kennedy-Platz. Tel: 783 30 35/30 34
Administration Office: Grünewaldstrasse 6–7, Room 5.

Pianistenschule Dounias-Sindermann
Seebergsteig 15–17. Tel: 89 39 43

Schiller College School of Music
European Address: Caspar-Theyss-Strasse 7, 1 Berlin 33.
American Address: 429 N.W. 48 Street, Oklahoma City, Okla. 73118
Tel: (405) 842 5979

Varied programs for winter and summer study: year-abroad-program; four-year Bachelor of Music degree program; summer workshops; United States college credit; instruction in English; inexpensive student travel to all parts of East and West Europe.

Musical Landmarks

Gravesites

So many famous personalities are buried in and around Berlin that the Verkehrsamt Berlin publishes a list of gravesites of artists, musicians, writers, and statesmen in the various cemeteries there. Further information may be obtained at the office at Fasanenstrasse 7–8.

In the center of Berlin you can locate the following:
Bach, Wilhelm Friedemann (1710–1784), the eldest son of J. S. Bach, is buried at Friedhof der Luisenstädtischen Kirche, Alte Jakobstrasse.

Brecht, Bertolt (1898–1956), dramatist and lyricist, known to many for his *Dreigroschenoper* (*Three-Penny Opera,* 1928) libretto which Kurt Weill set to music, rests in the Dorotheenstädtischer und Friedrichswerderscher Friedhof, Chausseestrasse.

Lortzing, Albert (1801–1851), composer of the operas *Zar und Zimmerman, Undine, Wildschütz,* and others is buried at the Friedhof in der Bergstrasse, east of Nordbahnhof (East Berlin).

Zelter, Karl Friedrich (1758–1832), Goethe's favorite musician, is buried at the Friedhof der Sophienkirche, Grosse Hamburgerstrasse.

In the Kreuzberg section there are others:
Hoffmann, E. T. A. (1776–1822), writer and musician, and **Felix Mendelssohn** (1809–1847), composer and pianist, are both buried at the Historische Friedhöfe am Halleschen Tor.

Tieck, Ludwig (1773–1853), whose poems were set to music by many lieder composers, is buried in the Historische Friedhof in der Bergmannstrasse.

In the Schöneberg section:
Bruch, Max (1838–1920), the well-known composer, is in the Matthäus-Friedhof am Südbahnhof Grossgörschenstrasse.

At Zehlendorf:
Humperdinck, Engelbert (1854–1921), opera composer, is buried at the Süd-west Friedhof in Stahnsdorf, formerly in West Berlin (now, in East Berlin).

Schreker, Franz (1878–1934), composer and teacher, lies buried at the Wald-friedhof Dahlem.

At Wedding:
Nicolai, Otto (1810–1849), composer of *The Merry Wives of Windsor,* rests in the cemetery of Dorotheenstädtische Friedhof II in der Liesenstrasse.

At Prenzlauer Berg:
Meyerbeer, Giacomo (1791–1864), composer of *Les Huguenots, Robert le diable, L'Africaine* and *Le Prophète,* is buried in the Friedhof der Jüdischen Gemeinde, Schönhauser Allee (East Berlin).

In the Tiergarten (Zoo), you will find monuments to **Haydn, Mozart, Beethoven, Wagner,** and **Lortzing.**

A monument to the Russian composer **Mikhail Glinka** (1804–1857) is located in the Friedhof der russische-orthodoxen Gemeinde (cemetery of the Russian Orthodox community). He died in Berlin, but was buried in St. Petersburg.

Musical Organizations

Arbeitsgemeinschaft der musikwissenschaftlichen Forschungsinstitut in Deutschland (Association of Musicological Research Institutes in Germany)
Bundesallee 1–12.

BACH: Bach Chor
Ev. Johannesstift.
Schönwalder Allee, 1 Berlin-Spandau. Tel: 36 10 05 337.

Berliner Barock-Orchester
Stölpchenweg 10b. Tel: 8 09 14 18.

Berliner Cappella

Berliner Motettenchor
Lodsweg 24. Tel: 661 44 77.

Berliner Philharmonisches Orchester
Philharmonie, Matthaikirchstrasse 1.

Bund Deutscher Liebhaberorchester (Association of German Amateur Orchestras)
Bundesalle 55, Berlin-Wilmersdorf.

This group also publishes a journal called *Das Liebhaberorchester.*

Collegium Musicum Vocale et Instrumentale der Berliner Universitäten
Höhmannstrasse.

Deutsche Gesellschaft für Musik des Orients (German Society for Oriental Music)
72–76 Reichpietschufer.

Deutsche Oper
Lagardestrasse 28, Berlin-Schlachtensee.

Gesellschaft für musikalische Aufführungs- und mechanische Vervielfaltigungsrechte GEMA, (Society for the Rights of Musical Performances and Mechanical Reproductions)
Bayreuther Strasse 37.

HAYDN: Haydn-Orchester Berlin

International Society for Contemporary Music
Winklerstrasse 20.

International Theater-Institute German Section
Bundesallee 23. Tel: 86 03 48.

MOZART: Berliner Mozart Chor
c/o Mozarteum Gesellschaft e.V.
Troppauer Strasse 23.

Philharmonischer Chor Berlin e.V.
Flenneburger Str. 21 Tel: 39 36 93.

Radio-Symphonie Orchester
Haus des Rundfunks.
Masurenallee 8.

Rias-Kammerchor Berlin
Kufsteiner Strasse 69.

Rundfunk in amerikanischen Sektor Berlin (RIAS)
Kufsteiner Strasse 69, Berlin-Schöneberg.

Sender Freies Berlin (SFB)
Masurenallee 8–14, Haus des Rundfunks, Berlin-Charlottenburg 9.

Singakademie
Reichsstrasse 8. Tel: 304 65 67.

The Singakademie was founded in 1791. Weber, Clara Schumann, Spontini, C. F. Zelter, Schlegel, Chamisso, Bettina von Arnim, Schiller, and Goethe, among others were members of this organization.

Mendelssohn had a long association with the Singakademie. He sang with them when he was a child, and they performed a psalm setting of his when he was 10 years old. His well-known revival of Bach's *St. Matthew Passion* in 1829 took place in the Singakademie.

Staats- und Dom Chor
Hardenburgstrasse 36. Tel: 3141.

Studio Berlin of the Norddeutscher Rundfunk (NDR)
Kufsteiner Strasse 69. Tel: 213 01.

Symphonisches Orchester Berlin
Dickhardstrasse 41.

Verband Deutscher Schulmusikerzieher e.V.
Bergstrasse 26. Tel: 0311/80 66 19.

Verband Deutscher Tonkünstler und Musiklehrer (Association of German Private Music Teachers)
Hähnelstrasse 9, Berlin-Friedenau

Verband Deutscher Geigenbauer e.V.
Ortsverband.
Kantstrasse 132. Tel: 3 12 16.

Zentralstelle für evangelische Kirchenmusik
Jebensstrasse 1. Tel: 0311/3 13 73 14.

Miscellaneous

Books About Berlin

Nelson, Walter Henry. *The Berliners: Their Saga and Their City.* (New York: David McKay, 1969).

Baedeker's *Handbook to Berlin* (New York, Macmillan, 1965), probably the best guidebook to the city.

International Clubs

Deutsche-Englische Gesellschaft (German-English Society)
Uhlandstrasse 7/8.

Deutsch-Amerikanischer Frauenclub (German American Women's Club)
c/o Succhi
Nymphenburgerstrasse 4.

International Institute for Comparative Music Studies

Winklerstrasse 20. Tel: 89 86 92.

Language Schools

Goethe Institute
Knesebeckerstrasse 38–49.

Although this is probably the most expensive course, it is definitely the best offered.

Deutsch für Ausländer (German for Foreigners)

Courses at both universities (Freie Universität and Technische Universität) are offered to foreigners; these are usually not for beginners.

In West Berlin, it is possible to attend all the lectures in the universities without anyone's permission, and although officially closed, the seminars may often be attended by permission of the professor.

Business of Music*

Ahn & Simrock
Meinkestrasse 10.

Apollo Verlag
Ostpreussendamm 26. Tel: 73 18 25.

*NOTE: *Inh.* is the abbreviation for proprietor.

Astoria Verlag
Brandenburgische Strasse 22.

Astra-Verlag
Am Bakequell 13.
1 Berlin-Steglitz.

Bading
Karl-Marx-Strasse 186.
Berlin-Neukölln. Tel: 62 44 11/62 76 66.

Bechstein, C.
Pianofortefabrik AG.
Reichenbergerstrasse 124.

Bennefeld, Albert
Schopenhauerstrasse 13.
1 Berlin-Schlachtensee.

Berliner Festwochen
Bundesallee 1–12. Tel: 881 04 41, Ext. 39.

Berliner Flohmarkt (Flea Market)
Wilmersdorfer Strasse 74. Tel: 885 67 80.
Good bargains may be available.

Berliner Klaviaturfabrik
C. Bohn & Co. KG.
Friedelstrasse 27.
1 Berlin-Neukölln.

Birnbach, Richard
Dürerstrasse 28a.
Berlin-Lichterfelde-West. Tel: 73 13 71.

Book, Curt
Sybelstrasse 29.
Berlin-Charlottenburg. Tel: 88 45 22.

Bote, E. & A. G. Bock
Hardenbergerstrasse 9a.
Berlin-Charlottenberg. Tel: 312 30 81.
Agent: Associated Music Publishers, U.S.A.; Schott, Britain.

Czichon, M.
Würzburgerstrasse 4. Tel: 42 23 65.
music, publishers, wholesale.

Drei Ringe Musikverlag GmbH
Hohenzollerndamm 54a.

Edition Canzonetta
Petzower Strasse 13.

Edition Corona
Hohenzollerndamm 54a.

Edition Corso GmbH
Reichsstrasse 4.

Edition Fortuna
Reichsstrasse 4.

Edition Majestic; E. Paesike
Helmstedter Strasse 27. Tel: 87 48 44.

Edition Meisel
Wittelsbacher Strasse 18.

Edition Metropol
Würzburger Strasse la.

Edition Primus KG
Hohenzollerndamm 54a.

Edition Record KG
Hohenzollerndamm 54a.

Edition Rhythmus
Hohenzollerndamm 54a.

Edition Standart Musikverlag
Nürnbergerstrasse 17.

Edition Tanzmelodie
Reichsstrasse 4.

Edition Takt und Ton GmbH
Hohenzollerndamm 54a.

Edition Tonleiter
Reichsstrasse 4.

Edition Vox
Hohenzollerndamm 54a.

Eschenbach, F.
Mittenwalderstrasse 7.
instruments

Fidelio Verlag
Lincke Ufer 41.

Fröhlich, Friedrich Wilhelm
Ansbacherstrasse 52.

Funke, H., Musikverlage
Lermooser Weg 3. Tel: 73 80 25.
1 Berlin-Lichterfeld 2.
music, books, records wholesale

Glas, A.
Promenadenstrasse 11
Berlin-Lichterfelde 45. Tel: 73 50 83.
books, musical instruments, records.

Gloria Musikverlag
Nürnbergerstrasse 17.

Grabau Kurt Musikverlag
Sachsenwaldstrasse 7.

Graf, Inh. Elsa Graf
Carl-Schurz-Strasse 29.
Berlin-Spandau 20. Tel: 37 36 64.
music, instruments, repairs, records.

Grünewald, Karl K.
Kantstrasse 107. Tel: 24 05 64.
music, instruments, repairs, records.

Gutheil, A. GmbH
Dessauerstrasse 17.
Agent: Boosey & Hawkes, Britain and U.S.A.

Harrison Musikverlag
Wittelsbacherstrasse 18.

Helbling-Production
Reichsstrasse 4.

Helvetia-Verlag, Ziessnitz & Sohn
Kreuzbergstrasse 7.

Hessling, Bruno
Rankestrasse 31. Tel: 24 34 69/24 59 82.

Hi-Fi-Musikverlag GmbH
Humboldtstrasse 42.

Idee-Musik-Verlag
Bornicher Strasse 39a.

Internationale Musikleihbibliothek
Brunnenstrasse 188/190.

Kiepenheuer, Gustav
Schweinfurthstrasse 60.

King Musikverlag
Hohenzollerndamm 54a.

Kirst, Inh. Bruno Kirst
Am Gesundbrunnen.
Brunnenstrasse 106a. Tel: 46 65 32.
books, music, instruments, records.

Kissel, Ernst
Togostrasse 77. Tel: 46 77 79.
instruments.

Klabunde, Alfred
Knesebeckstrasse 74.
1 Berlin-Charlottenburg 2.

Kollo, Willi
Hohmannstrasse 6.

Korber, Günter
Filandstrasse 29.
instruments.

Kuhn, Inh. Arnold Kuhn
Hauptstrasse 138.
Berlin-Schöneberg. Tel: 71 35 90.
music, instruments, records, repairs.

Lienau, Robert
Lankwitzerstrasse 9a.
Berlin-Lichterfelde-Ost.
Agents: Hinrichsen, Britain; Peters, U.S.A.

Löffler, Herman, Musikverlag
Schillerstrasse 115.

Manthey, Ferdinand
Klavierfabrik.
Reichenbergerstrasse 125.

May, Bernhard, L. Mors & Co.
Flügel- und Pianofortefabrik.
Maybach Ufer 40.
1 Berlin-Neukölln.

Meisel Gebr.; Edition Intro
Wittelsbacherstrasse 18.
1 Berlin-Nikolassee.

Merseburger Verlag
Alemannenstrasse 20.
1 Berlin-Nikolassee. Tel: 80 72 64.

Mills Musikverlag GmbH
Hohenzollerndamm 54a.

Monopol Verlag GmbH
Wittelsbacherstrasse 18.

Musik-Edition Europaton
Reichsstrasse 4.

Musik und Kunst
Carl-Schurz-Strasse 60.

Musikhaus am Zoo
Inh. Otto Simonovsky.
Nürnberger Strasse 24a. Tel: 211 64 26.
music, instruments, repairs.

Musik-"Schubert", Inh. Hans Duch
Wilmersdorferstrasse 161.
Berlin-Charlottenburg 1. Tel: 35 51 16.
music, instruments, repairs, records.

Musik-Wiebach
Gneisenaustrasse 18.
and
Forum Steglitz, 1–2 Schlossstrasse.
instruments.

Musikverlag Broadway GmbH
Reichsstrasse 4.

Musikverlage Rolf Budde
Hohenzollerndamm 54a.

Musikverlag Cordial
Hohenzollerndamm 54a.

Musikverlag Melodie, Froboess & Budde
Hohenzollerndamm 54a.
1 Berlin 33.

Neue Welt Musikverlag
Hohenzollerndamm 54a.

Neuköllner Musikhaus, Inh. Hertha Reeck
Hermannstrasse 201.
1 Berlin-Neukölln 44. Tel: 62 39 37.
music, instruments, repairs.

Oehme, Walter
Onkel-Tom-Strasse 3.
Berlin-Zehlendorf 37. Tel: 84 35 40.
music, instruments, records, repairs.

Pasold, Inh. E. und Ch. Pasold
Bismarckstrasse 39. Tel: 34 67 55.
books, music, instruments, records.

Paul-Gerhardt-Buchhandlung
Dr. Rudolf Elvers KG
Beymestrasse 8.
1 Berlin-Steglitz. Tel: 72 34 25.
books, music.

Pilar, Anton
Kleiststrasse 42.
instruments.

Plessow, Erich Musik-Edition
Nürnbergerstrasse 17.

Prokopius, Franz
Regensburgerstrasse 5.

Richter, Max Rudolph
Inh. Heinz Kliem Nachf. KG.
Sonnenallee 96.
Berlin-Neukölln. Tel: 62 57 56.
instruments, records, music, wholesale.

Riedel, Hans, Inh. Hans und Horst Riedel
Uhlandstrasse 38. Tel: 33 95/881 73 95.
books, music, instruments, records.

Ries und Erler Musikverlag
Charlottenbrunnenstrasse 42.
1 Berlin-Grünefeld.
Agents: Hinrichsen, Britain; Peters, U.S.A.

Risi-Ton-Verlag, G. Bode-Seidentopf
Caspar-Theuss-Strasse 29/II.

Schaeffers, Peter, Musikverlag
Reichsstrasse 4.

Schilling Musik, Inh. Gertrud Schilling
Molzstrasse 34. Tel: 24 43 51.

Schwartz, Alfred, Musikalienhandlung
Rheinstrasse 9.
1 Berlin-Friedenau 41. Tel: 83 54 52.
music, instruments, records, repairs.

Sirius-Verlag Berlin Margarita Katz
Wickhofstrasse 67.

Song-Edition Rolf Budde KG
Hohenzollerndamm 54a.

Spanka Musikverlag GmbH
Hohenzollerndamm 54a.

Steinway & Sons
Pianoforte-Fabrikanten.
Hardenbergstrasse 9.

Sulzbach, W., Inh. Margarete Limbach
Weddingen Weg 30.
1 Berlin-Lichterfelde 45. Tel: 73 56 73.
books, music, instruments, records.

Tauentzien Musikverlag
Sergious G. Safranow.
Humboldtstrasse 42.

Teichmann, Ingbert
Aachener Strasse 42.
instruments.

Verlag Alte und Neue Kunst
Reingaustrasse 3.

Viewer Verlag
Limonenstrasse 10.

Agents: Musica Rara, Britain, Peters, U.S.A.

Wetzel, Werner
Holsteinische Strasse 14.
instruments.

Wiebach, Inh. Paul Wiebach
Gneisenaustrasse 18. Tel: 66 87 34/66 36 65.
music, instruments, records, repairs, wholesale.

Wiedling, Hans, Inh. Margarethe Wiedling
Albrechtstrasse 120.
1 Berlin-Steglitz 41. Tel: 72 35 00.
books, music, records, instruments.

Woitschach, Radio- und Musikverlag
Artuswall 48.

Zielke, Erich
Beethovenstrasse 27–29.

EAST BERLIN

Just in case you'd like to try it, James Helme Sutcliffe in *Opera News* of February 28, 1970 explains the easiest way to get into East Berlin: Take the S-Bahn from Bahnhof Zoo to Friedrichstrasse, a seven-minute ride. Take your passport and about thirty marks. . . . At Friedrichstrasse, go down the steps to ground level and enter the door marked "Ausländer" (foreigners). Get in line and exchange your passport for a slip of paper with a number on it and a form that you have to fill out: name, Berlin address, how much money, cameras, or leather goods you have with you.

You'll have to change five West German marks for five East at the window; you're expected to use them up on food, books, or music before you come back. They cannot be reexchanged, but any amount over the five can be exchanged for West German marks again before you return. (Restaurants and box offices take West German money; be sure to get a receipt.) After a while, they'll call your number. . . . The customs man asks if you have anything to declare, and then you're through. Regulations are pretty much the same today, five years later.

Opera Houses and Concert Halls

Since you might take a chance, here are a few details on East Berlin theaters:

Deutsche Staatsoper

Unter den Linden 7. Tel: 20 04 91

Season: September to beginning of July; closed early July to end of August. Opera, ballet, and concerts are offered here.

Box Office: same location as above.

Hours: daily noon to 6:30 PM; Sunday and holidays 4:00 PM to 6:00 PM.

Authorized Ticket Agencies: Zentraler Besucherdienst der Berliner Bühnen.

Seating capacity: 1452

Customary Dress: Unlike the opera and concert halls of West Berlin, whose management suggests only street dress, the Deutsche Staatsoper prefers *festliche* (more festive) attire.

Built by Frederick the Great in 1742, the structure was remodeled, after various fires and bombings. Spontini directed the Staatsoper for twenty-two years. Otto Nicolai's *Merry Wives of Windsor* was given its premiere here in 1849. Alban Berg's *Wozzeck* also premiered here in 1925.

Komische Oper

Behrenstrasse (one parallel street beyond Unter den Linden).

According to James Helme Sutcliffe (see above) you see and hear best from the seats in the front of the second balcony. It's a smaller theater. (For more historical information on the three opera houses in Berlin, see "Berlin" in *Oxford Dictionary of Opera,* edited by Rosenthal and Warrack.)

Schauspielhaus

Gendarmenmarkt (Platz der Akademie).

This building, which opened in 1821 with Weber's *Der Freischütz,* is now being restored as a six-hundred-seat theater for chamber opera and concerts. An earlier building on the same site was the scene of the premiere of E. T. A. Hoffmann's *Undine* in 1816.

Maxim Gorki Theater

Unter den Linden.

Note: Box offices of East Berlin theaters are open from midday to the time of performance. Tickets go on sale ten days ahead. Tickets may be ordered from the box office on the Friedrichstrasse station platform (see above) without going into the East zone.

Originally the Singakademie, this is the theater in which Mendelssohn revived Bach's *St. Matthew Passion* in 1829. Corresponding to the Berliner Festwochen (see Festivals) the East Berliners have their Berliner Festtage of theater and music, held during the first two weeks in October in various theaters throughout the city. Tickets are available in September at the Zentral Besucherdienst (Central Visitors' Bureau) and the Pavillon on Friedrichstrasse (on the corner of Clara-Zetkin-Strasse), as well as at the box offices of the participating theaters.

Although we have not covered much of East Germany, there are numerous items of musical interest to be explored, especially in Leipzig and its environs. Visitors to all East German cities except East Berlin require a visa and advance hotel reservations. The inconveniences you may experience in making these arrangements will be amply rewarded by the opportunity to enjoy the musical offerings, past and present, among which are the following: the St. Thomas Church (and the Thomasschule) with which J. S. Bach was associated as Cantor for twenty-seven years, and where Wagner was baptized on August 16, 1813; the present Gewandhaus Orchestra, the best in East Germany, whose past history includes such musicians as Felix Mendelssohn, E. T. A. Hoffmann, Gustav Mahler, Bruno Walter, Wilhelm Furtwängler; the homes of Mahler, and Robert and Clara Schumann; the house where Schumann was born (now a museum) in Zwickau (an hour and forty-five minutes south of Leipzig by train); the new seventeen hundred-seat opera house at Karl-Marx Platz, home of what is generally considered the best all-around company in the Eastern zone and where an excellent seat costs little more than $2; the Bach Fest, held every four years (the last in 1974) in late May and early June; and East Germany's annual Wagner Festival, which takes place during early May in Dessau (an hour from Leipzig by train).

Libraries and Museums

Deutsche Staatsbibliothek

Unter den Linden 8.

Hours: Monday to Saturday 9:00 AM to 9:00 PM; Sundays 1:00 PM to 8:00 PM.

The library is open year-round.

Readers gain admission to the library by buying a library card. Representatives of scholarly institutions and students are not required to pay an entrance fee.

Included in this collection are the composer's manuscript scores of Acts I and II of *The Marriage of Figaro* and *Der Freischütz.*

Library of the Deutsche Staatsoper
Unter den Linden 7.
Hours: The library is open year-round. Readers may use it without special permission or other requirements. In certain special cases, the library may lend books and documents. Individual foreigners may borrow material through the cultural services of their embassies.

BONN

Tel. prefix: 2221

Through no fault of its own, modern Bonn is a city of paradoxes. Known today principally as the birthplace of Beethoven, Bonn was already of strategic importance during the Roman empire, when it emerged as a key point in the Roman fortification system along the Rhine river. In the thirteenth century, this city became the permanent home of the archbishops and prince-electors of Cologne. Their courts maintained the very best cultural traditions, and music was but one of the arts which flourished there.

Thrust into the political limelight in 1949, this quaint little city of approximately 135,000 inhabitants became the unwilling capital of the Federal Republic of Germany until such time as the two halves of the country will once again be unified. A visitor to Bonn never feels he is in the capital of *any* country, let alone that of a prominent western European nation. The old marketplace and its surroundings, the charming little cemetery on the outskirts of town, and even the great Rhineland university named after its founder, Friedrich Wilhelm III, King of Prussia, suggest instead a place somewhere in the hinterlands.

A magnificent baroque edifice, the Old Town Hall (1737) faces the open-air market looking much the same as it did when Beethoven's grandfather was alive. On a street off this square is the house where Beethoven was born in 1770. Numerous monuments, plaques, and memorials to the composer are located all over the city. The most impressive structure, however, is the famous Beethovenhalle, the concert hall which, together with the splendid Theater der Stadt Bonn, epitomize the best in contemporary concrete and glass architecture.

Opera Houses and Concert Halls

Beethovenhalle

Theaterstrasse 3 (Entrance at Wachsbleiche 17). Tel: 77 22 62/67

Seating capacity: Grosser Saal, 1476; studio, 387; Kammermusiksaal, 186.

Bonn's chief social and cultural center, the Beethovenhalle, a bold example of modern architecture, is the setting for the biennial Beethoven Festival here. Besides the large auditorium, the hall contains a studio for more intimate recitals and rooms for chamber music, lectures, and art exhibits. In the foyer can be found the well-known bust of Beethoven by Antoine Bourdelle.

Theater der Stadt Bonn (Bonn Municipal Theater)

Am Boeselagerhof 1, south of the Berliner Freiheit. Tel: 509 37-1

Box Office Hours: 9:00 AM to 2:00 PM and 4:00 PM to 8:00 PM.

Seating capacity: 1000

Städtische Bühnen

Kronprinzenstrasse 2, in the hall of the Bonner Bürgerverein.

Seating capacity: 770

This complex is used for opera, operetta and drama.

Stadttheater Bonn-Bad Godesberg

Theaterplatz 53, Bonn-Bad Godesberg. Tel: 6 32 02

Box Office Hours: Monday to Friday 4:00 PM to 7:00 PM.

Seating capacity: 729

Summer Concerts

Outdoor summer concerts are given in the courtyard of the Poppelsdorfer Schloss at Meckenheimer Allee and also in the Stadtgarten.

Ticket information for all events in Bonn may be obtained at the Informations-Pavillon, Städt. Verkehrsamt, Bahnhofstrasse 22 (Tel: BN 77466) and 53 Bonn-Bad Godesberg.

Information on concerts may be obtained from Kulturamt der Stadt Bonn, Rathaus, Kurfürstenstrasse 2, Bonn-Bad Godesberg. Tel: 8/600/645/663/628

Tickets may be obtained at the following box offices and agencies:

Städtische Konzertkasse
Mülheimer Platz 1. Tel: 65 68 00 or 7 76 66
Hours: Monday to Friday 9:00 AM to 2:00 PM; Saturday 9:00 AM to 1:00 PM.

Kasse des Stadttheaters
Theaterplatz, Bonn-Bad Godesberg. Tel: 8/6 3202
Hours: Monday to Friday 4:00 PM to 7:00 PM.

Subscriptions (*Abonnement*) to all theater and concert series are available at up to thirty percent savings for regular subscribers. If you turn in at the box office a ticket that you don't plan to use, an attempt will be made to sell it for you; also, you can pick up last-minute seats for performances in this way.

Libraries and Museums

Stadtbücherei, Städt. Musikbücherei, and Schumannhaus
Sebastianstrasse 182, D 53 Bonn-Endenich. Tel: 77 656
Hours: Monday to Saturday (except Tuesday) 10:00 AM to noon; Monday and Friday 4:00 PM to 7:00 PM; Wednesday and Thursday 3:00 PM to 6:00 PM. Closed Sunday and holidays.
(See Musical Landmarks, Schumannhaus.)

Universitätsbibliothek [Ben. 45]
Adenauerallee 37–41. Tel: 673 43 50
Hours: Monday to Friday 9:00 AM to 9:00 PM; Saturday 9:00 AM to noon.

Musikwissenschaftliches Seminar der Rheinischen Friedrich-Wilhelms-Universität Bonn [Ben. 44]
Am Hof 34. Tel: 73 45 81
Hours: Monday to Friday 9:00 AM to 1:00 PM and 3:00 PM to 6:00 PM. Closed August.

Beethoven-Archiv [Ben. 46]
Bonngasse 18. Tel: 6 351 88
Mailing Address: Postfach 73.
Hours: Monday to Friday 9:00 AM to 1:00 PM and 3:00 PM to 5:00 PM. Closed August.

This archive houses one of the finest Beethoven collections in the world. Only scholars and those doing research will be granted permission to use it. We therefore suggest obtaining a letter of recommendation in advance of your arrival in Bonn. (See Musical Landmarks, Beethovens Geburtshaus.)

Conservatories and Schools

Musikschule der Stadt Bonn
Kurfürstenstrasse 8, 53 Bonn-Bad Godesberg. Tel: 600 659

The school provides music instruction emphasizing instrumental proficiency.

Summer Courses

Internationale Meisterkurse Bonn
c/o Staatliche Hochschule für Musik Köln, "Meisterkurse"
Dagobertstrasse 38, 5 Cologne. Tel: 72 05 81
Dates: end of August through middle of September.

The courses in piano, violin, cello, voice, and chamber music are given by the State College of Music, Cologne, in cooperation with the city of Bonn and the Beethoven House Society, Bonn. For further information write to the above address.

Musical Landmarks

Beethovens Geburtshaus
Bonngasse 20. Tel: 63 51 88
Hours: summer weekdays 9:00 AM to 1:00 PM and 3:00 PM to 6:00 PM; Sunday and holidays 9:00 AM to 1:00 PM. Winter weekdays 10:00 AM to 1:00 PM and 2:00 PM to 5:00 PM; Sunday and holidays 10:00 AM to 1:00 PM.

This house, one of the best preserved *Geburtshäuser,* contains Beethoven documents and memorabilia, including manuscripts, portraits, and musical instruments. Slides and postcards are available for purchase here. Recordings made on Beethoven's original instruments are available next door from the Verlag Beethovenhaus, Bonngasse 18.

Schumannhaus
Sebastianstrasse 182, Bonn-Endenich 53. Tel: 77 656
Hours: Monday to Saturday (except Tuesday) 10:00 AM to noon; Monday and Friday 4:00 PM to 7:00 PM; Wednesday and Thursday 3:00 PM to 6:00 PM; Sunday and holidays only the *Gedenkzimmer* (memorial room) 11:00 AM to 1:00 PM.

The Schumannhaus contains both the Bonn municipal library (see Libraries) and the Schumann-Gedenkstätte.

This building was the asylum (partly rebuilt after World War II) where Schumann spent his last years. In the Schumann *Gedenkzimmer* there is a collection of approximately fifty documents and letters relating to the composer and his family and friends.

Max-Reger-Institut

Kurfürstenstrasse 6, Bonn-Bad Godesberg. Tel: 60 06 41
Hours: By appointment.

The Institute, founded in 1947 by Elsa Reger, manages Reger's estate and is preparing a scholarly edition of his complete works.

Beethovendenkmal (Beethoven Monument)

Münsterplatz.

In the center of the oldest part of town, not far from the railway station, stands a bronze statue of Beethoven, from 1845.

Alter Friedhof (Old Cemetery)

Bornheimerstrasse, northwest of the city center.

The graves of Robert and Clara Schumann are located on the main avenue of this cemetery leading to the west exit. Also buried here are Beethoven's mother and Charlotte von Lengefeld, Friedrich Schiller's wife. Their graves are immediately to the right beside the wall adjoining Bornheimerstrasse.

Another paramusical celebrity buried here is Mathilde Wesendonck, wife of the Swiss silk merchant Otto Wesendonck. Mathilde was Wagner's inspiration for Isolde in his opera *Tristan und Isolde.* Late in life, Frau Wesendonck became an active antivivisectionist and a close friend of Brahms, Wagner's archrival in musical circles.

Musical Organizations

Deutscher Musiakalienwirtschafts-Verband (Association of German Music Dealers)

Dahlmannstrasse 20.

They publish a periodical entitled *Fachblatt für den Handel mit Musikalien, Schallplatten, Musikinstrumenten und Zubehör.*

Deutscher Musikverleger-Verband (German Association of Music Publishers)

Dahlmannstrasse 20.

Inter Nationes
Kennedyallee 91–103, 53 Bonn-Bad Godesberg 2

This group is a music information center.

Deutscher Akademischer Austauschdienst (*German Academic Exchange Program*)
Kennedyallee 50, 532 Bad Godesberg.

Deutscher Musikrat—Sektion Bundesrepublik Deutschland im Internationalen Musikrat (*German Musical Council, Section of West Germany in the International Music Council*)
Director: Professor Dr. Siegfried Borris
Mailing Address: Michaelstrasse 4a, 53 Bonn-Bad Godesberg. Tel: 02229/63031

Gemeinschaft Deutscher Musik-Fachverbände (*Society of German Professional Musical Organizations*)
Dahlmannstrasse 2.

Miscellaneous

Information for foreign students

Akademisches Auslandsamt der Universität (*Foreign Students' Office*)
Nassestrasse 11. Tel.: 73 42 93

This office is designed to help foreigners connected with the University and to establish exchange contacts. It also runs a series of *Deutschkurse für Ausländer* (German courses for foreigners) at all levels from elementary to advanced, as well as *Internationale Ferienkurse* (vacation courses) during July and August. The latter cover German literature, culture, politics, etc., in addition to language training. During March and April the *Internationale Kurse für deutsche Sprache und Literatur* is designed primarily for foreign Germanists and German teachers. Excursions, concerts, and theater performances are included in the course.

For information on studying in Bonn:

For inquiries on courses, research facilities, registration, etc., contact the Rektorat der Universität, Liebfrauenweg 3. (*Mailing address:* 53 Bonn, Postfach 589).

In order to attend lectures or seminars at the University, it will probably suffice to register as a *Gasthörer* (visiting auditor). To find out what is being offered, one will need a *Vorlesungsverzeichnis* (catalog of courses) available at the university *Quästur* or any Bonn bookshop, about two months before the beginning of each new semester.

Books about Bonn

Bonn, Das Bild der Bundeshauptstadt (also in English). Available at any bookstore in town. A good introduction to the city, its history and geography.

Köln und Bonn von 7 bis 7, by W. Stahl and D. Wien. An excellent guide to all cultural points of interest, services, etc., in German.

The Business of Music

Publishers

Verlag Beethovenhaus
Bonngasse 18
This is the publishing organization of the Beethoven House (see Musical Landmarks and Libraries). It publishes facsimiles of Beethoven's works and also sells recordings of music played on Beethoven's original instruments.

COLOGNE (Köln)

Tel. prefix: 02 21

Cologne is over two thousand years old. Its exact age was unknown until 1968 when the keepers of the archives discovered too late that they had just overlooked the opportunity for a jubilee celebration. In this historical, cultural, and economic center of the Rhineland, which the Germans call "Köln," the inhabitants were too busy to notice the omission. After being informed, they accepted their lost opportunity with the utmost composure. The people of Cologne are not outgoing or warm; "proud, determined, and conscientious" are better adjectives to describe them.

This is a city of internationally famous industries, including automobile production, machine tools, cables, precision engineering, and, of course, Eau de Cologne! The largest German radio and television centers, including the West German Radio, Deutsche Welle, and Deutschlandfunk are located here.

Cologne, a showcase for international art, owns seven civic museums, about thirty private art galleries, a public art gallery (the *Kunsthalle*), and numerous auction houses. Its musical activities consist of opera, theater, and extensive series including the Gürzenich concerts, the Radio Symphony Orchestra concerts, as well as recitals presented by the city's Music Academy.

Another entertainment specialty, the Cologne Puppet Theater, offers plays in dialect, usually understood only by those whose German is fluent. The Gürzenich concerts are conducted by Professor Günter Wand or well-known guest conductors; the concerts broadcast by the West German Radio Orchestra promote contemporary music. Choral music is the province of the Philharmonic Choir and the Bach Society, and chamber music is the domain of the Chamber Orchestra of the Rhineland, which performs regularly in the city's museums. Cologne also has the second largest German university (founded in 1388), a teacher-training school, and many technical schools.

Cologne's history began with the Romans. By the time it had reached the status of a *colonia* (Latin for "colony" from which its name derives), the natives had already begun building the familiar city wall, some portions of which still survive. Cologne was bombed repeatedly during the war. Fortunately, despite the demolition of the entire area surrounding it, the famous Cologne Cathedral, tallest structure in the city (511 feet 6 inches), was practically unharmed. Curiously, while numerous air raid shelters were being dug around the city, many archeological treasures were discovered, some in the Cathedral itself. These are regularly on display for visitors to see. The Cathedral and a coronation figure prominently in Schumann's *Rhenish* Symphony; the Cathedral is also cited in Heine's poem (from his *Buch der Lieder*) with which Schumann concluded his *Dichterliebe.*

The public relations department at the Tourist Office here offers journalists and writers a particular service, a photoarchive with 8,000 items available for their (and your) inspection. Call 2 21 33 61 or visit their office, directly across from the Cathedral, and inquire about it in person.

Guides and Services

A weekly listing of concert programs and other cultural events appears in *Kölner Leben,* available at major hotels and at the City Tourist Office (Verkehrsamt der Stadt Köln, am Dom) opposite the west front of the Cathedral. Tel: 22 11 and 2 21 33 40. For last-minute concert information, phone 11 58.

Concert programs for the entire winter season are available at the end of August.

Advance tickets may be purchased at the Kartenvorverkauf of the Tourist

Office from Monday to Friday 10:00 AM to 12:30 PM and 1:00 PM to 6:00 PM; Saturday from 10:00 AM to noon. Closed Sunday.

For a tour of the city that takes in many of the culturally significant sites, phone 2 21 33 32 for details.

Articles on the musical and dramatic scene appear in the German review *Thema,* also available at the Tourist Office and the Neumarkt box office.

Opera Houses and Concert Halls

Opera House and Bühnen der Stadt Köln

Offenbachplatz 2. Tel: 21 43 15
Tel: (02 21) 23 32 31

Mailing address: Postfach 141, Cologne.
Season: September to July.
Seating capacity: Opernhaus: 1,346
Schauspielhaus: 920
Kammerspiel: 329
Box Office Hours: 8:00 AM to 8:00 PM.

This strikingly modern hall was built in 1957–62 from plans by W. Riphahn. The large hall opened in 1957 and the remaining sections of the building were completed by 1962. Workshops, prop shops, costume storage rooms, and rehearsal rooms are all contained within the complex. A covered passage connects the theater with the Opernterrassen (the theater restaurant), and another covered corridor links the house with a car-park building in the Kölner Ladenstadt (shopping center). Behind the Opera House is the Playhouse, a smaller theater also built to Riphahn's plans. The larger hall seats about fourteen hundred persons. The balcony-style boxes extend fanlike, high over the orchestra seats, and the orchestra, like many of those in other new halls in Germany, has no center aisle. Since nobody considers leaving a performance before its conclusion, this arrangement presents no difficulties.

Historically, this company's greatest years were those between 1917 and 1924 when the orchestra was conducted by Otto Klemperer. Premieres given then included Erich Korngold's *Die tote Stadt* (1920), and the first German performance of Jánaček's *Kátya Kabanova* (1922).

Kammeroper Köln

101 Perlengraben. Tel: 21 46 42 or 66 23 22

Opera and operetta are performed here.

Gürzenich

Gürzenichstrasse and Martinstrasse.

The Gürzenich has had a long and varied history. Built by the citizens as a banqueting hall in the mid-fifteenth century, it was the scene of a reception in 1520 attended by Emperor Charles V and Albrecht Dürer. In 1887, the Brahms Double Concerto had its premiere performance here with violinist Joseph Joachim and cellist Robert Hausmann as soloists. For a while the building was used as a warehouse and then, between 1952 and 1955, it was rebuilt under the direction of architects Karl Band and Rudolf Schwarz to serve as the city festival hall. The reconstruction joined it to the ruined church of St. Alban, extant parts of which date back to the seventeenth century. Today, festivals, concerts, and congresses all take place here at some time during the year.

The Gürzenich houses the Municipal Gürzenich Orchestra and the Gürzenich String Quartet as well as a rich variety of other performing organizations. It is the chief concert hall of Cologne. A restaurant and wine cellar are also to be found here.

Musikwissenschaftliches Institut der Universität

Albertus-Magnus-Platz, Cologne-Lindenthal. Tel: 20 24 249

Performances by the well-known Collegium Musicum of the Institute of Musicology take place in an auditorium here. This department has an excellent instrument collection, very well displayed and actually used for these performances.

Wallraf-Richartz-Museum

An der Rechtschule. Tel: 221 2379

Hours: daily 10:00 AM to 5:00 PM, Tuesday and Friday 10:00 AM to 10:00 PM.

Concerts are given in their auditorium. At the Tourist Office and at museum ticket offices, you can buy a pass that entitles you to an unlimited number of visits to the seven museums in Cologne on three consecutive days. If you are here for only a few days, you can visit them all for one low price. (Schoolchildren and students do not need a pass. Entry for them is always free.)

Westdeutscher Rundfunk

Wallrafplatz 5.

There is a concert hall in the Broadcasting House, home of the important Westdeutscher Rundfunk Orchestra concerts. A series of contemporary music concerts is regularly given here. The building also houses a studio for electronic music.

Marionette Theater

Puppenspiele der Stadt Köln (*Municipal Marionette Theater*)
2–4 Eisenmarkt. Tel: 21 63 71; for tickets only 23 32 31.

Puppet shows have been a Cologne specialty since the mid-nineteenth century. The plays are often given in Cologne dialect.

Cultural Institutes

The British Council (*Die Brücke*)
Hahnenstrasse 6.

America House (*United States Information Center*)
Apostelnkloster 13–15.

The Belgian House
Cäcilienstrasse 46.

The French Institute (*Institut Français*)
Sachsenring 77.

The Italian Cultural Institute
Universitätsstrasse 81.

The Finland Institute
Flandrischestrasse 13.

The Japanese Cultural Institute
near the Aachener Weiher, the lake just north of the University.

Concerts and lectures are offered at all of these cultural institutes.

Summer Concerts

Schloss Brühl
504 Brühl bei Cologne.
Transportation: by rail from central station or by suburban tram from Barbarossaplatz.

In Brühl, a suburb of Cologne, about ten miles out of the city, summer concerts are given from mid-May to October in the entrance hall of the Augustusburg, a rococo castle. (See also Conservatories, International Master Courses.)

Libraries and Museums

Universitäts- und Stadtbibliothek [Ben. 157]
Universitätsstrasse 33, 5 Cologne-Lindenthal. Tel: (0221) 470 Ext 22 14
Hours: Monday to Friday 9:00 AM to 8:00 PM, Saturday 9:00 AM to noon. Closed Christmas, New Year, one week at Pentecost, last week in September.

Staatliche Hochschule für Musik, Bibliothek [Ben. 156]
Dagobertstrasse 38. Tel: (0221) 72 05 81
Hours: Monday, Friday 10:00 AM to noon; Tuesday, Thursday 10:00 AM to noon and 2:00 PM to 4:00 PM. Closed semester vacations.

Musikbücherei der Stadt Köln (Music Library of the City of Cologne)
Jakordenstrasse 18–20, Jakordehaus. Tel: (0221) 3898
Hours: Monday, Tuesday, Thursday, Friday 11:00 AM to 1:00 PM and 3:00 PM to 6:00 PM.

Joseph Haydn Institute e.V. [Ben. 154]
Blumenthalstrasse 23. Tel: 73 37 96
Hours: Monday to Friday 9:00 AM to 6:00 PM; closed Saturday and Sunday, and legal holidays. Permission of Director is necessary for use of facilities.

The Institute was incorporated in 1955. It functions primarily as a research institute whose staff collects and sifts all sources of the works of Joseph Haydn in order to prepare a complete and historically authentic and accurate edition of same.

The collected edition is published by the G. Henle Verlag, Munich-Duisburg. This is not a continuation of the former fragmentary editions (Breitkopf & Härtel, Leipzig; Haydn Society, Boston-Vienna), but in every respect a completely new edition. The first volumes appeared in 1958. Since then, new volumes are in preparation and appear fairly regularly. A special catalog lists the works presently available.

The Institute also publishes *Haydn Studien* which includes articles on most recent Haydn research.

Musikwissenschaftliches Institut der Universität, Bibliothek [Ben. 155]
Albertus-Magnus Platz, 5 Cologne-Lindenthal. Tel: (0221) 470 Ext 22 49
Hours: Monday to Friday 8:30 AM to 7:00 PM; Saturday 9:00 AM to noon; semester vacations Monday to Friday 9:00 AM to 4:00 PM.

Erzbischöfliche Diözesan- und Dombibliothek [Ben. 153]
Gereonstrasse 2–4. Tel: (0221) 23 95 87

Hours: Monday to Friday 9:00 AM to 1:00 PM, 2:00 PM to 6:00 PM; Saturday 9:00 AM to 12:30 PM.

Rautenstrauch-Joest-Museum
Ubierring 45. Tel: 31 20 58
Hours: daily 10:00 AM to 5:00 PM; Monday and Thursday 7:00 PM to 10:00 PM.

A small instrument collection relating to non-Western music is on display here.

Museum für ostasiatische Kunst
Hahnentorburg, am Rudolfplatz. Tel: 23 16 21 and 21 38 63
Hours: daily 10:00 AM to 5:00 PM.

Chinese, Japanese, and Korean collections are here, including some musical instruments.

Kölnisches Stadtmuseum
Zeughausstrasse 1–3. Tel: 2 21 23 52
Hours: daily 10:00 AM to 5:00 PM and Thursday 10:00 AM to 10:00 PM.

This museum also has a small instrument collection.

Conservatories and Schools

Staatliche Hochschule für Musik, Köln
Dagobertstrasse 38. Tel: 720581

In mid-September, there are International Master Courses here in piano, voice, and violin. For information, write to the above address. Housing facilities available.

Musikwissenschaftliches Institut der Universität
Albertus-Magnus-Platz, Cologne-Lindenthal. Tel: 20 24 24 9

(See Libraries and Concert Halls.)

Kölner Kurse für neue Musik (*Cologne Courses on Contemporary Music*)
Rheinische Musikschule, Vogelsängerstrasse 28–32.

These occur in mid-October through November. Write for details.

International Master Courses of the State College of Music, Cologne (*Max Rostal Course*)
Information: write Staatliche Hochschule für Musik, Dagobertstrasse 38, D-5000 Cologne, Germany.

Courses for piano, voice, song interpretation for singer and pianist, violin; Hermann Reutter (song interpretation) and Max Rostal (violin).
Concerts and piano recitals given.

Musical Landmarks

In the Musical Academy located in Sternengasse, the eight-year-old **Beethoven** gave his first public concert in 1778. (Remember, he was born close by in Bonn.)

Jacques Offenbach, composer of light operas and operettas, was born at Grosser Griechermarkt 1 on June 20, 1819. The house is still standing.

Musical Organizations

Allgemeiner Cäcilien-Verband für die Länder der Deutschen Sprache (St. Caecilia Association for German-Speaking Countries)
Burgmauer 1.

Arbeitsgemeinschaft Deutscher Chorverbände (Association of German Choral Societies)
Burgmauer 68.

Deutsche UNESCO-Kommission
Komödienstrasse 40.

Verband Deutscher Schulmusikerzieher (Association of German Music Educators)
Manderscheider Strasse 35, Köln-Klettenberg.

Verbindungsstelle für Zwischenstaatliche Beziehungen (Office for the Promotion of International Relations in Musical Life)
Heumarkt 62.

Bund Deutscher Klavierbauer
Frankenwerft 35. Tel: 23 31 01

Bund Deutscher Orgelbaumeister
Hansaring 24. Tel: 21 98 28

DARMSTADT

Tel. prefix: 06151

Guides and Services

Lebendiges Darmstadt

The official program of events issued every two weeks by the Tourist Office is available free at the office or at major hotels and newsstands in the city.

Verkehrsamt (Tourist Office)
Wilhelminenstrasse 17½. Tel: 13780 and 13781

Opera Houses and Concert Halls

Landestheater Darmstadt (in Orangeriehaus; also called Staatstheater)
Bessungerstrasse 44. Tel: 122005
Seating capacity: 550
Box Office: same as above address
Hours: Monday, only if there is a performance that day, 10:00 AM to 1:30 PM; Tuesday to Saturday 10:00 AM to 1:30 PM; Sunday 11:00 AM to 1:00 PM; also at the Orangeriehaus box office, one hour before curtain.

Concerts, operas, and plays are performed here.

For further information on the Landestheater, try the Städtisches Kulturamt (Municipal Office for Cultural Activities), Kasinostrasse 3, Tel: 13432 and 13434.

Stadthalle Darmstadt (formerly Schulturn Halle)
Wilhelm Leuschnerstrasse.

Promenade concerts and jazz concerts are held in the Herrngarten, the Orangeriegarten, and on the Mathildenhöhe.

Marionette Theaters

Darmstädter Puppenspiele
Heinrichstrasse 181. Tel: 76337

Puppenbühne Hildenbrandt
Alicenstrasse 6. Tel: 25156

Additional ticket and concert information at:
Informationsdienst am Hauptbahnhof (main station)
Informationsdienst Stadtmitte (center city), 17 Wilhelminenstrasse 17. Tel: 7 39 38

Libraries and Museums

Hessische Landes- und Hochschulbibliothek, Musikabteilung [Ben. 57]
Schloss, Darmstadt. Tel: (06151) 12 44 22 and 12420
Hours: Reading Rooms: Monday to Friday 9:00 AM to 6:00 PM; Saturday 9:00 AM to 12:30 PM. Circulation Department: Monday to Friday 10:00 AM to 12:30 PM and 2:30 PM to 4:30 PM; Saturday 10:00 AM to 12:30 PM. Closed legal holidays, Christmas to New Year's, one week after Pentecost.

Internationales Musikinstitut Darmstadt, Bibliothek [Ben. 58]
Nieder-Ramstädterstrasse 190. Tel: (06151) 13416/13417
Hours: Tuesday and Thursday 9:00 AM to noon, 2:00 PM to 4:00 PM.

The Information Center for Contemporary Music (Informationszentrum für zeitgenössische Musik, formerly [from 1947–62] the Kranichsteiner Musikinstitut) is the country's headquarters for the International Society for Contemporary Music. During the Internationale Ferienkurse für Neue Musik in August and September, the Library allows only limited entry.

Conservatories and Schools

Städtische Akademie für Tonkunst
Hermannstrasse 4. Tel: 13 348/349

For further information write to Sekretariat der Städtischen Akademie für Tonkunst at above address.

Institut für Neue Musik und Musikerziehung (Music Education)
Artilleriestrasse 15. Tel: 24240

This organization sponsors an annual meeting for music educators.

Summer Courses

Internationale Ferienkurse für Neue Musik (*International Holiday Courses for Contemporary Music*)

Nieder-Ramstädterstrasse 190. Tel: (06151) 13416 or 13417

Sponsored by the Internationales Musikinstitut, the courses are usually held during the last two weeks of July and into the first week in August. After 1976, the courses will be held every other year, but their duration will be extended by half the time of their present length. For further information, apply to the Director of the *Ferienkurse.*

Kranichsteiner Musikpreis

Composers as well as performers qualify for this award of DM 4,000. The prize will also no longer be set in the form of a competition, but awarded as a premium. One of the conditions is that the composition or performance must be carried out during the vacation courses. Applicants must be under thirty years of age. The award will be determined by a jury consisting of professors of the vacation courses. The winner(s) will receive a diploma as well as the money premium fixed by the jury.

Musical Landmarks

Between Darmstadt and Heidelberg lies the Bergstrasse (Mountain Street). The *"strata montana"* of the old Romans, it leads you to the romantic valley of the river Neckar and the mysterious Odenwald. This is supposedly the land of the Nibelungen, the legendary medieval race who possessed a magic hoard of gold. Today, two roads from Lorsch to Amorbach remind us of the legend, the Nibelungen Road via Bensheim and Lindenfels and the Siegfried Road via Heppenheim. The Bergstrasse-Odenwald reserve protects the country of the Nibelungen from noise and keeps it quiet and serene for hikers. (You will find a parking place there for your car.)

Musical Organizations

Internationales Musikinstitut Darmstadt

Nieder-Ramstädterstrasse 190. Tel: 13416/13417

This information center for contemporary music has a tape archive, a recording studio, and a studio for electronic music (see Libraries also).

Deutsche Sektion der Internationalen Gesellschaft für Neue Musik e.V.
(*German Section of the International Society for Contemporary Music*)
Neider-Ramstädterstrasse 190. Tel: 134162

Darmstadt has been a center for contemporary music for some time now.

A visit to the Städtisches Kulturamt, 3 Kasinostrasse, Darmstadt, will provide more information on the Mozart Association, the Jazz Group, the Choral Association, and the Instrumental Association in the city.

DÜSSELDORF

Düsseldorf offers an embarrassment of riches. To the fashion conscious, Düsseldorf is an ersatz Paris—the fashion capital of Germany. To the humanist, this is Heine's city—the birthplace of Karl August Varnhagen von Ense (1785–1858), whose wife, Rachel, was Beethoven's friend; the site of the Thomas Mann collection and the Goethe Museum. Art historians associate the names of Peter von Cornelius (1783–1867), Oswald Aschenbach (1827–1905) and Anselm Feuerbach (1829–1880) with Düsseldorf; and musicians remember that Mendelssohn was Director of Music here from 1833 to 1835; that Robert Schumann held that post from 1850 to 1853; that Brahms was here with the Schumanns from 1853 to 1856; that Antonio Draghi, the double bass virtuoso, Ferdinand Hiller, Julius Rietz, Hans Pfitzner, and Georg Frideric Händel all lived and worked here, too.

Düsseldorf is a new city, risen from the ashes of World War II. An industrial and commercial center, the city was totally destroyed during the war. There has been no effort, however, to rebuild the past. Instead, Düsseldorf today is excitingly modern. Although at times the citizens of this bustling metropolis feel harassed (much the same as we here in the States), they know how to relax. Having once been on the brink of disaster, they now plan, with Germanic precision, to spend time on sports and entertainment.

By combining resources with the nearby city of Duisburg, Düsseldorf can support one of the finest opera companies in Germany—its Deutsche Oper am Rhein. Facilities here are excellent, with first-rate operatic and concert performances. The people of Düsseldorf will not settle for less than the best.

About ten miles outside the city lies the Neanderthal valley where the fossils of prehistoric man were first uncovered. Incorporated in 1288, Düsseldorf celebrated its six hundredth anniversary in 1888 with a *Festschrift* (commemorative album) by G. Wimmer that praised theater and music in Düsseldorf, because these two arts had become synonymous with the city itself.

As the home of the world famous Thyssen Foundation, whose building is a landmark on the skyline, Düsseldorf feels assured of industry's continuing support for her cultural centers. Visitors here for business need never look far for entertainment.

Guides and Services

For programs and hours of concerts, consult *Düsseldorf,* a daily publication with theater and concert information, as well as the official city theater guide, *Düsseldorfer Hefte,* and the announcements on kiosks around the city.

Concert information Tel: 1 15 16

Opera Houses and Concert Halls

Rheinhalle
Oeder Allee 1. Tel: 899 23 00
Season: concerts during the season from September to June.

Robert-Schumann-Saal
Ehrenhof 4. Tel: 899 41 25
Season: concerts mostly during the season from September to June.

In these two most important concert halls of the city, tickets may be purchased at the box office one hour before start of performance as well as at the authorized ticket agencies (see below).

*Deutsche Oper am Rhein (Theatergemeinschaft Düsseldorf-Duisburg**)
Heinrich Heine Allee 16a. Tel: 32 64 41
Season: mid-September to mid-July. Closed mid-July to mid-September; December 24 and May 1; presents operas, operettas, musicals, and ballets.
Box Office Hours: Monday to Friday 11:00 AM to 1:00 PM and 5:00 PM to 7:30 PM; Saturday and holidays 10:00 AM to 1:00 PM and 6:30 PM to 7:30 PM; Sunday 10:00 AM to 1:00 PM.
Seating capacity: 1344

The opera house was built in 1875 and renovated in 1956. The company is one of the finest in Germany today and tours fairly often, particularly in the summer in the Netherlands for the Holland Festival and in other neighboring countries as well.

*These two German industrial cities together sponsor the Deutsche Oper am Rhein. The Duisburg Stadttheater, built in 1912 and reconstructed again in 1950, has a seating capacity almost equal to that of the large Düsseldorf house.

Konzertsaal of the Robert-Schumann-Konservatorium
Fischerstrasse 110. Tel: 89 91

Marionette Theaters

Rheinischen Marionetten-Theater
Bilkerstrasse 7. Tel: 32 29 32; 1 28 22; 34 64 39

This marionette theater offers operas as well as traditional puppet shows.

Ticket Agencies

Verkehrsverein der Stadt Düsseldorf, Rheinbahnhaus (at Railroad Station). Tel: 35 05 05

Theater- und Konzertkasse Heinersdorff, Flingerpassage. Tel: 1 08 88

F. Fierlings Musikalienhandlung, Kaiserstrasse 30. Tel: 44 65 93

Libraries and Museums

Goethe Museum (Anton und Katharina Kippenberg Stiftung) [Ben. 66]
Jägerhofstrasse Hofgärtnerhaus. Tel: 44 69 35
Hours: Tuesdays to Sunday 10:00 AM to 5:00 PM. Closed Monday.

Although it is best to write the Director in advance of your coming, regular visiting hours are observed in this delightful, relatively modern building constructed according to the plans of a house that Goethe admired. An extensive collection of documents relating not only to Goethe but also to some of his contemporaries has not yet been completely cataloged. An important Hummel exhibition (the composer Johann Nepomuk Hummel and his son, the artist Carl Hummel) was on display in 1971 with material taken from their own treasures. Autographs and first editions of Zelter, Reichardt, Zumsteeg, Schubert, as well as Hummel can be found here.

Landes- und Stadtbibliothek [Ben. 67]
Grabbeplatz 7. Tel: (0211) 899 41 55
Hours: Monday, Tuesday, Thursday, Friday from 10:00 AM to 4:30 PM; Wednesday 10:00 AM to 6:30 PM; Saturday 10:00 AM to 1:00 PM.

This has been a depository library for official documents of the Düsseldorf area for over sixty years. The Heinrich Heine archives (see below) are located here.

Heinrich-Heine-Archiv
Grabbeplatz 7. Tel: 8 99 42 24/5
Hours: Monday to Friday 9:00 AM to 4:00 PM.

This remarkable collection of documents relating to Heine includes over 4,000 volumes (manuscripts of works and letters). The poet was born here in 1797 (see Musical Landmarks below).

Stadtbüchereien Düsseldorf, Musikbücherei [Ben. 69]
Berliner Allee 59. Tel: (0211) 899 43 94
Hours: circulation Monday and Friday from 11:00 AM to 1:00 PM and 4:00 PM to 7:00 PM; Wednesday from noon to 4:00 PM; the record studio is open Monday and Friday from 11:00 AM to 7:00 PM, Tuesday and Wednesday from 9:00 AM to 4:00 PM; and Thursday and Saturday from 9:00 AM to noon. Closed mid-August to mid-September.

This library has a special Schumann collection.

Schumann-Archiv
Bilkerstrasse.

Write above address for further information about archives not yet open to public.

Stadtarchiv, Düsseldorf
Heinrich-Ehrhardt-Strasse 61.

This archive contains musical memorabilia, autographs, and first editions, as well as musical instruments of importance in the history of Düsseldorf.

Sammlung-Thomas-Mann of the Universitätsbibliothek, Düsseldorf
Königsallee 22/III. Tel: 32 78 17

This important collection of first editions, photographs, and literature about the life and works of Thomas Mann can be seen by appointment. Write in advance to the Secretary of the Collection.

Dumont-Lindemann Archives
Ehrenhof 3. Tel: 44 56 97
Hours: Monday to Friday 9:00 AM to 2:00 PM.

This famous collection of German theater memorabilia was founded by Gustav Lindemann and his wife, who managed the Düsseldorf Theater from 1905 to 1932.

Conservatories and Schools

Robert-Schumann-Konservatorium der Stadt Düsseldorf
Fischerstrasse 110; other buildings at Hombergerstrasse 9 and Inselstrasse 27.
4 Düsseldorf-Nord. Tel: 44 63 32

Städtische Jugendmusikschule Düsseldorf
Bilkerstrasse 7. Tel: 1 46 31 and 899 24 91

Landeskirchenmusikschule der Evangelischen Kirche im Rheinland
Graf-Recke-Strasse 209. Tel: 68 41 40
Housing facilities available for students.

Musical Landmarks

Mendelssohn was Düsseldorf's Director of Musical Activities from 1833 to 1835. A statue of the composer by the Düsseldorf sculptor Clemens Buscher was placed in front of the Stadttheater in 1901. In August 1936 it was removed and, in 1940, melted down along with other statues of similar non-Aryans. In 1956, a new bronze bust by the sculptor Ivo Beucker was placed in the interior of the opera house.

In a similar incident, a bronze plaque on a house at Jan-Wellem-Platz 1 replaces one destroyed in 1937. The new plaque has a portrait in relief of the composer also done by Ivo Beucker in about 1959. In this house Mendelssohn composed the oratorio *Paulus,* in 1835.

A bronze relief of **Schumann** done by Ferdinand Heseding in 1949 stands in the lobby of the Schumann-Konzertsaal. A bronze bust of the composer stands in the Hofgarten behind the Opera. It is the work of Karl Hartung (1956), commemorating the centennial of Schumann's death. A plaque at Bilkerstrasse 15 marks the place where Robert and Clara Schumann lived from September 1, 1852, to March 4, 1854. The house is *not* open to the public.

A marble plaque at Haroldstrasse 14 (formerly Poststrasse 32) marks **Brahms'** home from 1856–1857. The house is *not* open to the public. (The previous plaque was destroyed during the war.)

At Bolkerstrasse 53, the modest house in which **Heinrich Heine** was born has been reconstructed and is now marked with a plaque. Another plaque can be seen at Bolkerstrasse 44, the house where Heine grew up. It is now the inn *Zum Goldenen Kessel.* Busts of the poet can be found in the courtyard of the Wirtschaftsmuseum (by Georg Kolbe) and in the Hofgarten (by Maillol). Also, a Heine monument stands on the Napoléonsberg.

Musical Organizations

Düsseldorf Symphoniker (Symphony Orchestra)
Rheinhalle, Oeder Allee 1.

This group offers several different series of concerts all available both on subscription and on an individual basis. The different types of concerts consist of a series of twelve orchestral concerts, eight chamber music concerts, twelve so-called *Meisterkonzerte* (the most costly), and in April two weeks known as *Düsseldorfer Tage für Neue Musik,* concerts of contemporary music for which the prices are lower.

Werkgemeinschaft Lied und Musik (Lied and Music Society)
Carl-Mosterts-Platz 1.

Deutsche Orchestervereinigung in der DAG
(German Association of Professional Orchestras and Choirs in the German Employees' Trade-Union)
Graf-Reckestrasse 26.

This group publishes a magazine, *Das Orchester.*

Deutscher Musikverband in der Gewerkschaft Kunst des DGB
(German Association of Musicians in the Trade Union for the Arts of the German Trade Union Federation)
Birkenstrasse 107.

Their publication is called *Der Musiker.*

FRANKFURT

Tel. prefix: 06 11

Since ancient times, the Hessian city of Frankfurt has been both a transit area and connecting link between north-south and east-west. Highways connect the North Sea with the Alps, and lead from the Rhine to the East. This area is well suited to industry, for the main northern industrial cities of Frankfurt, Offenbach, Hanau, Darmstadt, and Kassel are all situated between the Rhine and the Main rivers.

Frankfurt itself was just the city to produce two such eminent—yet entirely different—men as Goethe and Rothschild. Great names of finance as well as celebrities of theatrical history are associated with this cosmopolitan city, the least "German" of any of the larger cities in the Federal Republic. Goethe's parents' house on the Grosse Hirschgraben is only a few minutes away from the theater complex (the Städtische Bühnen), where operas, dramas, and intimate plays can be given simultaneously. A new opera house was completed by Christmas of 1951, but the old building on Opernplatz, destroyed during World War II, has still not been replaced.

Because of its position as the terminus of many transatlantic flights (Berlin's Tempelhof airport is too small for modern jets), Frankfurt necessarily receives many American visitors. The citizenry makes sure that they offer tourists great art collections, good opera, and fine theater. The Museum für Kunsthandwerk, located near the Romberg, has a famous collection of manuscripts and miniatures, while the art museum in the Städelschen Kunstinstitut houses an excellent group of German primitives, as well as works by Dürer, Cranach, and Holbein. Today the Frankfurters don't settle for the second-rate in music, either. Georg Solti worked here as General Director of Music for a long time before he went to Covent Garden in London. His successor was Lovro von Matacic.

In summary, Frankfurt is the quintessence of a modern metropolis in which the theater concentrates on contemporary developments and music is available to those who are interested in it.

Guides and Services

This Week in Germany

Rhine-Main edition, an English language guide to cultural events is available at hotels and newsstands. Considerably more than cultural information appears in this pocket-size booklet that is most popular among English-speaking tourists in Frankfurt. *Die Welt,* a Frankfurt newspaper for those foreigners who read German, publishes news of concerts; so, too, does the *Frankfurter Wochenschau.*

For advance bookings go to the Hauptwache (underground office located on the site of a centuries-old watch tower). The office is open Monday to Friday from 9:00 AM to 6:30 PM and Saturday from 9:00 AM to 4:30 PM; Sunday and holidays from 10:00 AM to noon. Tel: (06 11) 28 74 86.

Another place for advance booking is the Frankfurter Verkehrsverein, located in the main station, north side, opposite track 23. This office is open weekdays from 8:00 AM to 10:00 PM; Sunday and holidays from 2:00 PM to 8:00 PM. Tel: 23 11 08, 23 22 18, or 23 47 01.

For additional information about Frankfurt, write to the Deutsches Fremdenverkehrszentrale, Beethovenstrasse 60, 6000 Frankfurt/Main.

Two other cultural guides are *Das Programm*, published by Verlag August Oesterrieth of Mainzer Landstrasse 184 and the *Vorschau*, published by Verlag Bodet & Link at Wilhelm-Leuschner-Strasse 89.

Opera Houses and Concert Halls

Städtische Bühnen Frankfurt

Theaterplatz 3. Tel: 21 06 3 35

Box Office Hours: Monday to Saturday 10:30 AM to 1:30 PM; Sunday and holidays 11:00 AM to 1:00 PM. Four days before the day of the performance and one hour before curtain time, advance tickets are available for purchase. Tickets also available at Hauptwache (see Guides and Services).

Note: with a student ID, you may buy tickets at the box office one hour before a performance at a discount.

Seating capacity: 1430 (Grosses Haus)

The late nineteenth-century opera house, built between 1873–1880 in Renaissance style and located on what is called Opernplatz, was destroyed in World War II. Despite many attempts to restore it, nothing has yet been accomplished here. Instead, Frankfurters hear their operas, operettas, chamber music, recitals, and symphony concerts in their new complex known as the Städtische Bühnen (municipal theaters), while the old house is shown to visitors as the *Opernhausruine*. If you go to the opera in the new theater, which incidentally is excellent, don't fail to see the large Marc Chagall mural and the sketches for it on the terrace above the orchestra level.

Historically, the Frankfurt Opera's finest period of performances occurred between 1880 and 1933 under Weingartner and Clemens Krauss, among others. The best-known premieres held at the opera include Schoenberg's *Von Heute auf Morgen* (1930), Carl Orff's *Carmina Burana* (1937), and also his *Die Kluge* (1952).

Saal der Hochschule für Musik und darstellende Kunst

Eschersheimer Landstrasse 33. Tel: (0611) 55 08 26

(See also Conservatories and Schools.)

Church Concerts

Among numerous churches where concerts are presented, see particularly: Katharinenkirche, Hauptwache. *Abendmusik* (evening music) concerts occur here frequently. The composer Georg Philipp Telemann was kapellmeister at this church from 1712 to 1721. (The *Abendmusik* concerts famous in music history, however, were not given here, but in Lübeck, under Buxtehude!)

Ticket Agencies

Nanda Stock, Zeil 121.
Ludwig Schäfer, Schweizerstrasse 35.
Lotterie Beck, Bolongarostrasse 134.

Libraries and Museums

Stadt- und Universitätsbibliothek, Musik- und Theaterabteilung Manskopfisches Museum [Ben. 86]
Bockenheimer Landstrasse 134–138. Tel: (0611) 7 90 71
Hours: Monday to Friday 8:30 AM to 7:00 PM; Saturday 9:00 AM to 6:00 PM by previous arrangement. Closed holidays. (Hours are Monday to Friday 9:00 AM to noon for Schopenhauer archive, also on these premises.)

This very large library also has numerous catalogs available to assist the researcher. Its special collections include bequests from several individuals and societies, autograph letters of the singer Julius Stockhausen, and the composer Humperdinck, music of Telemann (see *Church Concerts*), music manuscripts from old Frankfurt cloisters, southwest German choral societies, and early opera material. The Opera House archive was destroyed during the war (see *Opera Houses*). The present library consists of the municipal library (Stadtbibliothek), the Manskopfisches Museum für Musik- und Theatergeschichte, Gymnasialbibliothek (school library), the Bibliothek für neue Sprachen und Kunst (formerly Freiherrlich Carl von Rothschild Bibliothek), and the libraries of the Peters- und Barfüsskirche.

Städtische Musikbibliothek
Goethestrasse 30/I. Tel: (0611) 2 12 44 00
Hours: inquiries and information Monday to Friday 8:00 AM to 6:00 PM; borrowing Monday to Friday noon to 6:00 PM.

Musikwissenschaftliches Institut der Johann-Wolfgang-Goethe-Universität [Ben. 85]
Senckenberganlage 224. Tel: (0611) 789 21 83
Hours: Monday to Friday 9:00 AM to 5:00 PM; apply in advance to Secretary's office.

Freies Deutsches Hochstift, Frankfurter Goethemuseum
Grosser Hirschgraben 23–25. Tel: (0611) 28 28 24
Hours: April to September, Monday to Saturday 9:00 AM to 6:00 PM, Sunday 10:00 AM to 1:00 PM; October to March, Monday to Saturday 9:00 AM to 4:00 PM; Sunday 10:00 AM to 1:00 PM. Closed January 1, Good Friday, Christmas.

The Library is in a building beside the restored Goethe House (see *Musical Landmarks*).

Lautarchiv der Arbeitsgemeinschaften der Deutschen Rundfunkanstalten (Sound Archives of the Study Groups of the German Broadcasting Stations)
Eschersheimer Landstrasse 25.

Historisches Museum und Münzkabinett (History Museum), Musikzimmer
Saalhofkapelle, Saalgasse 31 and Rothschild-Palais, Untermainkai 15.
Tel: 212 33 70 and 212 35 95
Hours: Tuesday to Saturday 10:00 AM to 4:00 PM, Sunday 10:00 AM to 1:00 PM.

The Musikzimmer with numerous musical instruments is located in the Rothschild-Palais. The Rothschild family originally came from Frankfurt, but their home, and the homes of many other prominent German Jews, were destroyed by the Nazis who decimated the entire old ghetto of Frankfurt. It had been one of the oldest in western Europe.

Hessischer Rundfunk
Postfach 3294, Bertramstrasse 8.

Admission is restricted to temporary or full-time employees of the radio and television broadcasting station. However, upon a serious request, it is possible to consult books, scores, and documents for reference, or to listen to recordings on the premises. The library owns 70,000 tapes and 10,000 records.

Conservatories and Schools

Staatliche Hochschule für Musik und darstellende Kunst (National School of Music and Performing Arts)
Eschersheimer Landstrasse 33. Tel: (0611) 55 08 26
Administration Building: Grüneburgweg 9, Postfach 2326.

The faculty here has at one time or another included such luminaries as Joachim Raff, Clara Schumann, Engelbert Humperdinck, and others, while the students numbered Hans Pfitzner, Otto Klemperer, and Paul Hindemith among them. The school has both a library and an auditorium.

Dr. Hochs Konservatorium
Eschersheimer Landstrasse 4. Tel: 59 56 97

Kirchenmusikschule der Evangelischen Kirche in Hessen und Nassau (School of Church Music of the Protestant Church in Hessen and Nassau)
Fürstenbergerstrasse 221. Tel: 59 08 88

Musikwissenschaftliches Institut der Johann-Wolfgang-Goethe-Universität
Senckenberganlage 224. Tel: 77 98 21 83

Musical Landmarks

Goethehaus
Grosser Hirschgraben 23–25 (near Hauptwache). Tel: 28 28 24
Hours: Monday to Friday 9:00 AM to 4:00 PM, Sunday 10:00 AM to 1:00 PM. From April through September, the weekday hours are 9:00 AM to 6:00 PM.

Goethe was born here on August 28, 1749. The original house on this site was built about 1590. It was destroyed completely on March 22, 1944 during the Second World War. Now rebuilt and refurnished in period furniture, it recaptures something of the ambience of the original, although little of Goethe's family belongings are here. (They were burned when the house was bombed.)

The Goethe Museum is annexed to the Goethehaus (see Libraries). The Freies deutsches Hochstift that is in charge of the Goethehaus and Museum owns about 25,000 autographed manuscripts including, besides Goethe's works, items by writers Novalis, Clemens Brentano, Bettina Brentano and her husband, Achim von Arnim, and the composers Carl Loewe and Franz Schubert. It is best to write in advance to the Director of the library, if you want to see any of the manuscripts. The Director of Goethe House is not in charge of the library.

Albert Schweitzer Archive and Memorial Rooms
Römerberg 9. Tel: 2 04 51
Hours: Monday, Wednesday, Thursday 8:00 AM to 4:30 PM; Tuesday 8:00 AM to 7:00 PM and Friday 8:00 AM to 4:00 PM.

Radio Hessen
Bertramstrasse 8.

The Hessisches Rundfunks Orchester and Radio Hessen are affiliated with one another. Radio Hessen programs a "Studio for New Music" festival of new music in association with the International Summer Course at Darmstadt, and a series, *"Das wohlverstandene Meisterwerk"* (Understanding the Masterpieces).

Musical Organizations

Deutscher allgemeiner Sängerbund (General Association of German Singers)
Weckmarkt 3.

This group publishes the periodical *Der Chor.*

Verband der Deutschen Konzertdirektionen (Association of German Concert Managers)
Stettenstrasse.

Bundesverband der Deutschen Musikinstrumenten-Hersteller e.V.
Bockenheimer Anlage 1a. Tel: 55 29 21

This organization publishes a list of instrument makers and repairers.

Other musical organizations include: Philharmonische Verein (Liebhaberorchester), founded in 1834; the Frankfurter Kunstgemeinde, for chamber music; Collegium Musicum Vocale; and Freunde der Kirchenmusik.

FREIBURG-IM-BREISGAU

Tel. prefix: 0761

Guides and Services

Freiburger Veranstaltungs-Kalender (Calendar of Events)

Published by the Kulturamt, Rathausplatz 2. Appears twice a year. Events from January through June are listed in one issue and those from July through

December in the second issue. The *Calendar* is available at Tourist Offices and hotels and newsstands.

Opera Houses and Concert Halls

Städtische Bühnen
Bertoldstrasse 46. Tel: 3 11 33
Box Office Hours: weekdays from 10:00 AM to 1:00 PM, 4:00 PM to 6:30 PM; Saturday (except August) 10:00 AM to 1:00 PM. Closed Sunday.

The Städtische Bühnen (Municipal Theaters) comprise three theaters: the Grosses Haus, the Podium, and the Kammertheater. The Grosses Haus is the setting for most major theatrical and operatic productions, as well as ballets and symphony orchestra concerts. *Aida, Faust,* and the ballet *Coppelia,* for example, are presented in this thousand-seat theater. The three hundred-seat Podium offers smaller operas or musical comedies, *Irma la douce* or Stravinsky's *Histoire du Soldat,* for example. Also contemporary plays like Beckett's *Waiting for Godot* appear here. The Kammertheater, seating only ninety-nine persons, stages very small, intimate productions and chamber music concerts.

Libraries and Museums

Deutsches Volksliedarchiv (German Folksong Archive)
Silberbachstrasse 13.
Hours: Monday to Friday 9:00 AM to noon, 2:00 PM to 5:00 PM; closed December 24 to January 2.

Städtische Musikbücherei (Municipal Music Library)
Münsterplatz 17.

Musikwissenschaftliches Seminar der Albert-Ludwigs-Universität, Bibliothek [Ben. 88]
Bellfortstrasse 11. Tel: 203 2058

Conservatories and Schools

Musikwissenschaftliches Seminar der Universität
Werthmannplatz. Tel: 203/2058

Staatliche Hochschule für Musik
Münsterplatz 30. Tel: 3 60 32/33

This is the school for applied music. The International Student Club (ISC) headquarters is next door.

Summer Courses

Summer Vocal Institute in Freiburg
American Institute of Musical Studies, Baylor University, Waco, Texas 76703.
Season dates: usually mid-June to mid-August.
Areas of instruction: voice, opera, art song, stage study, language. Housing available in economy hotels in central location. Catalog available at address above.

Internationale Meisterkurse für Musik Freiburg

Master courses in piano, violin, and conducting held here the first two weeks in September. For more information write Kulturamt, Rathausplatz 2, 78 Freiburg. The Internationale Meisterkurse is affiliated with the local Hochschule. For further information write Staatliche Hochschule für Musik, Münsterplatz 30, 78 Freiburg-im-Breisgau.

HAMBURG

Tel. prefix: 04 11

The leading West German press and communication center today is Hamburg, the old city-state on the North Sea coast. The greatest number of newspapers and periodicals appears in Hamburg, where every day some 8.2 million copies of daily newspapers are circulated and every month some 80 million copies of magazines and periodicals are produced by Hamburg publishers. These include well-known magazines like *Die Welt, Der Spiegel, Die Zeit,* and *Stern.* Hamburg developed into one of Europe's major press centers after the war, and certainly played its part in the German "economic miracle." Today the circulation of newspapers and magazines on Hamburg's presses, in some instances, makes up 70 to 90 percent of the total German circulation of such publications.

For more than 300 years Hamburg has ranked with the major cities of Europe. In 1650, its population of 60,000 made it one of the two largest German-speaking cities, the other being Vienna. Today it has a population of 1.8 million, and, if we include the suburbs, 2.6 million. The port of Hamburg is still Germany's gateway to the world, and even in this jet age, activity is intense: two hundred sixty-four shipping lines make more than 800 regular sailings a month to over 1,100 ports all over the globe. Hamburg is the largest German commercial city and as an economic center ranks third in Europe, after London and Paris. Of the ten greatest industrial enterprises in the world, five have their German headquarters here. With its 75 consulates, Hamburg is second only to New York.

Lively and stimulating Hamburg is both a city and a federal state, one of the ten federal states of West Germany. Its liberal tradition stems from two sources: its location on the coast and its historic role as a member of the Hanseatic League, a group of citizens in North Germany who banded together as early as the twelfth century for purposes of profit and protection. Hamburg even predates the League: it was founded in 811!

As a cultural center, Hamburg offers excellent theaters which are among the best in German-speaking lands, three symphony orchestras, Germany's largest music school, and research centers and art collections staffed with internationally famous scholars and artists. The oldest German opera house is located in this city on the Elbe. The repertoire of the Hamburg State Opera includes sixty-two operas and fifteen ballets. Since its beginnings, the company has shown a preference for classical ballet, but this attitude is balanced by the exciting innovations Rolf Liebermann has presented in his operatic productions. Nevertheless, Hamburg is undeniably a merchant city. The burghers have ruled here for centuries and no emperor or king ever gained sufficient influence to supplant them. After a visit, one can tell that their cultural taste is on the conservative side. As a matter of fact, their taste in cultural activities contrasts sharply with their taste in pornography. Hamburg's red-light district is one of the oldest, and still the most famous, in all Europe. Stage shows in these quarters are hardly conservative!

Guides and Services

Hamburger Vorschau

Appears every two weeks and is the most informative guide to cultural events in the city. Published at Hachmannplatz, it is available at the City Tourist Office, hotels and major newsstands. German language.

Where to go in Hamburg

The English counterpart of the above, also appears every two weeks and is available in just about the same places.

Hamburg hat Kultur für Alle

This monthly, and the newspapers *Vorschau* and *Journal* all carry concert and opera announcements.

In addition, *Hamburger Musikleben* is a monthly, carrying complete information about concerts, including programs, and is available at Steinway-Haus, Collonaden 29 (see *Business of Music*).

The telephone number for general information in Hamburg is: 11 5 15.

From June 15 on, a theater pass may be obtained by those under 21. Students who are older, but who have an ID card, may also obtain this pass from "Kulturring der Jugend" at Hamburgerstrasse. The pass contains four coupons for theater and four coupons for concerts, theaters, operas, and films. Other advantages of the theater pass are reduced prices on tickets for all events—sometimes more than fifty percent off.

The address for tourist information is: Fremdenverkehrs-Zentrale Hamburg e.V., Bieberhaus am Hauptbahnhof. Tel: 24 12 34.

Ticket Agencies

Kurt Collien
Eppendorfer Baum 25. Tel: 48 33 90

Konzertkasse Gerdes für Hamburger Symphoniker
Rothenbaumchausee 77. Tel: 45 33 26

Theaterkasse Alster
Hofweg 33. Tel: 22 17 97

Theaterkasse Altona
Neue Gr. Bergstrasse Pavillon 5a. Tel: 38 62 64

Opera Houses and Concert Halls

Hamburgische Staatsoper

Dammtorstrasse 28. Tel: 35 11 51
Season: middle of August to end of June; closed from July 1 to August 15.
Box Office: Grosse Theaterstrasse 35.
Seating capacity: 1679

Hamburg can actually boast that it is the site of the oldest-established permanent opera company in Germany. The Goosemarket Theater (Theater am Gänsemarkt) opened in 1678 with a Singspiel by Johann Theile. Before the building was destroyed in 1750, close to three hundred operas had been performed, many with German recitatives and Italian arias in one and the same piece. In this way, audiences could understand the plot and enjoy the Italianate music of the aria whose words they could not distinguish anyway.

The Hamburg Stadttheater, built in 1874, had various music directors, among them Mahler, Klemperer, and Böhm. Included among its most famous singers are Jenny Lind, Lilli Lehmann, Lauritz Melchior, and Hans Hotter.

The Opera House was destroyed in an air-raid in 1943, but by 1945 the portion of the old house that was formerly the stage was reconstructed to accommodate stage, orchestra, and auditorium. This auditorium was later enlarged, and by October 1955, a completely new house opened with a production of Mozart's *Die Zauberflöte,* produced by Gunther Rennert.

One of the outstanding opera companies of Europe, if not the world, is the Hamburgische Staatsoper. Rolf Liebermann, its director, has also just begun his tenure as head of the Paris Opera. The company offers more than sixty different works in its repertory and includes among its roster of stars, singers from all over the world, among them Martina Arroyo, Grace Bumbry, Montserrat Caballé, Mirella Freni, Gwyneth Jones, Anna Moffo, Birgit Nilsson, Joan Sutherland, Josephine Veasey, Boris Christoff, Franco Corelli, Placido Domingo, Luciano Pavarotti, and Gianni Raimondi. Conductors today include Karl Böhm, Rafael Kubelik, and Ferdinand Leitner.

Operettenhaus

Spielbudenplatz. Tel: 31 37 37, 31 31 88
Seating capacity: 1419

Operettas and musicals may be seen here, but no performances are given during the summer.

Musikhalle

Karl-Muck-Platz. (Karl-Muck-Platz is named after the man who, for many years, conducted the Boston Symphony Orchestra.)

Tel: 35 32 20

Box Office: opens one hour before performance time for the Grosser Saal and half an hour before performances for the Kleiner Saal.

Seating capacity: Grosser Saal has 2000 seats and is used for orchestral and other large-scale concerts. Kleiner Saal has 640 seats and is used for chamber music and intimate musical events.

The Musikhalle is the concert center for Hamburg. Tickets may be obtained at all concert ticket agencies (see below).

Brahms-Saal
Rosenstrasse 16 (near main station). Tel: 32 59 09

This hall also has an adjoining music library.

Staatliche Hochschule für Musik (See Schools)
Harvestehuder Weg 12. Tel: 44 19 51

Amerika-Haus (U.S. Information Center)
Tesdorpfstrasse 1. Tel: 44 10 61

Festhalle Planten und Blomen

These are exhibition grounds near Dammtor Station. The Planten und Blomen are Hamburg's botanical gardens.

Grosser Saal der Norddeutschen Rundfunk (NDR)
Oberstrasse.

This is the auditorium of the North German Radio Station.

Institut Français
Heimhuderstrasse 55. Tel: 45 56 60 after 12 noon

Istituto Italiano
Hansastrasse 6. Tel: 44 04 41

Altonaer Museum
Museumstrasse 23. Tel: 39 10 71

A series of concerts, *"Hauskonzerte,"* is given here.

Jazzhouse Hamburg
Brandstwiete 2–4. Tel: 32 49 33

This hall is open daily from 8:00 PM to 2:00 AM. During the summer it is closed Mondays and Tuesdays until September.

Museum für Hamburgische Geschichte
Holstenwall 24. Tel: 34 10 91

Concerts are given here on the instruments that form part of the museum's display of old instruments (see Libraries).

Summer Concerts

Bergedorf Schloss Concerts
Inner courtyard of the Bergedorf Schloss.
June, mid-August to end of September.
Seating capacity: 200 seats
Transportation: by S-Bahn Bergedorf, five minutes' walk.

Musikpavillon
Planten und Blomen Park.
Every afternoon and evening, and Sunday mornings. Light music.

Rathaus Concerts
Courtyard of the Hamburg Town Hall.
Announcements will be found in the daily press. In case of rain, the concerts are held in the Kaisersaal in the Town Hall.

Ratzburger Dommusiken
Varied concerts of instrumental and vocal music (madrigals, organ recitals, chamber music). Every Sunday at 6:00 PM.

Libraries and Museums

Hamburger öffentliche Bücherhalle, Musikbücherei [Ben. 109]
Rosenstrasse 16. Tel: 32 59 09
Hours: Monday, Thursday noon to 5:00 PM; Tuesday, Friday 1:00 PM to 7:00 PM; Saturday 11:00 PM to 1:00 PM. Closed Wednesday and Sunday.

Musikwissenschaftliches Institut der Universität [Ben. 112]
Neue Rabenstrasse 13. Tel: 44 19 78, Ext 65
Hours: Monday to Friday 8:00 AM to 7:00 PM.
Apply to Secretary for admission.

Staatsarchiv (BEN. 113)
Rathaus, Rathausmarkt 1.
Hours: Monday to Friday 8:30 AM to 4:00 PM.

Staats- und Universitätsbibliothek, Musikabteilung [Ben. 114]
Moorweidenstrasse 40. Tel: (0411) 44 19 71 or 72 ext. 213
Hours: Monday to Friday 9:00 AM to 4:00 PM; closed one week after Christmas, Easter, Pentecost.

Several significant personal collections are here; also a Brahms archive, documents of Frederick the Great and Albert Schweitzer.

Universität Hamburg, Theatersammlung [Ben. 115]
Rothenbaumchaussee 162. Tel: (0411) 44 19 78 26
Hours: Monday to Friday 9:00 AM to 4:00 PM; Tuesday 9:00 AM to 6:00 PM.

Museum für Hamburgische Geschichte
Holstenwall 24. Tel: 3 41 09 21 00 or 34 10 91
Hours: Tuesday to Sunday 10:00 AM to 5:00 PM; Saturday 10:00 AM to 1:00 PM.

Several old instruments are on display here.

Museum für Kunst und Gewerbe
Steintorplatz 1. Tel: 248 25 26 30 or 24 82 51
Hours: Tuesday to Sunday 10:00 AM to 5:00 PM; Wednesday 10:00 AM to 7:00 PM.

The museum owns a small instrument collection.

Museum für Völkerkunde und Vorgeschichte
Binderstrasse 14. Tel: 44 19 51
Hours: Tuesday to Sunday 10:00 AM to 4:00 PM; Saturday 10:00 AM to 1:00 PM.

This museum also has an instrument collection.

Conservatories and Schools

Staatliche Hochschule für Musik und darstellende Kunst
Harvestehuder Weg 12 (Milchstrasse). Tel: 44 19 55 79

Housing provisions are limited to a few rooms in dormitories. According to the concert guide *Hamburg hat Kultur* (see above) and the German Tourist Office, the Staatliche Hochschule is one of the most important contributors to the concert life of Hamburg. Students' final recitals, opera performances, and chamber music concerts of students and faculty are often held at the Musikhalle (see above). The school also sponsors the Internationale Meisterkurse (see below).

Hamburger Konservatorium für Musik
Bahnhofstrasse 35, 2 Hamburg 55 (Blankensee). Tel: 86 02 64

Musikwissenschaftliches Institut der Universität Hamburg
Neue Rabenstrasse 13. Tel: 44 19 7865

Summer Courses

Internationale Meisterkurse für Musik
Given in late summer, these international courses for advanced instrumentalists and vocalists are sponsored by the Staatliche Hochschule für Musik (see above).

Youth Study Group on Music
German-Scandinavian Music Festival, ten days in early April, Scheersberg near Flensburg. Orchestral, chamber and choral music, concerts. April to November.

Franco-German Festival for Guitar and Lute Playing
Bielefeld and Sennestadt. Wind instruments with accompaniment, accordions with accompaniment. Mid-April.

German-Danish Song and Music Festival
Reinbeck near Hamburg. European choral and instrumental music, Orff Instrumentarium, group playing of early and contemporary music, chamber music, European and American dance. Mid-July.

International Seminar on Rhythmics, Physical Formations and Dance
Remscheid. First week in November.

Information for all of the above available from Arbeitskreis für Musik in der Jugend, 5 Alsterglacis, Hamburg 36.

Musical Landmarks

Brahms Gedenkstätte (Brahms Memorials)
Alfred-Toepfer-Stiftung
Peterstrasse 39. Tel: 34 42 18, 34 29 71
Hours: Tuesday to Friday 11:00 AM to noon and by arrangement if you telephone ahead.

The house where Brahms was born was located at Speckstrasse 60 (originally no. 24). It was destroyed during World War II. Two rooms have been reconstructed, and this new memorial site was dedicated in 1971. The new Brahms Gedenkstätte is located at Peterstrasse 39. On display are changing exhibits of Brahms memorabilia, including Brahms' instruments, autograph manuscripts, letters, photographs, etc. Among the manuscripts are the Piano Sonata in f (op. 5), the Second Piano Concerto, and an autograph score of the piano reduction of his *Requiem.*

A Brahms memorial column stands in Caffamacherreihe at the corner of Speckstrasse (see above).

Musical Organizations

TELEMANN: Telemann-Gesellschaft Hamburg
Schlüterstrasse 44. Tel: 445481

BRAHMS: Brahms-Gesellschaft Hamburg
Bahnhofstrasse 35. Tel: 86 02 64

Deutsche Stiftung für Musikleben (Foundation to promote Musical Activities)
Jungfernstieg 51.

Philharmonisches Staatsorchester
Musikhalle, Karl-Muck-Platz 2.
Box Office: Grosse Theaterstrasse 34. Tel: 35 15 55

This box office is located behind the Staatsoper and is also the official box office for opera performances.

Norddeutscher Rundfunk
Oberstrasse.
Box Office: NDR-Konzertkasse, Rothenbaumchaussee 132. Tel: 4 13 25 04
Hours: daily 10:00 AM to 3:00 PM. Closed Saturday.

This orchestra society is as important as the BBC in England. It has its own orchestra, the second best in Hamburg (the best is mentioned above), its own chorus and a concert hall (see above).

Societies

Arbeitsgemeinschaft für Musikerziehung und Musikpflege (music education)
Grosse Burstah 50.

Arbeitskreis für Junge Musik (Association for Youth Orchestras and Choirs)
Feldbrünnenstrasse 56.

Deutsche Gesellschaft für Musik des Orients (German Society for Oriental Music)
Loogestieg 6.

Deutscher Musikrat (German Section of the International Music Council)
Feldbrünnenstrasse 56.

Deutsche Orchestervereinigung im Deutschen Gewerkschaftbund (DGB) (German Association of Professional Orchestras of the German Trade Union Congress)
Charlotte-Niese-Strasse 8.

Genossenschaft Deutscher Bühnenangehörigen (Theatrical Union)
Feldbrünnenstrasse 74.

The Business of Music

Steinway-Haus
Collonaden 29. Tel: 34 91 71

Piano manufacturers of international reputation, Steinway-Haus in Hamburg is the foremost music dealer in the city. Located in a six-storied building just off the fashionable Jungfern Stieg and very close to the Opera House, Steinway sells both classical and popular sheet music, stringed instruments as well as pianos, and, in general, supplies the public with information about cultural events of significance. Numerous advertisements and brochures are available at the store. Furthermore, a ticket agency there makes it easy to purchase tickets to concerts and shows in advance.

HANOVER (Hannover)

Tel. prefix: 05 11

Guides and Services

Konzert- und Theateranzeiger für Hannover (*Concert and Theater Announcements for Hanover. Note the different German spelling of the city's name.*)

Published by Alexander Stahlberg and available at major newsstands, hotels, and the city Tourist Office, it is the best guide to cultural events.

Opera Houses and Concert Halls

Opernhaus

Opernplatz. Tel: 16 81 (Rathaus)

Box Office Hours: Monday to Friday 8:00 AM to 5:00 PM; Saturday 9:00 AM to 1:00 PM and 6:00 PM to 8:00 PM.

Seating capacity: 1503

The first opera given in this city was probably Cesti's *Orontea* in 1649; and the first opera house opened in 1689 with Steffani's *Enrico Leone.* The present Opera House, built by Georg Ludwig Laves between 1845 and 1852, was burned during the Second World War, but reconstructed in 1960. It is now open nearly the entire year, with top-flight performances. Closed during July and August. There is also an opera museum in the building.

Kuppelsaal der Stadthalle

Trammplatz 2.

Seating capacity: 3670

This very large auditorium is open all year.

Beethovensaal der Stadthalle

Trammplatz 2.

Seating capacity: 767

Both the Beethovensaal and the Kuppelsaal (see above) belong to the Landestheater Hannover. The Beethovensaal is used for chamber concerts.

Galerie Herrenhausen in the Grossen Garten Herrenhausen

Arswaldstrasse 8. Tel: (0511) 2 61 98

Box Office: Monday to Friday 9:00 AM to 5:00 PM.
Seating capacity: 686

The Galerie was built in 1694–98. In the Barocksaal of the Galerie, Händel, kapellmeister at the Hanover court from 1710 to 1712, gave concerts. Today the annual festival, Musik und Theater in Herrenhausen, is held here.

Libraries and Museums

Kirchenmusikschule der Evangelisch-Lutherischen Landeskirche Hannovers, Bibliothek [Ben. 118]
Am Markt 45. Tel: (0511) 1 35 90

Stadtbibliothek, Musikabteilung [Ben. 121]
Hildesheimerstrasse 12. Tel: (0511) 16 81

Kestner Museum, Bibliothek [Ben. 117]
Trammplatz 3.
Hours: Tuesday to Friday 10:00 AM to 4:00 PM by appointment.

Music division of this private cultural museum was begun with a gift from Hermann Kestner (see above) in 1884. The museum itself was founded in 1889.

Niedersächsische Landesbibliothek [Ben. 120]
Am Archive 1. Tel: (0511) 1 36 61 or 62
Hours: Monday to Friday 9:00 AM to 1:00 PM, 2:00 PM to 6:00 PM; Saturday 9:00 AM to 1:00 PM.

Conservatories and Schools

Staatliche Hochschule für Musik und Theater
Walderseestrasse 100. Tel: 168 34 64

A large staff covers instruction in all areas of practical music and theater. This institution also has a Jugendmusikschule (Music School for Youngsters). Its library, open from 2:00 PM to 6:00 PM Monday through Friday, has a total of about 26,000 volumes.

Kirchenmusikschule der Evangelisch -Lutherischen Landeskirche Hannovers
Am Markt 45.

(See *Libraries* for this School of Sacred Music of the Protestant Luthern Church of Hanover.)

The Business of Music

Publishers

Erhardt Friedrich Publishing Co.
3001 Velber bei Hannover.

The Erhardt Friedrich Publishing Company is one of the most important theatrical publishers in Europe. The periodical *Opernwelt* is published here; *Theater Heute,* concerned with opera and ballet, also originates here. In addition, the company publishes monographs on significant artists.

KASSEL

Tel. prefix: 05 61

The city of Kassel is synonymous with the business of music and musicology in Germany. It is headquarters of the world-famous music publishing firm of Bärenreiter, located at Heinrich-Schütz-Allee 29–37.

The following societies, as well as the publishers Hinnenthal and Alkor-Edition, are all located at Heinrich-Schütz-Allee 33–35:

Gesellschaft für Musikforschung (Society for Musical Research); Handel Society; Schütz Society (see *Musical Organizations*); RISM headquarters and library; and a Johann Nepomuk Hummel Society.

Opera Houses and Concert Halls

Staatstheater Kassel
Friedrichsplatz 15.
Box Office Hours: Tuesday to Saturday 10:00 AM to 1:30 PM; Sunday 11:00 AM to noon; and one hour before the start of performances; closed Monday. Box Office Tel: Grosses Haus 15852; Kleines Haus 15853; Konzerte 15854.
Seating capacity: Grosses Haus: 950
Kleines Haus: 580

This new Staatstheater opened in 1959. In the nineteenth-century opera house in this city, Spohr was the conductor from 1822 to 1857, and Mahler was its leader for the two years 1883 to 1885.

Libraries and Museums

Deutsches Musikgeschichtliches Archiv [Ben. 141]
Ständeplatz 16. Tel: (0561) 1 22 77
Hours: Monday to Friday 9:00 AM to 12:30 PM and 2:30 PM to 4:30 PM. Closed holidays.
About 50,000 volumes; microfilm archive of primary source material for study of German musical history; manuscripts and early printed music. RISM is the acronym for Répertoire Internationale des Sources Musicales (International Repertory of Musical Sources), an organization that researches and locates early manuscripts and prints and publishes catalogs of their whereabouts. RISM replaces the Eitner Quellen-Lexikon.

Louis Spohr-Gedenk- und Forschungsstätte [Ben. 142]
Brüder Grimm-Platz 4a. Tel: (0561) 7 22 63
Hours: Friday 3:00 AM to 6:00 PM and by arrangement if you write or phone ahead.

Murhard'sche Bibliothek der Stadt Kassel und Landesbibliothek [Ben. 143]
Brüder Grimm-Platz 4a. Tel: (0561) 192 64 91
Hours: Monday to Friday 9:00 AM to 6:45 PM; Saturday 9:00 AM to 1:00 PM.

Musikakademie der Stadt Kassel, Bibliothek
Kölnischestrasse 36. Tel: 19 26 Ext. 596
Hours: Tuesday noon to 12:30 PM and Thursday noon to 1:00 PM. Closed school vacations.

Conservatories and Schools

Musikakademie der Stadt Kassel
Kölnischestrasse 32. Tel: 19161
(See also Libraries above.)

Summer Courses

Anglo-German Youth Week
Konigswinter.
Early August
Choir, orchestra, chamber music, improvisation.

Franco-German Seminar for Musicians and Music Teachers
Hardehausen near Scherfede/Westphalia.
Late July
Piano and chamber music; instrumental courses, analysis and interpretation; comparative music education.

Franco-German Youth Week
Michelbach near Schwabisch Hall.
Early April
Choir, orchestra, chamber music.

Franco-German Youth Week
Remscheid.
Second week in August
Choir, orchestra, chamber music.

International Study-Group on Music
Internationaler Arbeitskreis für Musik,
Heinrich-Schütz-Allee 33, D-3500 Kassel-Wilhelmshöhe.
April to August
This Kassel-based study group includes the following summer courses, youth weeks, and seminars taking place in various cities and towns throughout Germany. Information about any and all of them may be obtained at the address above.

International Youth Week
Schmie near Muhlacker/Württemberg.
Second week in April
Orchestra, choir, chamber music.

International Youth Week
Bad Waldsee/Württemberg.
Early August
Choir, orchestra, chamber music.

Musical Landmarks

Ludwig Spohr (1784–1859), German violinist, composer, and conductor. A monument to Spohr is located at Spohrplatz. He is buried at the Hauptfriedhof.

Musical Organizations

The Internationaler Arbeitskreis für Musik, the Gesellschaft für Musikforschung, and the Georg-Frideric-Händel Gesellschaft (Handel Society) have all been mentioned above in the introduction to Kassel.

Internationale Heinrich Schütz-Gesellschaft
Heinrich-Schütz-Allee 35, 35 Kassel-Wilhelmshöhe. Tel: (0561) 30013

This society sponsors the Schütz Festival (see Festivals). It also publishes the complete works of Schütz, Schein, Lechner, and others, and issues phonograph recordings of works by Schütz.

International Association of Music Libraries
Ständeplatz 16.

Viola-Forschungsgesellschaft
Schloss Bellevue, Schöne Aussicht 2. Tel: 3 95 6

Radio Station

Hessischer Rundfunk, Studio Kassel
Ahrensbergstrasse 22, 35 Kassel-Wilhelmshöhe. Tel: (05 61) 340 25

MUNICH (München) Tel. prefix: 08 11

Munich is Paris, New York, and Vienna rolled into one. Already a city of over a million inhabitants, whose permanent population increases every year by thirty thousand, Munich is the third largest metropolis in Germany after Berlin and Hamburg. Not just the center of commerce and industry, not exclusively baroque, renaissance, classical or even Biedermeier, Munich is unique because it is all of these and more; many feel it is the real capital of Germany.

Italian, Dutch, and French influences were absorbed at one time or another in Munich's history. Furthermore, bohemian Schwabing, the Viktualien Markt, the Hofbrauhaus, Karl Richter's church concerts, the Oktoberfest, opera festivals, the Bayerisches Rundfunk, the Cuvilliés-Theater, and English Gardens coexist in this remarkable city. Two dozen art museums, many private galleries, a host of castles and palaces from the rococo Amalienburg to the Lindenhof, Nymphenburg, and the slightly distant Neuschwanstein, all make Munich a special treat for visitors, both foreign and domestic alike.

This is the city where the medieval *Carmina Burana* were sung, where the original Tannhäuser and Walter von der Vogelweide wrote and sang their own songs, where Wagner saw four of his operas premiered in his lifetime (a fifth was done posthumously), where George, Rilke, and Wedekind were at home in Schwabing, and where the electrical engineer Oskar von Miller founded the Deutsches Museum, the largest technical and natural science museum in the world. (Incidentally, this museum's display of the evolution of the various families of instruments has never been duplicated anywhere.)

The tradition of Munich's musical life dates back to the sixteenth century, when its court orchestra under Orlando di Lasso was the best in Europe. Opera has been performed here since 1653. And the distinction of building the first opera house on German soil and presenting some of the first German-language operas offered in this country belongs to Munich. (Italian opera had been fairly common; opera in the vernacular was something new.) About a hundred years later, Mozart's *La Finta Giardiniera* and *Idomeneo* received their premieres here. The Cuvilliés-Theater, too, had already been built.

In 1811, two orchestras founded the Musical Academy to further the cause of symphonic music; and that year, too, Weber's *Abu Hassan* was premiered. Richard Strauss was born in Munich in 1864; his grandfather Pschorr was then one of the prominent brewers of the city. In 1911, having written *Der Rosenkavalier,* Strauss dedicated it "to my dear kinfolk, the Pschorr family in Munich." Strauss conducted the Munich orchestra for a total of seven years, and his works always get special attention when performed there. Max Reger taught for six years at the Academy of Musical Art and Hans Pfitzner entrusted the premiere of *Palestrina* to the Munich stage.

The Munich Philharmonic was founded before the turn of the century. Bruckner and Mahler's music was soon performed there. Von Bülow, Levi, Weingartner, Krauss, and Knappertsbusch were among the most prominent conductors. Today, three first-class orchestras as well as a brilliant opera company are based here; and many publishing concerns make Munich a focal point of intellectual activity that often rivals Berlin. There are now twenty-five theaters, not to mention literary and political cabarets, dialect theaters, small art stages, and four puppet theaters, all of which seem constantly full as tourists continue to pour into this extraordinary mecca for travelers.

Linked to the Alpine regions and towns like Garmisch-Partenkirchen, where the Strauss family still lives, and Oberammergau, scene of the Passion Play every ten years, Munich also offers its citizens the bucolic delights of nearby Salzkammergut.

Munich is a very German city, whose inhabitants are proud to live there, unlike Frankfurt, where everyone insists he works there, but "I assure you I'm *not* from here!" Almost totally destroyed during the war, Munich has not yet been completely rebuilt. What *has* been done is new and different. No attempt has been made to recapture yesterday's image. Probably the best we can say is that Munich exemplifies the coexistence of the diverse.

Guides and Services

München: Offizielles Monatsprogramm

Fremdenverkehrsamt der Landeshauptstadt München
Rindermarkt 5, "Haus 3 Rosen." Tel: 24 81

This remarkably comprehensive monthly is available at major hotels, bookstores, and newsstands throughout the city. It covers concerts, operas, theaters, museums, libraries, art exhibits, information centers at the airport and center city travel bureaus, foreign cultural institutes, airlines, consulates, theater and concert advance sale centers, banks, church centers, sightseeing tours, and exchange services. You name it and it's there. The *Monatsprogramm* also gives previews of things to come as well as current listings. Significant categories appear in three languages and unless your German is absolutely non-existent, this is the guide to use.

Münchner Woche (Munich Weekly)

Available every Friday at hotels and leading newsstands, this weekly provides information on theaters, concerts, movies, lectures, museums, exhibitions, sporting events, etc., for the coming week.

Three additional guidebooks to the city are E. Steinkopf's *Munich: A New Guide,* Frank Gordon's *Munich-Go-Round,* and Richard Kerler's *München-Wo?* or *Where in Munich* available in English translation. All can be obtained at Hugendubel, Salvatorplatz 2.

Note: Although tickets and listings for performances are available at various box offices throughout the city, a good idea might be to check listings at the Verkehrsbüro (Tourist Office) on arrival and then to purchase tickets immediately from the agent located behind track 21 at the main train station (Bahnhof) or at Maximilianstrasse 11 (Tel: 22 13 16). Open daily from 10:00 AM to 1:00 PM and from 3:00 PM to 5:00 PM; weekends from 10:00 AM to 1:00 PM. Tickets can also be obtained from the ABR Reisebüro on Stachus (Tel: 55 25 15).

You can obtain *Stehplatz* (standing room tickets) in advance for performances at the Nationaltheater (see below) at Maximilianstrasse 11.

Tickets for performances of light plays and opera can be purchased in advance at the box office of the Altes Residenztheater, Residenzstrasse 1.

Ticket Agencies

Because of the tremendous interest in music and drama in this city, the number of authorized ticket agencies is exceedingly high. It *is* customary to purchase tickets here in advance of a performance.

Abendzeitung–Kartenvorverkauf
Snedlingerstrasse 79. Tel: 2 60 72 23

Abendkasse Herkulessaal
(Box Office at the Herkulessaal after 7:00 PM).

ABR-Theaterkasse am Stachus (entrance on Sonnenstrasse).
Tel: 55 24 15

Radio-RIM
Theatinerstrasse 17. Tel: 22 65 03
Theater and concert tickets on sale here.

Radio Schutter
Einsteinstrasse 98. Tel: 47 92 44
Theater and concert tickets are on sale here in this shop near the Prinzregententheater.

Opera Houses and Concert Halls

Munich's opera houses deserve special attention. In the rococo Residenztheater (see below) designed by Cuvilliés, Mozart's *La Finta Giardiniera* (1775) and *Idomeneo* (1781) received their first performances. The famous Nationaltheater designed by Karl von Fischer opened in 1818, was burned, rebuilt, and finally bombed in 1943. Wagner's relationship with King Ludwig of Bavaria led to the premieres in this city of *Tristan, Meistersinger, Rheingold,* and *Walküre.* Among the foremost conductors here we can list von Bülow (1867–69), Hermann Levi (1872–96), Felix Mottl (1903–11), Bruno Walter (1911–22), Clemens Krauss (1937–44), Georg Solti (1946–52), and Ferenc Fricsay (1955–59). Munich's third opera house, von Possart's Prinzregententheater, designed on the same model as Bayreuth, was originally intended exclusively for Wagnerian operas. It became the home of the Bavarian State Opera until the Nationaltheater was rebuilt, but it is not now used for opera.

Nationaltheater or Bayerische Staatsoper München

Max Joseph Platz and Maximilianstrasse. Tel: 21851

Season: mid-September to end of June for opera, ballet and concerts. Closed August to mid-September; also Good Friday, May 1 and December 24.

Box Office: Maximilianstrasse 11, opposite the Nationaltheater. Tel: 22 13 16

Hours: Monday to Friday 10:00 AM to 1:00 PM and 3:00 PM to 6:00 PM; Saturday and Sunday 10:00 AM to 1:00 PM.

Authorized Ticket Agencies: ABR Theaterkass, München am Stachus, Max Hieber, etc. (see list of agencies p. 179).

Seating capacity: c. 1750; standing room: 320

Customary Dress: evening dress suggested.

Top-flight operatic performances here are all given in German, only rarely in the original language of the composition.

Cuvilliéstheater or Altes Residenztheater

Residenzstrasse 1.

Season: approximately the end of September to end of June. Closed from beginning of August to about September 21.

Box Office: advance sale at Maximilianstrasse 11. Tel: 22 13 16

Hours: Monday to Friday 10:00 AM to 1:00 PM and 3:00 PM to 5:00 PM; Saturday and Sunday 10:00 AM to 1:00 PM.

Seating capacity: 523

Visiting hours to see the theater itself are Monday to Saturday 2:00 PM to 5:00 PM; Sunday from 10:00 AM to 5:00 PM.

Gold, red, and ivory are the colors of this magnificent rococo theater built by François Cuvilliés (see Schloss Nymphenburg) during the period 1751–1753. Four richly-decorated tiers of boxes rise above the horseshoe-shaped ground floor. Each tier is ornamented differently. The theater is such an obvious gem that it is open to the public for viewing even when no performances are being given. It has superb acoustics. Destroyed during the war, it was rebuilt to the exact specifications of its original architect. The gold decorative work had been removed before the bombardments and stored in the mountains. At the end of the war, everything was available for the redecoration of the interior. This is the theater used for those very special performances of operas like Strauss' *Capriccio* or concerts given by the world famous Bayerische Rundfunkorchester.

Städtische Galerie im Lenbachhaus
Luisenstrasse 33. Tel: 52 14 31
Hours: daily except Monday from 9:00 AM to 4:40 PM for the gallery.

Tickets can be purchased here when concerts are programmed.

Grosser Sendesaal des Bayerischen Rundfunks
Rundfunkplatz 1.

This auditorium is on the homeground of the leading Bavarian orchestra.

Herkulessaal of the Residenz
Entrance on Max-Joseph-Platz 3. Tel: 22 45 55

Top-flight artists appear here regularly during the concert season. The hall is in the complex of buildings that had been the Royal Palace, former residence of the Bavarian kings.

Concert Hall of the Hochschule für Musik
Arcisstrasse 12. Tel: 55911 or 55912

Although this hall is in the Conservatory, it is one of the most important halls in the city. Check the *München Monatsprogramm* and the newspapers regularly for performances here.

Kongresssaal des Deutschen Museums (Congress Hall of the German Museum)
Mailing Address: Postfach 26.

This fabulous museum (see Libraries), located in the middle of the Isar River and reached via the Ludwigsbrücke, has concerts in its Congress Hall. It also has a remarkable instrument collection (see Libraries).

Museum Tel: 21791

Staatstheater am Gärtnerplatz
Gärtnerplatz 3. Tel: 60 32 32
Season: all year, offering opéra comique, operetta, etc. The theater maintains its own ballet ensemble and offers ballet evenings as well.
Box Office: for advance sale Monday to Friday 10:00 AM to 1:00 PM and 4:00 PM to 6:00 PM; Saturday and Sunday 10:00 AM to 1:00 PM.

The Nationaltheater and the Cuvilliés-Theater, as well as the concert halls in the Residenz complex are all situated close to one another in the center of the city. The Gärtnerplatz Theater, however, begun in 1864 as a Volkstheater or popular theater, was built in a workers' district. The aim of its founders was to bring entertainment to the people. The theater has retained this function to the present day. From 1900 to 1950, operettas were performed there, and gradually the repertory became what we might call exclusively "opéra comique." Its director has tried to stage some unusual items—for example, Rameau's *Platée,* Purcell's *Fairy Queen,* and Janáček's *Cunning Little Vixen,* as well as some basics that appear also at the Nationaltheater.

Deutsches Theater

Schwanthalerstrasse 13. Tel: 59 29 11

Season: all year, offering opera, operettas. The theater has no ensemble of its own, but it offers guest performances by outside ballet and opera companies.

Box Office: daily 10:00 AM to 7:00 PM.

Seating capacity: 1800 seats after its reconstruction after World War II.

Marionette Theaters

Münchner Marionettentheater

Blumenstrasse 29a at the Sendlinger-Tor-Platz. Tel: 26 57 12

Box Office: for advance sale, daily except Monday, 10:00 AM to noon and 1:00 PM to 4:30 PM.

The repertory here consists not only of German fairy tales and Punch and Judy shows, but also of operas by Mozart, Rossini, and Donizetti.

Marionettenstudio Kleines Spiel

Neureutherstrasse 12 (entrance on Arcisstrasse). Tel: 98 35 30

Free admission. Closed in August.

Münchner Puppentheater

Künstlerhaus, Lenbachplatz 8. Tel: 59 14 14

Box Office: daily except Monday, 10:00 AM to 1:00 PM and 4:00 PM to 6:00 PM.

Mechanisches Theater-Spieldose

Theater Münchner Studenten, also in the Künstlerhaus (see above).

Run exclusively by students. Closed in August. Tel: 59 13 37

(See Puppentheatersammlung in Münchner Stadtmuseum, the puppet collection in the Munich City Museum, under *Libraries.*)

Summer Concerts

A specialty of the city and its environs, particularly the various castles surrounding it, are the summer outdoor concerts offered in many different places.

Usually the evenings are pleasantly warm, not too hot. If it rains, postponements are inevitable.

Brunnenhof der Residenz
Entrance on Residenzstrasse 1. Tel: 22 42 29
Box Office Hours: Monday to Friday 10:00 AM to 1:00 PM and 3:00 PM to 7:00 PM; Saturday and Sunday 10:00 AM to 1:00 PM.
Seating capacity: 1240

Concerts as well as operas are offered here. We witnessed a delightful performance of Telemann's opera, *Pimpinone,* here in the courtyard.

Neues Schloss Schleissheim
Schloss- und Gartenverwaltung Schleissheim, 8042 Oberschleissheim.
Melanchthonstrasse 2. Tel: 315 1212
Season: in June and July about eighteen to twenty chamber music concerts are given.
Seating capacity: 569

Tickets available at the usual *Vorverkaufstellen* (authorized ticket agencies) starting in early May. Reduced prices for students.

Konzerte im Schloss Ameranger Arkadenhof
Amerang Südlich 8201 Wasserburg/Inn. Tel: 080 75/2 04

Tickets available for these castle concerts also at the Münchner Theatergemeinde, Goethestrasse 23. Tel: 53 08 46

Schloss Nymphenburg

Designed as a hunting lodge by François Cuvilliés (1695–1768), the French court architect who also designed the theater that bears his name, this is an excellent example of German secular rococo architecture. The castle with its many smaller buildings (Amalienburg, Badenburg, Pagodenburg, etc.) was built for the wife of the Elector Karl Albrecht. Summer concerts take place in the Steinerner Saal.

Nymphenburger Sommerspiele im Steinerner Saal
Freunde der Residenz, Zuccalistrasse 21. Tel: 17 21 61
Season: three weeks in July on Wednesday, Thursday, Saturday and Sunday, offering chamber music, chamber operas, oratorios.
Seating capacity: 380
Customary Dress: evening clothes are suggested.

Tickets available from above address either four weeks before start of concerts or at authorized agencies.

Münchner Kammeroper
Silvanastrasse 12. Tel: 95 52 33

Public Entrance: Residenzstrasse 1.
Season: About June 15 to August 20, specializing in eighteenth-century operas (see Brunnenhof der Residenz). Outdoor performance also in Münzhof (Mint courtyard) a good example of Renaissance architecture.
Box Office: same address or authorized agencies. Tel: 22 42 29
Hours: Monday to Friday 10:00 AM to 1:00 PM and 3:00 PM to 7:00 PM; Saturday and Sunday from 10:00 AM to 1:00 PM.
Seating capacity: 1240

Schloss Neuschwanstein

Built by King Ludwig II of Bavaria, this fantastic castle has several splendid royal apartments which contain pictures from German epic sagas and scenes from Richard Wagner's operas. The music hall itself is a duplicate of the hall in the Wartburg castle which figures so prominently in *Tannhäuser.* This medieval-style *Schloss* is the scene of orchestral concerts for one week in early September. Check at authorized ticket agencies in Munich for precise dates.

Münchner Kammerorchester

Zamboninistrasse 5b. Tel: 15 59 77

Summer concerts offered at Brunnenhof, Schleissheim, and Nymphenburg castles.

Schloss Herrenchiemsee

Every Saturday from mid-May to the end of September, chamber music performances are offered here at 7:30 PM. (At the height of the season, two performances are given, one at 7:30 PM and the second at 8:30 PM.) Herrenchiemsee is one of three of Mad King Ludwig's architectural extravaganzas, the other two being Neuschwanstein (see above) and Linderhof. The concert setting is particularly beautiful at Herrenchiemsee as the light of thousands of wax candles creates a fairytale ambience in this fantastically decorated section of the castle.

Tickets are best purchased in advance through the American Express Office in Munich (you can see this series caters to tourists). Buses leave Munich from Lenbach Platz 1 at 2:40 PM on Saturdays. Although tickets may be purchased at the castle, the number of tickets is limited and you have no guarantee of a ticket at the castle box office. Before the concert it is possible to visit the castle. The last guided visit is at 5:00 PM.

Festive Concerts of the Munich "Kammerorchester"

Mid-July.

Open-Air Performances of Munich "Kammeroper" in the "Münzhof"

Mid-July to mid-August..

Libraries and Museums

Bayerische Staatsbibliothek, Musiksammlung [Ben. 191]
Ludwigstrasse 16. Tel: 2 19 81
Hours: Monday to Friday 9:00 AM to 5:00 PM; the general reading room is also open Saturday morning; in August, open mornings only. Closed Holy Week.
Separate manuscript department at Meisterstrasse 10.

Musikwissenschaftliches Seminar der Ludwig-Maximilians-Universität, Bibliothek [Ben. 199]
Geschwister-Scholl-Platz 1. Tel: 21 80 Ext. 634
Hours: Monday to Friday 9:00 AM to 1:00 PM and 2:00 PM to 5:00 PM. Closed August.

Universitätsbibliothek der Ludwig-Maximilians-Universität [Ben. 203]
Geschwister-Scholl-Platz 1. Tel: 2 18 01 Ext. 431
Hours: Monday to Friday 8:00 AM to 8:00 PM; Saturday 8:00 AM to noon; University holidays 8:00 AM to 7:00 PM.

Deutsches Museum on the Isar Island (Ludwigsbrücke) [Ben. 195]
Tel: 2 17 91
Hours: daily including Sunday from 9:00 AM to 5:00 PM. Closed New Year's Day, Good Friday, Easter Sunday, May 1, Whitsunday, Corpus Christi Day, November 1 and Christmas Day.

This is the world's largest museum of exhibits of natural science and technology. Coal mining, hydro-electric power plants, steam engines, all types of scientific and technological work are demonstrated here with unbelievable attention to detailed explanations for all to understand. In addition, the acoustics section contains a remarkable collection of instruments displayed in groups according to their manner of sound production: reed instruments, percussion instruments, string instruments, etc. Mechanical instruments are also on display. Their Thalkirche organ (1630) is the oldest South German organ surviving in its original state.

Alongside several musical clocks in the Baroque music room, you will find keyboard instruments whose development from clavichord and cembalo to concert grand and electric organ is demonstrated by a supervisor who plays music of the respective periods on suitable instruments. (Records are available at the sales desk of the Museum. Be sure to purchase those that include about fifty different pieces on early keyboard instruments. They are unbelievably well done!)

Staatliche Hochschule für Musik, Bibliothek [Ben. 200]
Arcisstrasse 12. Tel: (0811) 55 91 Ext. 234
Hours: Monday to Friday 9:00 AM to 1:00 PM. Closed summer vacation.

Städtische Musikbibliothek [Ben. 201]
Salvatorplatz 1. Tel: 22 27 04
Hours: Monday 10:00 AM to 3:00 PM; Tuesday 3:00 PM to 7:00 PM; Wednesday 10:00 AM to 3:00 PM; Thursday 10:00 AM to 3:00 PM; Friday 3:00 PM to 7:00 PM; Saturday 10:00 AM to noon. Closed in August. (These are new opening hours.)

Founded in 1902, this is the largest public music library in Germany. Its iconographic collection consists of about thirteen hundred volumes; its folk song archive has about two thousand volumes, seven thousand records; it also owns two thousand autographs of Munich composers.

Münchner Stadtmuseum, Musikinstrumentensammlung (*Munich City Museum*)
St. Jakobsplatz 1. Tel: 2 48/23 67
Hours: daily except Monday from 9:00 AM to 4:30 PM (see Puppet Theater Collection).

This museum has a collection of musical instruments from all over the world with special emphasis on exotic (non-Western) instruments. This formerly private collection, the second largest in Europe, was presented to the city in 1940 by Dr. Neuner. Today, only part of the collection is on display.

Bayerisches Nationalmuseum, Bibliothek [Ben. 192]
Prinzregentenstrasse 3. Tel: 22 25 91
Hours: Monday to Friday 8:30 AM to 5:30 PM. Closed holidays.

Metropolitankapitel (*or Erzbischöfliches Ordinariat*) *Bibliothek* [Ben. 198]
Maxburgstrasse 2. Tel: 24 43 27
Mailing Address: Postfach 360.
Hours: by arrangement. For access, write to Musiksammlung, Bayerische Staatsbibliothek.

Amerika Haus Bibliothek (*U.S. Information Center Library*)
Karolinenplatz 3. Tel: 59 53 69
Hours: Monday to Friday noon to 7:30 PM; Saturday 10:00 AM to 5:00 PM. Closed German and American holidays.

British Council Music Library
Giselastrasse 10. Tel: 39 46 39

Theatermuseum der Clara-Ziegler-Stiftung (*Theater Museum of the Clara Ziegler Foundation*) [Ben. 202]
Galeriestrasse 4a (Hofgartenarkaden). Tel: 22 24 49
Hours: Tuesday to Friday 10:00 AM to noon and 1:00 PM to 5:00 PM.

Admission is free to this extensive collection of materials and books relating to the history of the theater. It's a must for opera buffs.

Puppentheatersammlung in Münchner Stadtmuseum (*Puppet Theater Collection in the Munich Stadtmuseum*)
St. Jakobsplatz 1.
Hours: daily except Monday from 9:00 AM to 4:30 PM.

Admission only to persons over 14 years of age. Students and artists are admitted at reduced prices; Sunday free. Puppets from all over the world are displayed here. There is also an international library of materials relating to the history of puppet theaters. Other documents and a picture archive dealing with puppets will be found here too. (See Marionette Theaters, under Concert Halls.)

Staatliches Museum für Völkerkunde
Maximilianstrasse 42. Tel: 22 48 44
Hours: daily except Monday from 9:30 AM to 4:30 PM.

This museum is a must for ethnomusicologists.

Conservatories and Schools

Staatliche Hochschule für Musik in München
Arcisstrasse 12. Tel: 55 911 or 5591/232

No provisions for housing of students. Foreigners are accepted here if they meet the same requirements set for Germans and if they are proficient in the German language.

Staatliche Berufsfachschule für Geigenbau (*National Trade School of Violinmaking*)
Mittenwald (74 miles from Munich).

In the Bavarian mountain village of Mittenwald, the art of violin-making has been cultivated for nearly three hundred years. This world-famous school was founded here in the middle of the nineteenth century. For further information, see Germany, General, Schools, Mittenwald.

Richard-Strauss-Konservatorium der Stadt München mit Sing- und Musikschule
Ismaningerstrasse 29. Tel: 44 38 06

Housing arrangements must be made privately. The Richard-Strauss-Konservatorium was founded through the merger of various institutions: Städtische Singschule, Städtische Berufsschule für Musiker und Tänzer, Städtische Orchestervorschule, Jugendmusikschule and the Trapp'sche Konservatorium. In 1962, it had the title "Konservatorium und Musikschule der Landeshauptstadt München." In 1964 it received its present name in conjunction with the hundredth anniversary of the birth of Richard Strauss, the composer most closely associated with the city.

Musikwissenschaftliches Seminar der Ludwig-Maximilians-Universität
Geschwister-Scholl-Platz 1. Tel: 21 80 23 64.

Federation of German-American Clubs
Birnauerstrasse 6.

Twenty scholarships are available to nationals of the United States for study in West Germany. American candidates must have completed at least two years of college. Candidates must possess outstanding scholastic and personal qualities and be highly recommended. They must be unmarried and under 25. Awards are offered on an exchange basis between the Federation and American universities and colleges. Write by December 1 to Frau H. Brandenstein, Verband der Deutsch-Amerikanischen Clubs at above address.

Summer Courses

Chamber Music Course, with interpretation course on contemporary music
Three weeks in August.

(See below, International Summer School.)

Festival of Contemporary Music
Hanover.
Late January.

International Study Group on Chamber Music and Orchestral Music
Klappholtal/Sylt.
Two weeks in July.

International Summer School
Schloss Weikersheim, c/o Musikalische Jugend Deutschlands Hirschgarten-allee 19.

August to mid-September.

Write to above address for further information on courses in conducting and courses in opera, etc.

Musical Youth of Germany
Generalsekretariat der Musikalischen Jugend Deutschlands
Hirschgartenallee 19.

Musical Youth of Germany is the title given to a group of courses and festivals held throughout the year in various cities and towns throughout Germany. Information about all of the courses listed above as well as the one-week Congress in mid-August of the International Jeunesses Musicales may be obtained by writing to the address given above.

Musical Organizations

Some of these organizations are merely listed to give you an idea of the considerable musical activity in Munich. For a few, we have given additional information.

Arbeitsgemeinschaft der Akademien, Hochschulinstitut und Konservatorien der Musik
c/o R. Strauss-Konservatorium, Ismaninger Strasse 29. Tel: 0811/44 38 06.

Bläserquintett

Cappella Antiqua

Cappella Monacensis

Chor- und Orchestergemeinschaft des Münchner Siemens-Werkes

Hidegheti Trio
Internationaler Musikwettbewerb der Rundfunkanstalten der Bundesrepublik (ARD)
Rundfunkplatz 1. Tel: 0811/59 00–24 71.

Internationale Vereinigung der Musikbibliotheken-Deutsche Sektion (International Association of Music Libraries, German Section)
Salvatorplatz 1.

Jugend Musiziert-Wettbewerbe für das instrumentale Musizieren der Jugend
Hirschgartenallee 19. Tel: 17 45 81.

Münchner Choruben

Münchner Kammerchor

Münchner Kammerorchester
Zamboninistrasse 5b. Tel: 15 59 77.

This group of 15 string players and a harpsichordist, directed by Hans Stadlmair, presents winter concerts in the Herkulessaal or the Grosses Konzertsaal of the Hochschule für Musik. In the summer, they perform at various castles including Schleissheim, Nymphenburg, and the Brunnenhof in the center of town.

Münchner Nonett

Münchner Oktett

Münchner Philharmoniker

Münchner Posaunenquartett

Munich Bach Choir and Orchestra

Musica-Viva-Konzerte
Clemensstrasse 60. Tel: 30 19 56

PFITZNER: Hans Pfitzner Gesellschaft
Steffanistrasse 13.

This group publishes the *Mitteilungen der Hans Pfitzner Gesellschaft* approximately three times a year. It contains original articles about the composer and his works.

Philharmonischer Chor

Rundfunkchor

Studio der frühen Musik

Studio für elektronische Musik

Studio für neue Musik

Symphonieorchester des Bayerischen Rundfunks
Rundfunkplatz 1.

Verband Deutscher Musikerzieher und Konzertierender Künstler (Association of Private Music Tutors and Concert Artists)
Hirschgartenallee 19.

Wilde Gung'l

This organization is the oldest and best known of the amateur orchestras.

The Business of Music

Antiquariats

Musikantiquariat Hans Schneider
Mozartweg 1, D-8132 Tutzing near Munich. Tel: 08158/475

In a magnificent contemporary home with a beautiful view over the surrounding countryside, you will find the virtual king of musical antiquarians, Hans Schneider. Of the thousands of items listed in his numerous yearly catalogs (all of which are prepared on the premises by Schneider and two of his assistants), only the most precious items are stored (and lovingly shown) at his home. The balance are kept in about five warehouses nearby. Schneider was infected with collector's mania as a child. He has never stopped buying. Lately, he has also accumulated a magnificent collection of old keyboard instruments. His prices are high, but if you simply must have an item, Schneider is your best source.

Schneider also publishes facsimiles of some of his priceless manuscripts and early editions as well as reprints of significant works.

Walter Ricke, Musikantiquariat
St.-Anna-Platz 1a, Munich 22. Tel: 08 11/22 11 82

Upstairs on the "first floor" of an old building near the Stadtbibliothek is Walter Ricke's place of business. His prices are reasonable and he has a large stock of new as well as second-hand books. On occasion, Ricke also publishes some musical material. He issues several catalogs annually.

Dr. Emil Katzbichler, Musikantiquariat
D-8210 Giebing, Post Prien am Chiemsee. Tel: Prien (08051) 2595

Katzbichler handles records, books, and scores, and deals with universities as well as individuals. He can readily take care of large orders. He publishes about two catalogs a year.

J. Kitzinger, Buchhandlung/Antiquariat
Schellingstrasse 25.

NUREMBERG (Nürnberg)

Tel. prefix: 0911

Guides and Services

Summer in Nuremberg

Lists all musical activities, theaters, and exhibits. It may be obtained at the Verkehrsverein, Eilgutstrasse 5. Tel: 22 64 34. You can also obtain it at the Hauptbahnhof (main station).

Ticket Agencies

Konzertdirektion Wolf
The main agency has several locations:
Ludwigstrasse 1; Karolinestrasse 11;
and Theatergasse 17. Tel: 55 80 03 and 22 51 88

Konzertdirektion Martin
Vordere Sterngasse 28. Tel: 22 78 21

Note: Written reservations from abroad should be sent to: Verkehrsverein Nuremberg, P.O. Box 2980, 85 Nuremberg.

Opera Houses and Concert Halls

Opernhaus
Administration: Lessingstrasse 1. Tel: 20 45 85
Public Entrance: Richard-Wagner-Platz.
Season Dates: September to July.
Box Office Hours: 9:00 AM to 6:00 PM.
Seating capacity: 1456

The Städtische Bühnen Nuremburg-Fürth comprise the Opernhaus, the Schauspielhaus (924 seats), and the Kammerspiel (197 seats), also located in the Schauspielhaus.

Although situated to the left of the main railroad station, the Opera House is one of the few center-city buildings not destroyed or seriously damaged during the Second World War. A plush-looking structure which dates from

1905, it is used for operas and operettas, and in size it resembles the Frankfurt Opera House, which still stands in ruins awaiting reconstruction by that city.

Note: Seelewig, the earliest German opera for which we still have the music, was given a private performance in Nuremberg in 1644.

Meistersingerhalle

Platz der Opfer des Fascismus.

Situated on the square dedicated to the victims of fascism, this modern multipurpose building was erected in 1963. It has two concert halls and an excellent restaurant, and like many new cultural buildings in Germany today, it functions for business and cultural purposes alike. Concerts, including those of the Nuremberg Philharmonic and the Frankisches Landesorchester, are presented here.

Städtisches Konservatorium der Musik

Am Katharinenkloster 6. Tel: (0911) 20 251

Concerts are given in the auditorium of the school.

Organ recitals are offered in St. Sebaldus and St. Lorenz churches.

Summer Concerts

Outdoor concerts are given in the Schwedenhof of the Imperial Castle, from the end of May to the beginning of August. Chamber music concerts are offered in the Rittersaal of the Kaiserburg during the summer months. Advance sale at Konzertdirektion Wolf (see Agencies).

Music in Nuremberg Patrician Houses

Pellerhaus Konzerte

Stadtbibliothek Pellerhaus (Municipal Library in Peller House)
Egidienberg, Nuremberg.
Concerts start at 8:00 PM.

Fembohaus Konzerte

Stadtmuseum Fembohaus
Burgstrasse 15.

Same information as for Pellerhaus Konzerte above.

Music in Nuremberg Courtyards

Konzerte im Kreuzigungshof des Heilig-Geist-Spitals (*Concerts in the Holy Ghost Hospital Courtyard*)

Concerts held indoors in case of inclement weather.

Matineen in Rathaushof (*Matinees in Town Hall Courtyard*)
Entrance at Rathausplatz 2.
Concerts given only in good weather at 11:00 AM. Free admission.

Musik in Langwasser
Glogauerstrasse 50.
Concerts given in Parish Hall, Langwasser.

Music in the Planetarium
Planetarium, Am Plärrer 41.
Concerts begin at 8:00 PM.

Additional performing organizations giving concerts here are the Nürnberger Solisten-Ensemble, the Hans-Sachs Kammerchor im Verein Merkur, Die Nürnberger Philharmoniker, Die Nürnberger Symphoniker, and Der Chor des Lehrergesangvereins.

Libraries and Museums

Stadtbibliothek [Ben. 218]
Egidienplatz 23. Tel: (0911) 20 25 or 27 90
Hours. Monday to Friday 10:00 AM to 8:00 PM; Saturday 9:00 AM to noon. Closed end of July to early September.

Musikabteilung des Amerika-Hauses
Gleissbühlstrasse 13. Tel: 20 33 27
Hours: Monday to Friday noon to 8:00 PM; closed German holidays, Fourth of July and Thanksgiving.

Germanisches Nationalmuseum, Bibliothek [Ben. 216]
Kornmarkt 1. Tel: (0911) 20 39 71
Mailing address: Postfach 9301.
Hours: Tuesday, Thursday 9:00 AM to 5:00 PM; Wednesday 1:00 PM to 9:00 PM; Friday 9:00 AM to 4:00 PM; Saturday 9:00 AM to 1:00 PM. Closed holidays.

This library is important because of its musical manuscripts of the ninth to the twentieth centuries, including Wagner's *Die Meistersinger,* and also because it owns the remarkable Ulrich Rück historical instrument collection, one of the finest in Germany. All items are magnificently displayed.

Conservatories and Schools

Städtische Konservatorium der Musik
Am Katherinenkloster 6.

Staatlich genehmigte Ausbildungsstätte für Ton- und Fernsehtechnik der Rundfunk-Betriebstechnik (Official Technical Institute for Television and Radio Personnel)
Tillystrasse 42. Tel: 66 10 48

Musical Landmarks

In the center of the city, a late nineteenth-century bronze monument to Hans Sachs commemorates this sixteenth-century cobbler-meistersinger who lived his entire life here from 1494 to 1576. Sachs's house still stood in the square named for him until it was bombed on January 2, 1945. The *Goldenes Posthorn,* an inn near St. Sebaldus Church, was founded in 1498 and became a favorite spot for refreshments of both Sachs and Albrecht Dürer, another former citizen of Nuremberg.

Miscellaneous

St. Katherine's Church, specified by Wagner for Act I of *Die Meistersinger,* could not actually have been used by the meistersinger because of a law forbidding the use of churches by meistersingers. The law was eventually rescinded, but the real Sachs died half a century before this occurred, and churches were not yet in use.

The church, on Peter Vischerstrasse near the Pegnitz, was destroyed during World War II, except for its shell. The floor has since been covered with cement, and it is used for open-air concerts by the Nuremberg Conservatory of Music.

The Theater in der Klosterruine St. Katharina (Open-Air Theater in the Ruins of St. Katherine's Convent) offers performances by the Hans-Sachs-Theater Group of Nuremberg Volkshochschule. Plays by Hans Sachs and others are presented. In the event of inclement weather, these plays are given in the auditorium of the Conservatory.

STUTTGART

Tel. prefix: 07 11

Guides and Services

Stuttgarter Wochenspiegel, appearing weekly, published and distributed by the Verkehrsamt der Stadt Stuttgart, Lautenschlagerstrasse 3, Stuttgart 1, is the best guide to cultural events in Stuttgart. Most concerts and recitals begin at 8:00 PM. Phone 24 91 63 35, 24 91 33 95 or 24 91 37 42 for information about concerts.

Musik in Stuttgart, Veranstaltungskalendar has a list of concerts for the entire year, particularly if they are handled by the Südwest-deutsche Konzertdirektion, Erwin Russ, Charlottenplatz 17, Stuttgart 1 Tel: 29 03 49. You may write for it.

Ticket Agencies

Verkehrsverein Stuttgart in Verkehrsamt, Hauptbahnhof (Tourist Office)
Unter den Arkaden. Tel: 29 29 73
Hours: Monday to Friday 8:30 AM to 6:30 PM, Saturday 8:30 AM to 2:00 PM.

Kartenhäusle
Kleiner Schlossplatz Tel: 29 55 83
Hours: Monday to Friday and Saturday same as above; additionally, the first Saturday of the month until 5:00 PM.

Opera Houses and Concert Halls

Württembergisches Staatstheater
Oberer Schlossgarten 5. Tel: 24 951
Mailing Address: Postfach 982, D-7000 Stuttgart.
Season: mid-September to mid-July. Closed August, May 1, and Christmas.
Box Office Hours: daily except Monday from 10:30 AM to 1:00 PM and 5:00 PM to 6:30 PM; also a half-hour before evening performances. Telephone reservations accepted on weekdays from 10:30 AM to 6:30 PM and on Sunday 10:30 AM to 1:00 PM.

Seating capacity: Grosses Haus (Opernhaus) 1424
Kleines Haus (Schauspielhaus) 841
Kammertheater i. Grossen Haus 400
no standing room

Although known today primarily as a commercial center, Stuttgart had already given operatic performances at its Neues Lusthaus in the final years of the sixteenth century. The composer Jommelli was kapellmeister to the Duke of Württemberg between 1753 and 1771, thus assuring the natives of a supply of good music. Reconstructed about 1812, the Lusthaus became the Hoftheater, unfortunately destroyed by fire in 1902. The present theater opened in 1912, and in that year offered the premiere of Strauss's *Ariadne auf Naxos.*

Concert Hall in the Musikhochschule

Urbansplatz 2. Tel: 24 60 41 and 24 60 42

Villa Berg (*home of the Süddeutscher Rundfunk*)

Neckarstrasse 145.

Stuttgarter Liederhalle

Berliner Platz 1. Tel: 29 13 67
Public Entrance: Breitscheidstrasse.
Season: all year.
Box Office: at the main entrance on Breitscheidstrasse; guided tours on Monday, Wednesday, Friday at 11:00 AM; no tours in August.
Seating capacity: Beethovenhalle 2013
Mozarthalle 752
Silcherhalle 355

Stuttgart's main concert hall was opened in 1956. It was built on the site of its famous predecessor, the Liederhalle, which was constructed in the 1860s and 1870s by the Stuttgart Lieder Society and destroyed in 1943. Architects Adolf Abel and Rolf Gutbrod have designed a structure that comprises three halls of different sizes, all of which have excellent acoustics and are air-conditioned throughout. The halls represent different components of the same overall structure and are connected to each other by a two-storied foyer. There is an underground garage to accommodate two hundred cars, and additional car parks are nearby.

Gustav-Siegel-Haus

Leonhardsplatz 28.

Stuttgart's next important concert hall after the Liederhalle, the Gustav-Siegel-Haus, was rebuilt in 1954 after being bombed in the war. It is located in the Stuttgarter Musikschule.

Stuttgarter Marionetten-Theater
Wanner-Saal of the Linden Museum für Völkerkunde, Hegelplatz 1.
Mailing Address: Postfach 3006, 7 Stuttgart. Tel: 24 22 80
Box Office: open forty-five minutes before each performance. Performances usually begin at 2:00 PM on Sundays only, between October and April.

Summer Concerts

Ludwigsburger Schlossfestspiele
Season: May to October, concerts every Saturday at 8:00 PM in Schloss Ludwigsburg; chamber music and recitals in the Ordenssaal of the castle; church music in the Schloss Barockkirche; serenades in the Innenhof of the castle; and plays in the Schlosstheater
Box Office: information from the Städt. Verkehrsamt Ludwigsburg, Wilhelmstrasse 24, Stuttgart, or American Express and Cooks'.
Tel: 61252 and 22211

The Ludwigsburger Schloss is the largest baroque castle in Germany. Summer concerts here are very well attended.

Summer concerts are also given in the Höhenpark Killesberg on Sunday afternoons.

Libraries and Museums

Württembergische Landesbibliothek [Ben. 258]
Konrad-Adenauer-Strasse 8. Tel: (0711) 20 21
Public Entrance: Urbanstrasse.
Hours: Monday to Friday 9:00 AM to 5:00 PM, Saturday 9:00 AM to 1:00 PM. Closed August 1 to 15.

Music literature and libretti of 1930–44 were destroyed during the war. The library currently has twelfth to sixteenth-century chant and choir books, operas, manuscripts, cantatas, dance music, and bequests of Württemberg composers, including holdings of the former Royal Library (Kgl. Hofbibliothek); receives Württemberg depository copies since 1817.

Staatliche Hochschule für Musik und darstellende Kunst, Bibliothek [Ben. 257]
Urbansplatz 2. Tel: (0711) 24 60 41/42
Hours: Monday to Thursday and during school vacations by appointment. Closed for a month end of August to end of September.

Stadtbücherei, mit Musikbücherei (*Municipal Library*)
Zentralbücherei in Wilhelmspalais, Konrad-Adenauer-Strasse 2.
Public Entrance: Urbanstrasse 5. Tel: 23 34 34
Hours: Monday to Friday 10:00 AM to 7:00 PM; Saturday 10:00 AM to 4:00 PM.

Württembergische Landesmuseum (*State Museum of Württemberg*)
Altes Schloss. Tel: 29 92 21
Hours: daily except Monday from 10:00 AM to 4:00 PM.

Instrument collection here.

Stadtgeschichtliche Sammlungen der Stadt Stuttgart (*Historical Collections of the City of Stuttgart*)
Wilhelmspalais, Konrad-Adenauer-Strasse 2. Tel: 23 34 34
Hours: Tuesday to Friday 11:00 AM to 6:00 PM, Saturday and Sunday 10:00 AM to 4:00 PM. Closed Monday.

The poet Eduard Mörike (1804–1875) is buried in Stuttgart in the Prag cemetery. The municipal museum has manuscripts, pictures, books, and personal mementos of Mörike and his friends from Stuttgart. Mörike's poems were set to music by many composers, but Wolf is the musician most closely associated with him.

Bibelmuseum der Württembergischen Bibelanstalt (*Bible Museum*)
Hauptstätter Strasse 51 B. Tel: 24 29 45
Hours: Monday to Friday 8:00 AM to 4:00 PM.

This museum has on display charts of old Bible manuscripts, early Luther Bibles, illustrations from the Gutenberg Psalter, etc.

Landesgewerbeamt Baden-Württemberg (*State Trade Board of Baden-Württemberg*)
Kanzleistrasse 19. Tel: 20 11
Hours: Tuesday, Thursday, Sunday 11:00 AM to 6:00 PM; Wednesday 11:00 AM to 7:00 PM; closed Monday.

A collection illustrating the history of piano construction can be found here.

Schiller-Nationalmuseum Marbach and Schillers Geburtshaus
Stuttgart-Marbach.
Hours: October to March 9:00 AM to 5:00 PM; April to September 8:00 AM to 6:00 PM.

Friedrich Schiller (1759–1805), Germany's famous poet and dramatist, was born in this town.

Conservatories and Schools

Staatliche Hochschule für Musik und darstellende Kunst
Urbansplatz 2. Tel: 24 60 41/42

Stuttgarter Musikschule
Leonhardsplatz 28.

Universität Stuttgart (Technische Hochschule)
Huberstrasse 16. Tel: 2 07 31

Lectures on musical history and theory are included here in general studies in the department of arts.

Meisterschule für Orgel- Klavier- und Harmoniumbauer (Training School for the Construction of Keyboard Instruments)
Hohenzollernstrasse 30.

Musikwissenschaftliches Institut der Universität Tübingen
Schulberg 2 Pfleghof, 74 Tübingen (about thirty-nine miles from Stuttgart).
Tel: 71 22 380

Musical Organizations

Süddeutscher Rundfunk (SDR)
Neckarstrasse 145. Tel: 72 34 56

Verband Deutscher Geigenbauer e.V.
Bebelstrasse 30. Tel: 63 22 15

For complete information on the more than one hundred choral groups in Stuttgart, see Erwin Schwarz's *Chor in Stuttgart,* available through

Stadt Stuttgart Kulturamt
Stuttgart Mitte
Rathaus
Mailing Address: Postfach 161, 7 Stuttgart 1.
Tel: 2491-2847

WIESBADEN

Tel. prefix: 0 61 21

Opera Houses and Concert Halls

Hessisches Staatstheater (*Hessian State Theater*)

Tel: 3 93 31

Public Entrance: Theater Colonnade.
Season: September 15 to July 15 for opera, operetta, drama, ballet, concerts.
Box office: on premises in foyers of large and small houses.

Tel: 37 09 91 for large house;
30 09 14 for small house

Hours: weekdays except Monday, 10:00 AM to 1:00 PM; 6:30 PM to 8:00 PM; Sunday and holidays 11:00 AM to 1:00 PM and 6:30 PM to 8:00 PM.
Seating capacity: 1258 in large house; 346 in small house; 98 in the studio.
Authorized Ticket Agencies: Cigar House Witte; Theater Colonnade Bookshop; and N. Windfelder, Paracelsusstrasse 4, Mainz.

Libraries and Museums

Hessische Landesbibliothek [Ben. 282]
Rheinstrasse 55–57. Tel: (06121) 36 81 Ext. 730 or 742.
Hours: Monday to Friday 9:00 AM to 7:00 PM except Wednesday 9:00 AM to 1:00 PM; Saturday 9:00 AM to 12:30 PM. Closed one week after Pentecost and last full week in September.

Breitkopf & Härtel Archives
Walkmühlstrasse 52. Tel: (06121) 4 70 45
Hours: open by appointment only; write in advance.

Conservatories and Schools

Wiesbaden Conservatory and Music Seminar
Bodenstadtstrasse 2/Ecke Parkstrasse 16. Tel: 37 05 96

WÜRZBURG

Tel. prefix: 0931

Opera Houses and Concert Halls

Konzertsaal des Bayerischen Staatskonservatoriums für Musik
Hofstallstrasse 6–8. Tel: 50 641 (for Conservatory, see below)
Seating capacity: 862

Stadttheater Würzburg
Theaterstrasse 21. Tel: 5 86 86
Season: September to June, presenting opera, operetta and drama.
Box Office: Open Monday to Friday 10:00 AM to 1:00 PM and 5:00 PM to 7:00 PM.
Seating capacity: 756

Palace Concerts

Bishop's Residence

The famous Würzburg Mozart Festival is held yearly in this beautiful palace.

Schloss Weissenstein
8602 Pommersfelden bei Würzburg.

Chamber music concerts are held here.

Libraries and Museums

Stadtbücherei (Max-Heim-Bücherei)
Haus zum Falken Marktplatz 9. Tel: 37 444
Hours: Monday to Friday 9:00 AM to 7:00 PM; Saturday 9:00 AM to 4:00 PM; closed legal holidays.

Musikwissenschaftliches Seminar der Bayerischen Julius-Maximilians-Universität [Ben. 288]
Residenzplatz 2 (south wing). Tel: 50 128
Hours: Monday to Friday 8:00 AM to 6:00 PM; Saturday 8:00 AM to 1:00 PM (closed Saturday on school holidays).

Universitätsbibliothek der Julius-Maximilians-Universität [Ben. 289]
Domerschulstrasse 16. Tel: (0931) 3 13 74
Hours: Monday to Friday 9:00 AM to 8:00 PM (holidays 9:00 AM to 5:00 PM); Saturday 9:00 AM to noon.

Conservatories and Schools

Bayerisches Staatskonservatorium für Musik
Hofstallstrasse 6–8. Tel: (0931) 50 641

Dating back to 1797, this conservatory is the oldest school of music in Germany.

Musikwissenschaftliches Seminar der Bayerischen Julius-Maximilians-Universität
Residenzplatz 2. Tel: 50 128

GERMANY (GENERAL)

Opera Houses and Concert Halls

A staggering number of German cities and even towns have their own theaters, concert halls, and/or opera houses. Some of these facilities might even be considered cultural complexes in that they comprise several auditoriums (a small experimental theater as well as a larger hall) in one building; to cite but two, the Stadttheater in Bremerhaven and the Staatstheater in Brunswick. (*Stadt* or *Städtische Bühnen* refer to municipally-run theaters; *Staatstheater* are state or national theaters. In every instance, federal, state, and municipal governments contribute to the maintenance of these institutions.) The following cities have sizable theaters, many with a staff that includes a general manager, dramaturg, and music director:

Aachen, Augsburg, Bielefeld, Bochum, Bremen, Bremerhaven, Brunswick (Braunschweig), Detmold, Dortmund, Duisburg, Erlangen, Essen, Esslingen, Gelsenkirchen, Giessen, Göttingen, Hagen, Heidelberg, Hildesheim, Kaiserlautern, Karlsruhe, Kiel, Koblenz, Krefeld and Mönchengladbach, Lübeck, Mainz, Mannheim, Münster, Neuss, Oberhausen, Oldenburg, Osnabrück, Passau, Recklinghausen, Regensburg, Remscheid, Saarbrücken, Trier, Tübingen, Wuppertal.

Summer concerts in castles and/or cloisters, cathedrals, or open-air theaters are given in Alpirsbach, Annweiler, Augsburg, Bad Dürkheim, Bad Gandersheim, Bad Hersfeld, Bruhl/Rhine, Detmold, Heidelberg, Koblenz, Leitheim, Lübeck, Ludwigsburg, Meersburg, Neustadt, Pommersfelden, Recklinghausen, Regensburg, Schwangau, Zweibrücken.

The main season usually starts in September and ends by August 1. Of course, in some cities the theaters operate all year long; and in a few, like Augsburg, the hall is closed until October 15. It is best to check in advance. Most box offices are open daily; hours will vary. Always write or visit the Verkehrsverein (Tourist Office) for most up-to-date information.

Libraries and Museums

Germany is particularly rich in libraries that contain substantial collections of music books, printed music, and music manuscripts. Furthermore, numbers of ecclesiastical institutions such as monasteries and cloisters, as well as Landesbibliotheken (the central library of a province) also possess fine collections of music. The best source for detailed information about these libraries is *Benton*.

The newest German guide to music libraries is Richard Schaal's *Führer durch deutsche Musikbibliotheken* (*Taschenbücher zur Musikwissenschaft* 7; Wilhelmshaven-Heinrichshofen, 1971).

The following cities have significant music libraries or music collections in their main libraries; some have instrument collections:

Aschaffenburg, Augsburg, Bamberg, Bochum, Bremen, Brunswick (Braunschweig), Detmold, Donaueschingen, Duisburg, Eichstatt, Erlangen, Essen, Flensburg, Fulda, Göttingen, Harburg über Donauwerth, Heidelberg, Karlsruhe, Kiel, Lübeck, Mainz, Mannheim, Marburg/Lahn, Münster, Offenbach am Main, Ratzeburg, Saarbrücken, Speyer, Tübingen, Wolfenbüttel, Wuppertal.

Opening days and hours vary; so do the credentials required. Where possible, write in advance and also have good identification with you on your arrival.

Conservatories and Schools

German universities can look back on a proud tradition: the University of Prague was founded by a German emperor in 1348 and the oldest universities on the territory of the Federal Republic of Germany today are those in Heidelberg (1385) and Cologne (1388). Currently, many German universities are undergoing reforms; their reorganization, however, is not our concern here. We should like merely to cite the largest and most representative of the state colleges, because many of them have departments that are active in musicological research. Besides Berlin University, there are universities at Detmold, Essen, Frankfurt, Freiburg, Hamburg, Hanover, Cologne, Munich, Saarbrücken, and Stuttgart. There are also music schools partly supported by the state and partly by the municipality. Various designations such as "college," "academy," and "conservatory" do *not* indicate differences in rank. Their names simply derive from local customs and traditions. Often their teaching staffs enjoy international reputations. The basic difference between a college or academy and a state college is that only the state colleges (universities in American parlance) grant degrees. Applied music and musicology are not taught at the same institutions. Musicology is the domain of the university; applied music, whether preparation for a professional performance career, a teaching position, or a church position, is taught in the conservatory, college, or academy. Lectures on music are also given in some of the technical schools.

Another unusual area of instruction is the course for training instrument makers. Violin-maker Matthias Klotz founded a celebrated school for violin-makers in Mittenwald, near Munich. Fussen am Lech was once the European center for the production of lutes and other stringed instruments. (Klingenthal and Markneukirchen are today important centers of this craft in East Germany.) After the schools of instrument-making came the factories where these instruments were mass-produced. Steinweg in Brunswick, Bechstein in Berlin, Blüthner in Leipzig, and Steingräber in Bayreuth are known the world over for their fine pianos. Heckel made Wiesbaden a center for bassoons and heckelphones. Alexander brass instruments came from Mainz, and Hohner harmonicas from Trossingen.

Some schools specialize in making older instruments: harpsichords, clavichords, spinets, etc: Neupert in Nuremberg/Bamberg, Wittmayer in Gotenberg, Sperrhake in Passau, and Schütze in Heidelberg are all famous makers. Organ builders are particularly numerous in Germany: Dr. Walcker in Ludwigsburg, Klemper in Lübeck, Steinmeyer in Ottingen, and Schuke in Berlin are all top-flight specialists in their field.

For all these crafts, the Germans have established schools to train young people who are later apprenticed to master craftsmen. In our list below, however, we cite principally the cities with schools and conservatories that train musicians and/or music historians:

Aachen (Aix-la-Chapelle), Augsburg, Brunswick (Braunschweig), Bremen, Bubenreuth, Detmold, Duisburg, Erlangen, Essen, Esslingen, Göttingen, Heidelberg, Herford, Karlsruhe, Kiel, Lübeck, Ludwigsburg, Mainz, Mannheim, Marburg an der Lahn, Mittenwald, Münster, Osnabrück, Regensburg, Rottenburg, Saarbrücken, Schlüchtern, Speyer, Trier, Trossingen, Tübingen, Wuppertal.

Recently, German schools have undergone a series of reforms making it possible for them to reduce and in many instances eliminate their tuition fees. The situation is still flexible. Always write in advance for the latest information concerning fees and foreign students, and also investigate the possibility of going over as an exchange student.

Note: a special booklet, *Ausländischer Student in Deutschland* (The Foreign Student in Germany), published by the Deutscher Akademischer Austauschdienst (German Academic Exchange Service), lists all kinds of music schools —as well as other schools—and their requirements. This booklet is available on request from the German Consulate General, 460 Park Avenue, New York. It is extremely helpful even for those with a limited knowledge of German.

Summer Courses

The Internationaler Arbeitskreis für Musik, a society for the musical education of both young people and adults, organizes about a hundred music courses and festivals a year. Most of these are intended for amateurs, but some are for professional musicians as well. Courses are offered in choral singing and conducting, orchestra, chamber music, etc. Below is a selection of cities where summer courses are given.

Augsburg, Bad Hersfeld, Bad Waldsee/Württemberg, Calw/Württemberg, Fredeburg/Westfalen, Fürsteneck/Hessen, Klappholttal/Sylt, Trossingen, Weikersheim (near Munich).

For further information write to Internationaler Arbeitskreis für Musik, Heinrich-Schütz-Allee 33, D-3500 Kassel-Wilhelmshohe. A catalog, *Musiklehrgänge,* which lists all the courses, is available at the above address.

Miscellaneous

Baden-Baden

Brahmsgesellschaft Baden-Baden e.V.

Postfach (P.O. Box) 10034, 757 Baden-Baden. Tel: 70172

The Brahmsgesellschaft (Brahms Society) is housed in the Brahmshaus, whose public entrance is at Maximilianstrasse 85.

Hours: Monday, Wednesday, Friday 10:00 AM to noon and 3:00 PM to 5:00 PM;

Sunday 10:00 AM to 1:00 PM. Other visiting hours must be arranged in advance.

The Brahmshaus in Baden-Baden is the only home of the composer that has been preserved in Germany. The inscription on a memorial tablet on the door reads: "Brahms lived here 1865–1874, during which time he completed parts of several of his most significant works, including the Second Symphony, The *German Requiem,* the *Alto Rhapsody,* the *Schicksalslied,* the Horn Trio, the Sextet, Op. 36, two string quartets and several lieder." The house contains two display rooms for changing exhibitions of Brahmsiana.

Important Information for Travelers

The following four official offices of the Federal Republic of Germany should be helpful in answering your questions:

German Information Center, 410 Park Avenue, New York City.
German Consulate General, 560 Park Avenue, New York City.
German National Tourist Office, 500 Fifth Avenue, New York City.
German-American Chamber of Commerce, Inc., 666 Fifth Avenue, New York City.

The *Bühnenjahrbücher* (Theater Annuals), although issued somewhat irregularly, should nevertheless be consulted for information on theaters, opera houses, etc., for the various cities.

For a listing of instrument dealers in Germany, consult the *Mitglieder-Verzeichnis* published by the Bundesverband der deutschen Musikinstrumenten-Hersteller e.V., Bockenheimer Anlage 1a, 6 Frankfurt am Main 1. Tel: (0611) 55 29 21.

German Information Center

410 Park Avenue, New York City. Tel: (212) PL 2-5020

This office provides cultural, political, economic, travel, and tourist information.

Cultural News from Germany

A monthly publication, free upon written request to: Inter-Nationes, Kennedyallee 91, 53 Bonn-Bad Godesberg, West Germany.

Books about Germany

Two books on German cultural history:

Ernst Johann and Jörg Junker. *German Cultural History of the Last Hundred Years.* (Munich: Nymphenburger Verlagshandlung, 1970.)
Paul Schallück, ed. *Germany: Cultural Developments since 1945.* (Munich: Max Hueber, 1971.)

Festivals

Ansbach

Bachwoche Ansbach
Geschäfsstelle der Bachwoche Ansbach,
P.O. Box 41, 88 Ansbach. Tel: 0229/64780
Mailing Address: 1 Fasanenstrasse, 53 Bonn-Bad Godesberg 1.
Dates: every two years in odd-numbered years at the end of July. Concerts of the sacred and secular works of Johann Sebastian Bach.
Box Office: Haus der Volksbildung, Promenade 29. Tel: 0981/2559
Hours: open seven days a week, 2:30 PM to 8:30 PM.
Customary Dress: for morning concerts, daytime dress; for evening concerts, dressy clothes; for church concerts, dark clothes.
Seating capacity: Five separate concert rooms in various places; all together approx. 5,000 seats.

For housing accommodations, write to Stadtisches Reise- und Verkehrsbüro Ansbach, Quartieramt, Postfach 41, 88 Ansbach.

Augsburg

Festspiele am Roten Tor
Städtisches Verkehrsamt, 89 Augsburg.
Dates: July to beginning of September.
Open air opera performances.

Deutsches Mozartfest
Mailing Address: 11 Bahnhofstrasse, 8900 Augsburg. Tel: (0821) 25588
Dates: variable; usually during the month of May. Chamber music, orchestral and vocal music by Mozart.
Authorized Ticket Agency: Fa. Anton Böhm & Sohn, Ludwigstrasse, 89 Augsburg.

For housing information, write to Deutsches Mozartfest, 12 Halderstrasse, 89 Augsburg.

This festival is held annually, but not in the same location. The Festival headquarters, however, is located in Augsburg. The concept behind the idea of a traveling festival is to acquaint as large an audience as possible with the music of Mozart. The Festival has been located in the following cities: Ansbach, Augsburg, Berlin, Bremen, Köln-Brühl, Düsseldorf, Hanover (twice), Cologne, Ludwigsburg (three times), Regensburg, Stuttgart, Wuppertal, and Zweibrücken.

Baden-Baden

Brahmstage

Maximilianstrasse 85, Baden-Lichtental. Tel: 70172
Mailing Address: Postfach 1003, 757 Baden-Baden.
Dates: three days in May.

Chamber and orchestral concerts of the works of Brahms and Schumann.

The Brahmstage annual festival was started in 1968 by the Brahms-Gesellschaft (Brahms Society). Performances are held in the Weinbrennersaal and the Kurhaus-Empfangszimmer. The performers donate their time, and the proceeds go to the upkeep of the Brahmshaus.

Bayreuth

Bayreuther Festspiele at the Festspielhaus

Luitpoldplatz. Tel: Bayreuth 5722
Mailing Address: Bayreuther Festspiele, Postfach 2320, 8580 Bayreuth 2.
Dates: mid-July to the end of August. Wagner operas.
Box Office: Festspielhaus (mailing address as above). Tel: Bayreuth 5722
Hours: Tuesday 3:00 PM to 5:00 PM.
Seating capacity: 1,930

Housing accommodations are handled through the city's housing bureau, with priority given to ticketholders. Address: Gastedienst des Fremdenverkehrsvereins, 858 Bayreuth. There are also excellent accommodations available outside of Bayreuth.

Evening dress is customary at all, even afternoon, performances.

Every Bayreuth Festival opens with the first performance of the annual new production, and attracts an audience which has been compared with the opening night audience at the Met for glamor. Most performances at the Festival begin at about 4:00 PM, in keeping with the local tradition of ending operas by 10:00 PM. There are usually two intermissions of between forty-five minutes and an hour long each, during every opera, allowing the audience to flock to the snack bar in another building or to consume more substantial fare (ordered in advance) at the Festival restaurant. Getting tickets for performances poses a problem, and it may be easier to obtain them on this side of the Atlantic, since those sold in Bayreuth disappear very early. In America, both American Express and Cook's receive allotments of tickets.

Frankische Festwoche

Markgräfliches Opernhaus, Bayreuth Tel: 0921/65313
Mailing Address: Schloss- und Gartenverwaltung, Bayreuth, Hofgarten.
Dates: one week at the end of May. Opera, ballet, concerts, drama.

Box Office Mailing Address: 9 Luitpoldplatz, Bayreuth. Tel: (0921) 69001
Customary Dress: street dress.
Seating capacity: 500

International Youth Festival Meeting in Bayreuth

(See Bayreuth, Summer Courses.)

Berlin

Bach Tage

9 Hahnelstrasse, 1 Berlin 41 (Friedenau). Tel: (0311) 851 83 24
Dates: one week in mid-July.

Various concerts, lectures. Mainly Bach, although there are also concerts of music of other composers.

Box Office: address above. Tickets are also obtainable from the Verkehrsamt.

Concerts are held in Kaiser-Wilhelm-Gedächtniskirche; Akademie der Kunste; Schloss Charlottenburg; Grosser Sendesaal of the Haus des Rundfunks; St. Ansgar-Kirche; St. Matthäus-Kirche; Neue Nationalgalerie; Musikinstrumenten-Museum Berlin. Concerts are given by the Münchner Kammerorchester, Bach-Collegium Berlin, Kölner Kammerorchester, and various organists and chamber players.

There are also lectures, e.g., "Bach und das Problem des musikalischen Zyklus" by Prof. R. Stephan of Berlin; "Von Dufay zu Bach" by Dr. W. Nitschke of Berlin. There is also a tour of the musical instrument museum.

Berliner Festwochen (International Festival of Berlin)

Berliner Festwochen, 1–12 Bundesallee, 1 Berlin 15. Tel: 8 81 04 41
Dates: early September to early October.

Opera, theater, ballet, orchestral concerts, chamber music, solo recitals.

Box Office: at the above address. Mail orders are taken up to July 31. No phone orders are accepted. Tickets can also be obtained through all German travel bureaus. In addition, Berliners can purchase tickets at the box office and other authorized ticket agencies starting August 29.

For housing accommodations, write to Verkehrsamt Berlin, 7–8 Fasanenstrasse, 1 Berlin 12, or contact any travel bureau. Tel: (0311) 24 01 11

The Berlin Festival is held in theaters throughout the city. Many international artists, orchestras, and conductors make special appearances during the Festival. It includes the Berliner Jazz-Tage, a jazz festival held during the first week of November.

Festival of Non-Western Music

Winklerstrasse 20, 1 Berlin 33. Tel: 89 28 53

Dates: one week at the end of May or the beginning of June.

This festival is sponsored by the Internationales Institut für vergleichende Musikstudien und Dokumentation (see Libraries, Institutes).

Bonn

Internationales Beethovenfest

c/o Kulturamt der Stadt Bonn
Kurfürstenstrasse 2–3, 52 Bonn-Bad Godesberg. Tel: 8/60 06 45, 8/6006 63
Dates: every three years (1970, 1973, 1976, etc.) in mid-September.

Braunschweig (Brunswick)

Festliche Tage Neuer Kammermusik der Stadt Braunschweig

Stadthalle Braunschweig.
Mailing Address: Steintorwall 3, 33 Braunschweig.
Dates: at the end of November. Three concerts, one lecture.
Box Office: Konzertdirektion Walter Ernst Schmidt, 1 Zeppelinstrasse, 33 Braunschweig.
Customary Dress: as one wishes.
Seating capacity: 500

For housing information, write to Städt. Verkehrsbüro, Hauptbahnhof, 33 Braunschweig.

Bremen

German Bach Festival

Bachfestbüro, 7 Böttcherstrasse, D-2800 Bremen.
Dates: one week early in June.

Concerts of works by Bach and his contemporaries; exhibitions.

Cologne

Ballet Week

Städtische Bühnen Köln, 5 Cologne.
Dates: July.

Constance

Internationale Musiktage

Verkehrsamt der Stadt Konstanz, 6 Bahnhofplatz, D-7750 Konstanz.
Dates: mid-June to mid-July.

Orchestral and chamber music concerts. Various visiting orchestras and conductors.

Donaueschingen

Musiktage für Zeitgenössische Tonkunst (Festival of Contemporary Music)
Städtisches Verkehrsamt, Rathaus, D-7710 Donaueschingen.
Dates: two days in mid-October.
Modern and avant-garde music.

Elmau

Schloss Elmau Festival
Schlossverwaltung Elmau, D-8010 Post Kleiss, Oberbayern.
Dates: one week early in June.
Chamber music. Works by composers ranging from J. S. Bach to Bartók.

Göttingen

Göttingen Händel Festival
Göttinger Händel Gesellschaft, Herzberger Landstrasse 105, D-3400 Göttingen.
Dates: first week in July.
Chamber music, orchestral, and choral concerts of the music of Händel and his contemporaries.

Hamburg

International Music Festival of the International Society for Contemporary Music
Deutscher Musikrat, Weltmusikfestbüro, Feldbrunnenstrasse 56, 2 Hamburg 13.
Dates: June.

Hanover

Tage der Neuen Musik
Norddeutscher Rundfunk, 3 Hanover.
Dates: end of January.
Contemporary music.

Musik und Theater in Herrenhausen
Herrenhäuserstrasse 3A. Tel: Durchwahl 168 4817

Mailing Address: 2 Trammplatz, Rathaus, 3 Hanover.
Dates: end of May to mid-September.

Opera, ballet, symphony orchestras, jazz, chamber, and choral concerts, plays.

Box Office: 3A Herrenhäuserstrasse, 3 Hanover. Tel: 168 3490; evening box office 168 5872.
Hours: Monday to Friday from 2:00 PM; Saturday, Sunday and holidays from 11:00 AM.
Authorized ticket agency: Verkehrsbüro, 8 Ernst-August-Platz, Hanover. Also, Besucherring, 36 Georgstrasse, Hanover.
Customary dress: according to the weather.
Seating capacity: interior theater, 704; garden theater, 952.

For housing information write to Verkehrsbüro, 8 Ernst-August-Platz, D-3000 Hanover (Hauptbahnhof).

After evening performances the "Great Garden" will be illuminated for the visitors at these performances only.

Heidelberg

German Bach Festival

Neue Bachgesellschaft, Rumannstrasse 10–11, 3 Hanover.
Dates: held in June.

Hitzacker/Elbe

Sommerliche Musiktage Hitzacker

Hitzacker/Elbe 3139. Tel: Hitzacker 518
Dates: last week in July.

Concerts, chamber music, song recitals, and solo recitals.

Seating capacity: approx. 400
Box Office: For advance tickets, Bücherecke Berndt, 23 Drawehnertorstrasse, 3139 Hitzacker/Elbe. Tel: 05862/398.

This festival is sponsored by the Gesellschaft der Freunde der Sommerlichen Musiktage.

Kassel

Internationales Heinrich Schütz-Fest

Internationale Heinrich Schütz-Gesellschaft e.V., 35 Heinrich Schütz-Allee, 35 Kassel-Wilhelmshöhe Tel: 0561/30013
Dates: variable; usually the first week in October, every other year.
Concerts: primarily a musicological gathering.

This festival has been taking place every other year (without complete regularity) since 1930. It is not based in one particular city, although its headquarters is based in Kassel; every two years it is located in a new city, not always in Germany (Berlin, Uppsala, Amsterdam, Bern, London, etc.).

International Weeks Devoted to Contemporary Sacred Music (Internationale Wochen für Geistliche Musik der Gegenwart)
Kantorei am St. Martin, Mittelgasse 20, D-3500 Kassel.
Dates: one week in mid-April.
Includes both concerts and a congress.

Kassel Music Festival
Geschäftsstelle der Kasseler Musiktage, Heinrich Schütz-Allee 33, D-3500 Kassel-Wilhelmshöhe.
Dates: two days at the end of October.
Chamber music, jazz concerts, and contemporary chamber music. World premieres of contemporary music.

Kiel

Kiel Week
Städtisches Verkehrsamt, 23 Kiel.
Dates: June.
Theater, operas, concerts.

Lüdenscheid

Little Music Festival
Geschäftsstelle der Kleinen Musikfeste, Wilhelmstrasse 37, D-5880 Lüdenscheid.
Dates: two days in May.
Renaissance and baroque music.

Marburg

Palace Festival
Städtisches Verkehrsamt, 355 Marburg/Lahn.
Dates: June and July.
Classical music.

Munich

Münchener Bach-Fest (Munich Bach Festival)
Bayerische Konzertdirektion, Marienplatz 2, D-8000 Munich 2.

Dates: one week in June.
Concerts: vocal and instrumental chamber music.
Box Office: for foreign reservations and orders: Amtliche Bayer. Reisebüro, 12 Karlsplatz, 8 Munich 2.

Concerts take place at various halls throughout Munich: Herkulessaal, Markuskirche, Hochschule, Kongresssaal. Guest artists frequently perform.

Munich Ballet Festival

Bayerische Staatsoper München, Ballettdirektion, Maximilianstrasse 11, 8 Munich 1.
Dates: one week in mid-May.

Various ballets.

Munich Opera Festival

Nationaltheater, Munich
Mailing Address: Bayerische Staatsoper, Dramaturgie, Brieffach, D-8000 Munich 1.
Dates: second week in July through first week in August.

Operas by various composers.

Box Office: Festspielkasse der Bayerischen Staatsoper, Brieffach, 8 Munich 1, for ticket orders in writing. Tel: 22 13 16 (for ticket order by phone)
Hours: Monday to Friday, 9:00 AM to 6:00 PM; Saturday, Sunday, and holidays, 9:00 AM to 1:00 PM.
Agency for advance booking in Munich: box office of the Bayerische Staatsoper, 11 Maximilianstrasse.

Tickets can also be ordered at the following agencies: Karl Hardach Travel Service, Inc., 500 Fifth Avenue, New York 10036 and Mayfair Travel Service, Inc., 119 West 57th Street, New York 10019.

Customary Dress: dark suit; street clothing.

For housing information, write to Kongress- und Verkehrsstelle München GMBH, Fremdenverkehrsamt München, 2 Bahnhofplatz, Munich 2.

The Munich Opera Festival is more than sixty years old. It is dedicated to four composers: Mozart, Wagner, Strauss, and Pfitzner. Consequently, many of their works are usually performed. This is not to the exclusion of compositions by Verdi, Donizetti, Orff, and Britten, as well as other new composers, who are frequently represented. In addition, the Munich Opera Festival draws many guest orchestras, conductors, and performers.

Festival Concerts of the Munich Philharmonic Orchestra

Münchner Philharmoniker, 3–4/III Rindermarkt, D-8000 Munich 2.
Dates: June and July.

Symphony concerts.

Nuremberg

International Organ Festival

Internationale Orgelwoche Nürnberg, Menschelstrasse 38, 85 Nuremberg.
Dates: one week in June.

Organ recitals, as well as orchestra, chorus, and soloists. A concert by the prizewinning contestants of the previous year's Composers' Competition.

Passau

Europäische Wochen Passau

Nibelungenhalle, Neubergerstrasse, 839 Passau. Tel: 0851/2143
Dates: mid-June to mid-July.

Ballet, opera, concerts, plays.

Box Office: Nibelungenhalle.
Mailing Address: Nibelungenhalle, Passau. Tel: 0851/7966
Hours: 9:00 AM to noon; 5:00 PM to 7:00 PM.
Customary Dress: evening clothes.
Seating capacity: 1250

For housing information, please write to Nibelungenhalle, Fremdenverkehrsverein, Passau.

Schwetzingen

Schwetzingen Festival

Schwetzinger Festspiele, Verkehrsverein, Schlosspark, D-6830 Schwetzingen.
Dates: end of April to the end of May.

Chamber music and solo performances featuring artists from all over the world.

The Festival is set in the rustic locale of Prince-Elector Carl Theodor's summer residence. Both traditional and contemporary music are performed.

Staufen-im-Breisgau

Staufener Musikwochen

Verkehrsamt, 7813 Staufen-im-Breisgau. Tel: 5446
Dates: one week at the end of July.
Highly varied concerts; everything from medieval songs to twentieth-century chamber music.
Seating capacity: Approx. 400

For housing accommodations, write to Verkehrsamt, 7813 Staufen-im-Breisgau.

Stuttgart

Stuttgart Ballet Festival

Württembergisches Staatstheater, Dramaturgie, Postfach 982, 7 Stuttgart 1.
Dates: May.

Wiesbaden

International May Festival

Hessisches Staatstheater, Dramaturgie, Postfach, D-6200 Wiesbaden.
Tel: 3 9331
Dates: late April to late May.
Opera and Ballet.
This festival has been a tradition since 1896.

Würzburg

International Music Weeks

Verkehrsamt, Bad Mergentheim (near Würzburg).
Dates: August and September.

Mozart Fest

Mozart-Fest Würzburg, Haus zum Falken, D-8700 Würzburg.
Tel: 0931/54100 and 52277
Dates: two weeks in late June.
Opera and concerts.
Box Office: same as above address.
Hours: weekdays from 8:00 AM to noon.
Standing room: places are obtainable only at the box office, if it is not raining.
Seating capacity: 800
Tickets may be reserved by mail, and will be held for foreign patrons at the Mozart Festival office.
For housing information, write to Fremdenverkehramt, Haus zum Falken, 8700 Würzburg.

Concerts are held at the Residence, in this palace's gardens, and in its Imperial Hall. If the weather is poor, evening concerts scheduled to be held outdoors are held in the Residence. The Festival's high artistic standards are maintained through the cooperation of international artists.

Competitions

Berlin

Von Karajan International Conductors' Competition
Herbert Von Karajan Stiftung, Internationaler Dirigenten-Wettbewerb
Bundesallee 1–12.
Biennial.
Deadline: June 1. Apply to the address above. Only those conductors between 20 and 30 years of age are eligible.

The Von Karajan International Conductors' Competition is held in the concert hall of the Academy of Music. Each contestant is asked to select three works from each of the groups (classical, romantic, and modern), which he will be prepared to conduct. The selection is limited by a repertory list available from the organizers, from which the contestant must make his selections. If the participant elects not to choose specific works himself, the jury will then select the works.

Awards: First Prize is the Herbert von Karajan Gold Medal, DM 10,000, possible assistant conductorship under Herbert von Karajan, concert and recording engagements, and an appearance with the Berlin Philharmonic Orchestra at the end of the competition; Second Prize is the Herbert von Karajan Silver Medal and DM 7,500. Third Prize is the Herbert von Karajan Bronze Medal and DM 5,000.

Von Karajan International Meeting of Youth Orchestras
Herbert Von Karajan Stiftung, Internationale Begegnung für Jugendorchester
Bundesallee 1–12.
Biennial. It alternates yearly with the Von Karajan International Conductors' Competition (see above).

The competition is open only to non-professional youth orchestras; orchestras of colleges of music, conservatories, music academies, universities, and other youth orchestras, provided that their members are not older than 25 years of age.

This competition comprises two categories: chamber orchestra and symphony orchestra. Each orchestra is asked to present a two-hour concert with individually chosen programs, including works by contemporary composers of the orchestra's country, and one set work.

Prizes: Herbert von Karajan Gold Medal for the best interpretation and performance in each category. In addition, other medals and certificates are awarded.

For information and applications, apply to the above address.

Von Karajan International Youth Orchestra Composition Prize

Herbert von Karajan Stiftung, Kompositionspreis, Internationale Begegnung

Bundesallee 1–12.

Biennial. This contest is held concurrently with the International Meeting of Youth Orchestras (see above).

Composers entering this competition are asked to write a composition suitable for youth orchestras, with a maximum duration of eighteen minutes.

Awards: First Prize is DM 5,000; Second Prize, DM 3,000. The winner's composition is performed by Herbert von Karajan and the Berlin Philharmonic Orchestra.

For information and applications, write to the above address.

Bonn-Bad Godesberg

Kulturbrief

Published by Inter Nationes, a German association for promotion of international relations. An English version by Timothy Nevill offers information on Festivals, Competitions, Lectures, Congresses, and articles of interest. For further information address inquiries to Inter Nationes, D-53, Bonn-Bad Godesberg.

Freiburg-im-Breisgau

Wettbewerb der Staatlichen Hochschulen für Musik (Competition of the State Academies of Music)

c/o Staatliche Hochschule für Musik, Münsterplatz 30, Freiburg-im-Breisgau.

Kiel

Internationaler Orgel-Wettbewerb

Klosterkirchhof 8, D-2300 Kiel 1.

Held in September.

This is a recently-created competition which is open to organists of any nationality under thirty years of age who have proven their ability by achieving an A certificate in church music, or a concert examination, or by possessing a certificate from a recognized organist. Contestants are asked to prepare a program including several works by J. S. Bach, as well as compositions by Max Reger, Paul Hindemith, and other contemporary composers.

Awards: Three prizes of DM 2,500, 2,000 and 1,500, as well as a special prize for improvisation, will be awarded.

For information and applications, write to the above address.

Munich

Internationaler Musikwettbewerb (International Competition)

Bayerischer Rundfunk, Rundfunkplatz 1, D-8000 Munich 2.

Annual. Held the first three weeks in September.

Categories change. In 1971: voice, piano, organ, viola, trumpet, duo for violin and piano. In 1972: voice, piano, violin, oboe.

Deadline: July 1. Age limits vary with category, usually between ages seventeen or twenty and thirty. Musicians of all nationalities are admitted.

All sessions are open to the public free of charge.

Awards: there are three prizes in each category, ranging from DM 6,000 to DM 1,500.

This competition is sponsored by the Broadcasting Corporations of the German Federal Republic (ARD). For information and applications write to the above address.

Periodicals

Abhandlungen zur Kunst, Musik und Literaturwissenschaft
H. Bouvier and Co. Verlag, Postfach 346, Am Hof 32, 53 Bonn
Irregular

Acta Mozartiana
Deutsche Mozart Gesellschaft V., Maximilianstr. 89-1, 89 Augsburg
Quarterly

Acta Musicologica (Periodical of the International Musicological Society)
Institut der Johannes-Gutenberg-Universität, Postfach 606,
Saarstrasse 21, Mainz
Quarterly

Acta Sagittariana (Reports of the International Heinrich Schütz Society)
Heinrich-Schütz-Allee 35, 35 Kassel-Wilhelmshöhe
Two to three issues a year

Ad Marginem
Breite Strasse 96, 404 Neuss

Allgemeine Volksmusik-Zeitung
Bund Dt. Volksmusikverbände V., Postfach 1527, 7800 Freiburg

Archiv für Musikwissenschaft
Franz Steiner Verlag GmbH., Bahnhofstr. 39, Wiesbaden
Quarterly

Ars Organi (Periodical for Organists)
Verlag Merseburger Berlin GmbH., Alemannenstr. 20, Postfach 130, 1 Berlin 38
Two or three issues annually

Der Artist (Newsletter for the Popular Arts)
Louise-Dumont-Strasse 25, Postfach 5208, 4, Düsseldorf 1
Twice monthly

BLGV-Nachrichten
Berliner-Lehrer-Gesängverein e.V., Machnower Strasse 43a, 1000 Berlin 37

Die Bayerische Volksmusik
Josef Rietzler, Kolpingstr. 2, 8938 Buchloe

Berliner Jazz-Programm
Konzertdirektion Wolfgang Jänicke, Cicerostrasse 13, 1 Berlin-Halensee
Monthly

Bielefelder Katalog
Bielefelder Verlagsanstalt KG, Ulmenstr. 8, 48 Bielefeld
Semi-Annual

Blaetter und Bilder (Journal of Poetry, Music and Painting)
Verlag Andreas Zettner, Würzberg
Bi-monthly

Chordirigent (Newsletter for Choral Conductors)
B. Schott's Söhne, Postfach 3640, D 6500 Mainz
Two to three times annually

Der Chor
Dt. Allgemeine Sängerbund e.V., Wechmarkt 3, 6000 Frankfurt

Der Chorleiter
Christlichen Sängerbund, Westfalenweg 207, 56 Wuppertal 1
Bi-monthly

Der Chorsanger
Weber & Weidemeyer, Sandershauser Strasse, 3500 Kassel

Country Corner
Eichenstrasse 54, 29 Oldenburg
Five times yearly

Darmstaedter Beitraege zur Neuen Musik
B. Schott's Söhne, Mainz
Annual

Deutsche Saengerschaft
Hauptausschuss der Deutschen Sängerschaft, (Weimarer CC), Geschäftsfuehrung, Schmidenerstrasse 14, 7012 Fellbach
Bi-monthly

Der Deutsche Volksmusiker (*Official Organ of the German Folk Music Association*)
Anton Ehmer, Pelagiusgasse 5, Rottweil-Alstadt
Monthly

Deutscher Musikrat
Feldbrunnenstrasse 56, 2 Hamburg 13

Euro Piano
Verlag Das Musikinstrument, Klueberstrasse 9, D-6000 Frankfurt-am-Main
Quarterly

Film-Ton-Magazin
Heering-Verlag, Ortlerstrasse 8, 8000 Munich 25

Folk-Letter (*Organ of the Workers' Circle of the Interfolk Festival*)
Sitz Osnabrück, 4420 Coesfeld

Fono-Forum (*Periodical of Records, Music and Recording Technique*)
Bielefelder Verlagsanstalt KG., Ulmenstrasse 8, 4800 Bielefeld
Monthly

Fontes Artis Musicae (*Review of the International Association of Music Libraries*)
Secretariat of IAML, Ständeplatz 16, 3500 Kassel
Irregular; available only to members

Geistliche Chormusik Gesamtverzeichnis
Haenssler Verlag, 7000 Stuttgart-Hohensheim
Annual

Gema-Nachrichten
Bayreuther Strasse 37, 1000 Berlin 30

Der Gemeindechor
Christlichen Sängerbund e.V., Westfalenweg 209, 5600 Wuppertal 1
Bi-monthly

Gottesdienst und Kirchenmusik (*Journal of Church Music and Liturgy*)
Dr. Friedrich Kalb, Wilhelminenstr. 9, 858 Bayreuth
Bi-monthly

Hamburger Musikleben
Werbevlog. Glottbek, Sohrhof 2, 2000 Hamburg 52
Nine issues yearly

Hans Pfitzner-Gesellschaft, Mitteilungen
Hans Pfitzner-Gesellschaft e.V., Steffanistrasse 13, Munich-Obermenzing
Irregular

Harmonia Mundi Journal
Bärenreiter, Heinrich-Schütz-Allee 35, 35 Kassel-Wilhelmshöhe

Harmonie in Lied und Leben (*Newsletter of the Esslinger Lieder Circle*)
Wilhelm Lutz, Hellerweg 26/2, Esslingen am Neckar

Der Harmonika Lehrer
Löhrstrasse 32, 7217 Trossingen
Bi-monthly

Harmonika-Revue
Verlag die Harmonika, Mozartstrasse 17, 7217 Trossingen/Württemburg
Bi-monthly

Hausmusik
Bärenreiter Verlag, Heinrich-Schütz-Allee 29/37, 35 Kassel-Wilhelmshöhe
Monthly

***Haydn-Studien** (**Publication of the Joseph Haydn Institute**)*
G. Henle Verlag, Schongauerstr. 24, 8 Munich 55
Irregular

***Hifi Stereophonie** (**Official Organ of the German High Fidelity Institute**)*
Verlag G. Braun, Karl-Friedrich-Strasse 14/18, 75 Karlsruhe 1
Monthly

ISO Information
Geschaeftsstelle, D 7128, Postfach 234, Lauffen/Neckar

Instrumentenbau Zeitschrift
F. Schmitt, Kaiserstr. 99–101, Postfach 243, 52 Siegburg
Monthly

International Music Educator (Journal of the International Society for Music Education)
International Society for Music Education, Egon Kraus, Sec'y-General, Wallgraben 5, 29 Oldenburg
Semi-annual

Das Internationale Podium (Journal of Music, Film, Radio, Television and Recordings)
Postfach 527, 678 Pirmassens
Monthly

Internationale Richard Strauss Gesellschaft Mitteilungen (Text in English, French and German)
Richard-Wagner-Strasse 8–10, 1 Berlin 10
Quarterly

Intervalle
Bargteheider Str. 189, 2 Hamburg 73
Bi-monthly

Jahrbuch für Musikalische Volks und Völkerkunde
Walter de Gruyter & Co., Genthinerstr. 13, 1 Berlin 30
Annual

Jazz Bazaar
Hans W. Ewert, Hoehenweg 10, 5461 Rotterheide
Monthly

Jazz-Podium
Vogelsangstr. 32, 7 Stuttgart
Monthly

Jazzbrief
Radio Bremen, Heinrich-Hertz-Strasse 13, 2800 Bremen

Der Jazzfreund
Schlesienstrasse 11, 575 Menden (Sauerland)
Quarterly

***Jugendmusik* (*Publishers' Reports for all those involved with Young Musicians*)**
B. Schott's Söhne, Weihergarten 1–9, 65 Mainz

Der Junge Musikfreunde
Möseler Verlag, Hoffmann-von-Fallersleben-Strasse 8, Postfach 460, 3340 Wolfenbüttel

Kammerspiele München
EMHA-Verlag, Sendlinger-Tor-Platz 8, Munich 2

***Der Kirchenchor* (*Essays of the Association of German Protestant Church Choirs*)**
Bärenreiter-Verlag, Heinrich-Schütz-Allee 35, 3500 Kassel-Wilhelmshöhe
Bi-monthly

Kirchenmusikalische Mitteilungen
Domplatz 5, 6720 Speyer

***Kirchenmusikalische Nachrichten* (*Newsletter of the Society for Church Music of the Protestant Church in Hesse and Nassau*)**
Miquel-Allee 7, Frankfurt/M.
Quarterly

***Der Kirchenmusiker* (*Newsletter of the Central Office for Protestant Church Music*)**
Verlag Merseburger Berlin GmbH., Alemannenstrasse 20, Postfach 130, 1 Berlin 38
Bi-monthly

***Das Klavierspiel* (*Journal for Pianists and Friends of Piano Music*)**
Dr. P. Schnath, Hofweg 98, Hamburg 22 (Uhlenhorst)
Quarterly

***Kontakte* (*Journal for Music and Youth*)**
Möseler Verlag, Wolfenbüttel
Bi-monthly

Konzerte Mit Neuer Musik
Bayerischer Rundfunk, Rundfunkplatz 1, 8 Munich 2
Quarterly

Landesverbandes der Tonkünstler und Musiklehrer, Mitteilungsblatt
Hagedornstrasse 6, Hamburg 13

Lehren und Lernen
Verlag Hermann Wolfgang v. Waltershausen-Gesellschaft
Unertlstrasse 2, 8 Munich 23

Das Liebhaberorchester
Bund Deutscher Liebhaberorchester e.V., Schwachhauser Ring 52, 28 Bremen 1
Quarterly

Lied und Chor
Verlag Deutscher Sängerbund GmbH, Luepertzenderstr. 157–163, 4050 Mönchengladbach
Monthly

Der Liederkranz
Gesang-Verein Liederkranz, Heimstättenstrasse 62, 8720 Schweinfurt

Mein Saitenspiel
Zithermusikverband, Wartburgstrasse 3, 463 Bochum-Langendreer
Monthly

***Melos* (*Journal of New Music*)**
Melos-Verlag, Weihergarten, Postfach 3640, 65 Mainz
Monthly

Mitteilungen der Hans Pfitzner-Gesellschaft
Steffanistrasse 13, München-Obermenzing

Mitteilungen der Pfalzischen Musikgesellschaft
Prinzregentenstrasse 18, 6700 Ludwigshafen

Mitteilungen des Max-Reger-Instituts, Bonn
Max-Reger-Institut, Schumannhaus, Sebastianstrasse 182,
53 Bonn-Endenich
Irregular

Mitteilungsblatt der Gesellschaft für Bayerische Musikgeschichte e.V.
Schliessfach 731, Munich 1

Mitteilungsblatt des Landesverbandes der Tonkünstler und Musiklehrer, LTM Hauptgruppe Hamburg e.V.
Hagedornstrasse 6, 2000 Hamburg

Mitteilungsblatt des Post-Männerchors
Post-Männerchor, Fleischstrasse 57, 5500 Trier

Mitteilungsblatt für die Kirchenmusiker in der Evangelischen Kirche im Rheinland
Merseburger Verlag, Alemannenstrasse 20, Postfach 130, 1000 Berlin 38

Music
Das Dt. Musikmagazin
Music-Verlag Sybill Ptach KG, Am Rosenplatz 8, 2057 Reinbek bei Hamburg

Musica
Bärenreiter-Verlag, Heinrich-Schütz-Allee 31–37, 3500 Kassel-Wilhelmshöhe
Bi-monthly

Musica Sacra
Cäcilien-Verbands-Organ, Kalker Hauptstrasse 280, 5 Cologne
Bi-monthly

Musik im Unterricht
Weihergarten 12, 65 Mainz
Eleven issues per year

Musik-Informationen
Sigert-Verlag GmbH., Ekbertstrasse 14, 33 Braunschweig
Monthly

Musik Parade
Heinrich Bauer Verlag, Burchardstrasse 11, Hamburg 1
Bi-weekly

Musik und Altar **(*Journal of Music in Church and School, Youth and Home*)**
Tennenbacher Strasse 4, 7800 Freiburg i. Br.
Quarterly

Musik und Bildung **(*Journal of the Theory and Practice of Music Education*)**
Verlag G. Schott's Söhne, Weihergarten 1–9, Postfach 3640, D-65 Mainz
Monthly

Musik und Kirche **(*Journal of Protestant Church Music*)**
Bärenreiter-Verlag, Heinrich-Schütz-Allee 29–37, 35 Kassel-Wilhelmshöhe
Bi-monthly

Musik und Theaterzeitung
Jean Terhöven, Kaiserplatz 13, 516 Düren

Musikalische Jugend
Jeunesses Musicales, Landshuterstrasse 14 A, 84 Regensburg
Bi-monthly

Der Musiker
Deutscher Musikerverband, Besenbinderhof 56, Hamburg 1
Monthly

Die Musikforschung
Universität, Musikwissenschaftliches Institut, 66 Saarbrücken
Quarterly

Musikhandel **(*Official Newsletter for Dealers of Records, Musical Instruments, and Accessories*)**
Musikhandel Verlagsgesellschaft m.b.H., Dahlmannstrasse 24, Bonn
Eight issues per year

Das Musikinstrument
Klüberstrasse 9, 6000 Frankfurt/M.
Thirteen issues per year

Der Musikmarkt
Josef Keller Verlag, Postfach 40, 8130 Starnberg (Oberbayern)
Monthly

Musikpädagogik **(*Newsletter of Breitkopf & Härtel Publishers*)**
Breitkopf & Härtel, Wiesbaden

Die Musikwoche
Parrhysius, Baden-Allee 20, 1 Berlin-Charlottenburg 9
Monthly

Neue Musikzeitung (*Journal of the Musical Youth of Austria*)
Gustav Bosse Verlag, Landshuter Strasse 14a, 84 Regensburg
Bi-monthly

Neue Zeitschrift für Musik
Verlag B. Schott's Söhne, Postfach 3640, 6500 Mainz/Rhein
Monthly

Die Oper (*Journal of Bavarian National Opera*)
Nationaltheater München, Max-Joseph-Platz, Munich

Oper und Konzert
Magdalenenweg 3, Munich/Planegg
Monthly

Oper und Tanz (*Journal of Opera, Chorus, and Dance*)
Walter Kane, Georgstr. 2, 5043 Erftstadt-Lechenich

Opera International Journal
Residenzstr. 13/IV, 8 Munich 2
Bi-monthly

Opern Journal
Hauszeitschrift der Deutschen Oper Berlin-W., Richard-Wagner-Strasse 10
Berlin 10
Monthly

Opern Welt
Erhard Friedrich Verlag, 3001 Velber, Hannover
Thirteen issues per year

Das Orchester (*Journal for the Members of German Orchestras and Broadcasting Choruses*)
Verlag B. Schott's Söhne, Postfach 3640, 65 Mainz
Monthly

Pfälzer Sänger (*Periodical of the Vocalists of Pfälz*)
Südwestdeutsche Verlagsdruckerei Georg Hornberger, Postfach 31,
6757 Waldfischbach-Pfälz
Monthly

***Phonoprisma* (*Journal for the Friends of Records and Tapes*)**
Bärenreiter-Verlag, Heinrich-Schütz-Allee 29–37, Kassel-Wilhelmshöhe
Bi-Monthly

Die Posaune
S. H. Waitzmann, Nikolaus-Hofmann Str. 5, 8720 Schweinfurt

Pro Musica
Hohner-Verlag und Möseler-Verlag, Karlstrasse 2, 7217 Trossingen

Saar-Sänger-Bund
Preussenstrasse 42, 6600 Saarbrücken

Saitenspiel
Deutscher Zithermusik Bund, e.V., Nuremberg
Eight issues a year

***Salve Hospes* (*Brunswick Musical News*)**
Braunschweigische Musikges e.V., Lessingplatz 12, 3300 Braunschweig

Sammlung Musikwissenschaftlicher Abhandlungen
Verlag Heitz GmbH., Postfach 304, Yburgstrasse 36, 757 Baden-Baden
Irregular

***Sang und Klang* (*Singers' Association of the German Police Force*)**
Polizeipräsidium, 4650 Gelsenkirchen

Der Sänger am Linken Niederrhein
Albert Höntages & Söhne, Weyerhofstrasse 85, 4150 Krefeld

***Sänger-Musikantenzeitung* (*Bi-monthly for the Promotion of Folk Music*)**
Postfach 430, Lothstrasse 29, 8 Munich 13
Bi-monthly

Sänger- und Musikanten-Zeitung
Bayr. Landwirtschaftsverlag GmbH., Lothstrasse 29, 8 Munich 13
Bi-monthly

Sängergruss
Verlag Christl. Sängerbund, Kr. Moers, Schliessf. 122,
4133 Neukirchen-Vluyn
Bi-monthly

Schallplattenring-Illustrierte
Bertelsmann GmbH., Eickhoffstr. 14–15, Gütersloh

Das Schlagzeug (Jazz Magazine)
Aquator-Verlag GmbH., Galvanistrasse 6, 1 Berlin-Charlottenburg 1
Monthly

Schott-Kurier (Reports of the Theater and Concert Divisions)
Verlag B. Schott's Söhne, Weihergarten 1–9, 6500 Mainz
Irregular

Singende Woterkant
Herrengraben 70, 2000 Hamburg 11

Singendes Niedersachsen
Sängerbund Nordwestdeutschland im D S B, Violenstrasse 7, Bremen

Singet dem Herrn (Newsletter of the Protestant Singers' Association)
Bremer Strasse 2, 56 Wuppertal-Elberfeld

Spielet dem Herrn
Gütersloher Verlagshaus G. Mohn, Zweigerstrasse 9, 43 Essen
Quarterly

Spielplan (Monthly Theater Preview)
Bärenreiter-Verlag Karl Vötterle KG, Heinrich-Schütz-Allee 29–37, 35 Kassel-Wilhelmshöhe

Süddeutsche Sängerzeitung
Musikverlag Hochstein & Co., Fried.-Ebert-Anlage 28, 69 Heidelberg
Monthly

Das Tanzarchiv
"Das Tanzarchiv," Blumenstrasse 38a, 2 Hamburg 39
Monthly

Theater Heute
Erhard Friedrich Verlag, 3001 Velber bei Hannover
Monthly

Ton Magazin
Heering-Verlag, Ortlerstrasse 8, Munich 25
Bi-monthly

Tonband
G. Braun GmbH., Karl-Friedrich-Strasse 14–18, Postfach 129, 75 Karlsruhe 1
Bi-monthly

Tonband Schallplatte (*European Magazine for Hi-Fi Buffs*)
ELA-Verlag, Burgschmiestrasse 42, 85 Nürnberg
Monthly

Vereinszeitung des AGV München
Philisterverband des Akademischen Gesängvereins München e.V., Ledererstrasse 5, 8000 Munich 2

Volksmusiklehrer
Löhrstr. 32, Postfach 94, 7217 Trossingen/Württemberg
Bi-monthly

Volkstanz im Tanzarchiv
Verlag "Das Tanzarchiv," Blumenstrasse 38a, 2 Hamburg 39
Bi-monthly

The World of Music—Le Monde de la Musique—Die Welt der Musik (*Quarterly Journal of the International Music Council* [*UNESCO*] *in association with the International Institute for Comparative Music Studies & Documentation. Each issue in English- French- German*)
Bärenreiter-Verlag, Heinrich-Schütz-Allee 31–37, 3500 Kassel-Wilhelmshöhe
Quarterly

Württembergische Blätter für Kirchenmusik (*Newsletter of the Association of Protestant Church Choruses and Protestant Church Musicians in Württemberg*)
Birkenwaldstrasse 26, 7 Stuttgart-N
Bi-monthly

Zeitschrift für Spielmusik
Verlag Moeck, Postfach 143, 31 Celle
Three times a year

Zeitschrift für Volkskunde (*Official Organ of the Society for Folklore*)
W. Kohlhammer, Urbanstr. 12, 7000 Stuttgart-O.
Irregular

Zu Gottes Lob und Ehre (Report for Trombonists)
Im Druseltal 8, 35 Kassel-Wilhelmshöhe
Quarterly

Zugange
Fono Verlag, Bismarckallee, 78 Freiburg/Breisgau
Quarterly

Die Zupfmusik
Oertel & Spörer, Burgstrasse 1, Postfach 35, 741 Reutlingen
Quarterly

The Business of Music

Very often in a smaller city in a country like Germany, the proprietor of a music store may also do some music publishing on the side. He may deal in instruments as well as sheet music; he will certainly be able to direct you to an instrument repair shop or craftsman, even if he doesn't do that work in his own place. He will also be about your best local source of information on musical activities in his city. In order for you to be able to consult him or even to write in advance of a visit, the following information should prove helpful.

Aachen, Bad

Dealers

Hogrebe, Inh. Paul Hogrebe
Dahmengraben 7. Tel: 3 63 29.
Music, instruments, records, repairs, books.

Jerusalem, Inh. Franz Jerusalem
Komphausbadstrasse 36/38. Tel: 3 24 65.
Music, instruments, repairs, records, manufacturers.

Niessen, Mathias
Annastrasse 11/13. Tel: 3 57 39.
Music, instruments, repairs, manufacturers.

Rödiger, Otto & Sohn
Wilhelmstrasse 17. Tel: 2 03 13.
Music, instruments, repairs, manufacturers.

Wigger, Franz
Beverstrasse 5. Tel: 3 33 61.
Music, instruments, records, repairs, manufacturers.

Augsburg

Dealers

Bauderer, Inh. Hanns u. Hermann Bauderer
Tunnelstrasse 44, Augsburg 8900. Tel: 4 15 32.
Music, instruments, repairs, records.

Böhm, Anton & Sohn, KG
Sortiment Ludwigstrasse 15, Postfach 209. Tel: 2 48 77.
Books, music, records, publishers.

Braun, Hans
Frauentorstrasse 8.
Music, instruments.

Durner, Inh. Frau Sophie Kreppel
Phil.-Welser-Strasse Ecke Kanzleigässchen. Tel: 2 44 48.
Music, instruments, repairs, records, books.

Graf, Inh. Hanns Graf
Hl.-Kreuz-Strasse 18. Tel: 2 54 49.
Music, instruments, repairs.

Probst und Breidenstein
Lange Gasse 20. Tel: 73 67.
Music, instruments, records.

Publishers

Böhm, Anton & Sohn
Sortiment Ludwigstrasse 15, Postfach 209. Tel: 2 48 77.
Agent: Hinrichsen, Britain.

Finale Bühnen und Musikverlag
8900 Augsburg, Schalbeneck 13

Bamberg

Instrument Makers

Neubert J. C. Workshops for historic keyboard instruments
Am Knöcklein 9. Tel: 23683.
Museum since 1968 in Nürnberg.

Bielefeld

Dealers

Robert Bachauf Druckerei, Inh. Ludwig und Emma Bachauf
Friedrichstrasse 48, Postfach 8822. Tel: 7 85 71.
Books, records.

Böhme, Kurt
Altstädter Kirchstrasse 14 (am Ratscafé), Postfach 6008. Tel: 6 15 74.
Books, music, instruments, records, repairs.

Hofmeister, Wilhelm Inh. Gerhard Hofmeister
Obernstrasse 15, Postfach 4140. Tel: 6 15 79.
Music, instruments, records, repairs.

Kayser, Erich OHG, Inh. Erich Simonis und Ingrid Simonis
Waldeckstrasse 6, Postfach 4605. Tel: 6 85 09, 6 78 26.
Instruments, records, music (wholesale).

Niemeyer, Inh. Erna und Dieter Gehner
Niedernstrasse 41. Tel: 6 13 70.
Music, instruments, records, repairs.

Pfeffersche Buchhandlung, Inh. Gustav Werk
Alter Markt 7. Tel: 6 27 27.
Books, music, records.

Tönsmann, Carl Inh. G. Welscher
An der Stiftskirche 14, Bielefeld-Schildesche. Tel: 6 69 86.
Books, music, instruments, records.

Wehling, A. Victor, Buch-und Zeitschriften-Grosshandlung
Alfred-Bori-Strasse 12, Postfach 9040. Tel: 6 16 06, 6 16 07.
Books, music, records wholesale.

Publishers

Hinnenthal, J. P.
Königsbrügg 22.
Agent: Musica Rara, Britain.

Bochum

Dealers

Kühl, Inh. Karl H. Kühl
Kortumstrasse 102–104. Tel: 6 50 60.
Books, music, instruments, records, repairs.

Bottrop

Dealers

Bieling, Johann Inh. Ww. Gertrud Bieling
Horster Strasse 297. Tel: 31 54.
Music, instruments, repairs, manufacturing.

Erlenkämper, Horst
Osterfelder Strasse 25. Tel: 67 57.
Books, music, instruments, records.

Braunschweig (Brunswick)

Dealers

Bartels, Fritz Inh. Gertrud Bartels
Schlosspassage 6. Tel: 2 72 91.
Music, instruments.

Försterling & Poser, Inh. Fritz Försterling
Steinweg 1–3, Postfach 30. Tel: 2 60 41.
Records.

Maul, Inh. Richard Maul
Neue Strasse 3. Tel: 4 05 48.
Music, instruments, records, publishing, repairs.

Musikhaus Krause
Kattreppeln 19–21.
Music, instruments.

Musica, Inh. Dieter Argenton
Schlosspassage. Tel: 4 36 65.
Records.

Mewes, Inh. Otto Mewes.
Kohlmarkt 5, Postfach 698. Tel: 2 54 43.
Music, instruments, records, repairs.

Rautmann.
Schöppenstedter Strasse 42. Tel: 2 77 60.
Music, instruments, repairs, manufacturing.

Publishers

Maul
Neue Strasse 3. Tel: 4 05 48.

Instrument Makers

Grotrian-Steinway
Zim. Strasse 24. Tel: 30933.
Piano manufacturers.

Schimmel
Hamburger Strasse 273. Tel: 333277.
Piano manufacturers.

Bredstedt

Dealers

Günther
Markt 36, Postfach 17. Tel: 22 52.
Books, music, instruments, records.

Bremen

Dealers

Georg Bartels
Hinter dem Schütting. Tel: 32 59 89.
Books, music.

Bivour, Arnold
Ostendeich 130. Tel: 44 19 87.
Instruments (wholesale).

"Hanseat," Ed. Rostal
Waller Heerstrasse 44. Tel: 38 38 93.
Books, music, instruments, records, repairs.

Praeger & Meier, Inh. Werner Lutz
Böttcherstrasse 7. Tel: 32 51 73, 32 51 93.
Music, concert management.

Räke, Walter
Sielwall 7. Tel: 32 51 94.
Books, music, instruments, records, repairs.

Warnke, Friedrich
Hutfilterstrasse 9–13. Tel: 31 09 81.
Books, manufacturing, music, instruments, records, repairs.

Werner, Albert
Hillmann-Passage. Tel: 30 20 57, 38 06 84.
Music, instruments, records, repairs.

Bremerhaven

Dealers

Eidner, Carl Inh. Hans u. Wilhelm Eidner
Hafenstrasse 167–169. Tel: 4 28 16.
Music, instruments, records, repairs.

Junghanns, Inh. Paulus Meidenbauer
Potsdamer Strasse 15. Tel: 4 23 63.
Books, music, instruments, repairs, records.

Morisse, Fr. Inh. Hans Eschemann und Hermann Jelten
Bürgermeister-Smidt-Strasse 57a, Postfach 2045. Tel: 4 36 54.
Books, music.

Sadowsky
Georgstrasse 61. Tel: 2 26 50.
Music, instruments.

Detmold

Dealers

Musikhaus Harke
Allee 14.

Dortmund

Dealers

Althoff, Willi
Schlossstrasse 49. Tel: 1 32 32.
Music, instruments, publishing.

Buchhandlung des Ev. Mädchenwerkes
Haus Husen. Tel: 4 97 47.
Books, music.

Grosch, Inh. Fritz Bischoff
Kuckelke 10. Tel: 57 19 29.
Music, instruments, repairs.

Hellweg
Lütgendortmunder Hellweg 12, Postfach 101. Tel: 6 25 62.
Music, instruments, records (wholesale).

Jellinghaus
Wissstrasse 22. Tel: 52 57 71.
Music, instruments, repairs, records.

Köhler, Hugo
Limbecker Strasse 22, Postfach 42. Tel: 6 21 17.
Books, music, instruments, records.

Merkur, Inh. Bruno Steger
Münsterstrasse 57. Tel: 8 23 23.
Music, instruments.

"Mozart," Inh. Egmont Bach
Königswall 18. Tel: 3 57 38.
Music, instruments, records, repairs.

"Die Schallplatte" Kurt Nopens KG
Kampstrasse 30, Postfach 133. Tel: 3 48 50.
Records.

Schlüter, Irmgard
Westfalenhaus-Hansastrasse. Tel: 3 33 66.
Music, instruments, records, repairs.

Voss-Musikinstrumente, GmbH, Inh. Eckart Müller-Voss
Moltkestrasse 19. Tel: 52 72 88/89.
Instruments (wholesale).

Wildt's Musikverlag
Chemnitzer Strasse 10, Postfach 283. Tel: 52 53 11.
Music, publishing.

Publishers

Althoff, Willi
Schlossstrasse 49. Tel: 1 32 32.

Wildt's Musikverlag
Chenmitzer Strasse 10, Postfach 283. Tel: 52 53 11.

Duisburg

Dealers

Leigraf, Hugo
Wanheimer Strasse 119. Tel: 2 00 13.
Books, music.

Michael & Co.
Sittardsberger Allee 95/99, Postfach 520. Tel: 77 16 34/35, 77 19 11.
Affiliates: Koblenz, Rheinstrasse 30, München 19, Nibelungenstrasse 32.
Records (wholesale).

Pielka, Ruth
Mercatorstrasse 4. Tel: 2 35 16.
Music, instruments, records, books.

Scheuermann, Hermann Inh. Karl Schubert
Düsseldorfer Strasse 100. Tel: 2 03 59.
Books, music, records.

Essen

Dealers

Dietsch, A., Inh. Dietsch-Erben
Hachestrasse 19. Tel: 3 16 84.
Books, music, instruments, repairs, records.

Karstadt AG
Limbecker Platz, Postfach 72. Tel: 2 17 11.
Books, music, records.

Petri, Wilhelm, Inh. H. u. K. Wetzig
Altenessen, Altenessener Strasse 323, Postfach 223. Tel: 29 08 17.
Books, music, records.

Podehl, Gustav
Frintroper Strasse 131. Tel: 6 27 30.
Music, instruments.

Schmachtenberg, Egon
Huyssenallee 3, Postfach 1542. Tel: 3 86 33.
Affiliates: Alfredstrasse 1, Roacherstrasse 18.
Music, instruments, repairs.

Schmemann, O.
Limbecker Strasse 1. Tel: 3 26 16.
Affiliates: Alfredstrasse 1, Raadterstrasse 18.
Books, music.

Webels, Willi
Bochumer Strasse 55, Postfach 101. Tel: 5 03 73.
Books, music, publishing, records.

Publishing

Webels, Willi
Bochumer Strasse 55, Postfach 101. Tel: 5 03 73.

Gelsenkirchen

Dealers

Glüsel
Gildenstrasse 12. Tel: 2 42 76.
Music, instruments, records, repairs, manufacturing.

Hermuth, Heinrich
Hauptstrasse 5. Tel: 2 42 53.
Music, instruments, repairs, records, manufacturing.

Kohl, K., & Co., Inh. Ursula Tesch
Weberstrasse 19. Tel: 2 17 07.
Affiliates: Bad Wildungen, Brunenallee 20a.
Books, music, instruments, records, repairs.

Rating
Husemannstrasse 5, Postfach 1667. Tel: 2 39 27.
Affiliates: Marl-Hüls, Lipperweg 32.
Music, instruments, records, repairs, books.

Wittenberg, Karl
Marienstrasse 14. Tel: 3 21 26.
Books, music, instruments.

Hagen/Westf.

Dealers

Köhler, Fritz
Neumarktstrasse 22. Tel: 2 82 82.
Books, music, instruments, repairs, records.

Köhler
Kölner Strasse 28. Tel: 4 11 60.
Music, instruments, records.

Köhler, Haus der Musik, Inh. Richard
Konkordiastrasse 1. Tel: 2 71 64.
Music, instruments, repairs.

Schade, Otto KG
Kampstrasse 2. Tel: 2 88 30.
Music, instruments, repairs.

Hanau/Main

Dealers

Bayer, Gabriele Th.
Langstrasse 47. Tel: 2 31 94.
Music, instruments, repairs, records.

Klenk, KG
Rosentrasse 6. Tel: 2 29 72.
Books, music, instruments, repairs, records.

Heidelberg

Dealers

Hochstein
Hauptstrasse 86, Postfach 720. Tel: 2 01 68.
Music, instruments, repairs, records.

Neuenheimer Musikhaus Reiher & Kurth
Brückenstrasse 51. Tel: 2 24 11.
Books, music, instruments, repairs, records.

Pfeiffer, Eugen
Hauptstrasse 92. Tel: 2 24 32.
Books, music, instruments, repairs, records.

Zimmermann, Arthur
Bahnhofstrasse 15. Tel: 2 34 90.
Music, instruments, repairs.

Publishers

Hochstein & Co.
Friedrich-Ebert-Anlage 28, Postfach 1260. Tel: 2 23 35.

Willy Müller; Süddeutscher Musikverlag.
Mäzgasse 5.

Karlsruhe

Dealers

Bauer, Georg
Luisenstrasse 47/49. Tel: 6 42 04.
Music, publishing.

Halter, Wilhelm
Sophienstr. 246 (corner Nultsstr.). Tel: 5 33 34.
Music, publishing.

Müller, Erich
Durlach, Pfinztalstrasse 87, Postfach 44. Tel: 4 23 92.
Music, instruments, records, books.

Schlaile GmbH
Odeon-Haus, Kaiserstrasse 175, Postfach 1606. Tel: 2 78 11.
Music, instruments, records, repairs.

Publishers

Bauer, Georg
Luisenstrasse 47/49. Tel: 6 42 04.

Halter, Wilhelm
Sophienstr. 246 (corner Nultsstr.). Tel: 5 33 34.

Instrument Dealers and Makers

Bechstein Pianofortefabrik
Wachhausstrasse 6. Tel: 43421.

Deimer, Karl
Adlerstr. 18a. Tel: 66730.
Wind and percussion instruments.

Diehr, Werner
Elbingerstr. 4a. Tel: 64676.

Dörrwächter, Hans
Sophienstr. 180. Tel: 592560.

Engstle, Frz.
Imbertstr. 32. Tel: 42997.
Organ builder.

Hager, Rolf
Waldstrasse 95. Tel: 21030.

Maurer, Pianohaus
Douglasstrasse 15. Tel: 2 70 02.

Merzdorf, Eckehart
7531 Wilferdingen bei Pforzheim.
Bahnhofstrasse 6. Tel: (0 72 32) 95 33.
Keyboard instruments.

Padewet, Musikhaus J.
Kaiserstrasse 132. Tel: 2 37.33.
Music, instruments (specializes in violins).

Schlaile, GmbH
Kaiserstr. 175. Tel: 27811.

Thibaut, Musik
Waldstr. 93. Tel: 24712.

Wahl, Gerhard
Mathystrasse 40. Tel: 2 30 11.
Violins, recorders, guitars.

Kiel

Dealers

Bernhard
Iltisstrasse 37. Tel: 7 36 67.
Music, instruments, repairs.

Kihr-Goebel, GmbH
Holstenstrasse 24, Postfach 607. Tel: 4 72 62.
Affiliates: Schönberg/Holstein, Knüll 1 u. Rendsburg, Stegen.
Instruments, records.

Mühlau, Walter G., Inh. Dr. Waltraud Hunke
Holtenauer Strasse 116. Tel: 4 75 28/29.
Books, music, publishing.

"Musiksalon Sphinx"
Hermann Alt, Flämische Strasse 9. Tel: 4 34 88.
Music, instruments, records, repairs.

Streiber, Musikhaus Robert
Holstenstrasse 88/90 Howehaus. Tel: 4 14 16.
Music, instruments, records.

Publishers

Mühlau, Walter G.
Holtenauer Strasse 116. Tel: 4 75 28/29.

Krefeld

Dealers

Greven, J.
Hochstrasse 52. Tel: 2 32 85.
Books, music.

Jösch, Hans
Hochstrasse 118. Tel: 2 49 38.
Records, publishing, manufacturing (wholesale).

Kreyer, Ernst Paul
Hansa-Ecke Neusser Strasse, Postfach 3101. Tel: 3 44 59.
Music, instruments.

Kreyer, Otto, Inh. Geschw. A. u. H. Fischer
Neusser Strasse 53. Tel: 3 40 16.
Music, instruments, repairs, manufacturing.

Scherzer, Helmut
Friedrichstrasse 38. Tel: 2 89 07.
Music, instruments, repairs, manufacturing.

Publishing

Jösch, Hans
Hochstrasse 118. Tel: 2 49 38.

Lübeck

Dealers

Lehmensiek, Adolf L.
Königstrasse 65–67, Postfach 1801. Tel: 7 13 05–09.
Affiliates in: Lübeck-Kücknitz, Lübeck-Travemünde u. Timmendorfer Strand.
Records.

Meyer & Eggert, Inh. Walter Porsche
Aegidienstrasse 43. Tel: 7 33 03.
Books, music, instruments, records, repairs.

Ernst Robert, Inh. Erwin Lüddecke
Breite Strasse 29, Postfach 1885. Tel: 7 60 86.
Music, instruments, records, repairs.

Instrument Makers

Hellwig, Günther
Burgtor, Lübeck
Violin maker.

Kemper, E.
Kaninchenborn 7, Lübeck
Organ builder.

Ludwigshafen/Rhein

Dealers

Blatz, Inh. Georg Schmuck
Prinzregentenstrasse 44. Tel: 6 27 79.
Books, music, instruments, records, repairs.

Dr. Jaegersche Buchhandlung, Inh. Heinrich Hornung
Bismarckstrasse 112. Tel: 6 26 87.
Books, music, records.

Knoll, Otto
Bismarckstrasse 76. Tel: 6 34 53.
Music, instruments, records, repairs.

Mainz

Dealers

Gebr. Alexander GmbH
Bahnhofstrasse 9. Tel: 2 44 70.
Music, instruments, records, repairs, manufacturing (wholesale).

Sachs, Hans
Schillerstrasse 16. Tel: 2 23 91.
Music, instruments.

B. Schott & Sons, Musikverlag
Weihergarten 1–11. Tel: 24341, 20672.

Instrument Makers

Alexander Gebr. Rhein Musikinstrumentenfbr. GmbH
Bahnhofstrasse 9. Tel: 24470.

Publishers

Matthias-Grünewald-Verlag KG
Bischofsplatz 6, Postfach 847. Tel: 2 63 41.

Mannheim

Dealers

Musik-Blatz GmbH
S2,8. Tel: 6 27 79.
Books, music, instruments, repairs, records.

Dell & Stoffel OHG
G 6,15, Postfach 528. Tel: 2 28 88.
Manufacturing, records.

Ehret OHG
R 1, 7. Tel: 2 50 62.
Books, music, instruments, repairs, records.

Heckel, K. Ferdinand
O 3,9, Postfach 1020. Tel: 2 12 16.
Music, instruments, repairs, records.

Planken
P 5,8 (Fressgasse). Tel: 2 25 59.
Books, music, instruments, records.

Publishers

Badenia-Produktion
6800 Mannheim, Reinkaistrasse 14.

Mannheimer Musikverlag GmbH
6800 Mannheim, Postfach 1504.

Marburg an Der Lahn

Instrument Dealers

G. Meyer
Cölber Strasse, 3551 Wehrda (near Marburg an der Lahn).

Mönchengladbach

Dealers

Hogrebe's Musikhaus, Inh. Kurt u. Maria Géronne
Bismarckstrasse 22, Postfach 410. Tel: 2 29 68.
Music, instruments, records, repairs.

Mülheim/Ruhr

Dealers

Bohnes, H. W.
Bruchstrasse 31. Tel: 4 13 73.
Music, instruments, publishing.

Engels, Carl
Bülowstrasse 44, Postfach 529. Tel: 5 25 92.
Music, publishing.

Haubrich, Heinz
Monningstrasse 53. Tel: 5 26 96.
Music, publishing.

Matthay
Velauerstrasse 9. Tel: 47 90 63.
Records, instruments.

Riemann, Inh. Bernh. Mengede
Wallstrasse 22, Postfach 64. Tel: 4 57 65.
Music, instruments, repairs, records.

Gebr. Wellershaus OHG
Friedrichstrasse 1. Tel: 4 59 32.
Music, instruments, records, repairs, manufacturing.

Publishers

Bohnes, H. W.
Bruchstrasse 13. Tel: 4 13 73.

Engels, Carl
Bülowstrasse 44, Postfach 529. Tel: 5 25 92.

Haubrich, Heinz
Monningstrasse 53. Tel: 5 26 96.

Münster im Westfalen

Dealers

Kissel, Hans
Rothenburg 31, Postfach 708. Tel: 4 30 78.
Music, instruments, records.

Lyra-Musikhaus "Am Kiepenkerl," Inh. Hedwig Viegener
Am Spiekerhof 2, Postfach 892. Tel: 4 30 77.
Music, instruments, records, repairs, publishing.

Marcus, M.
Alter Fischmarkt 22. Tel: 4 33 00.
Music, instruments.

Schneider, Alfred
Königstrasse 12/14. Tel: 4 31 01.
Music, instruments, repairs.

Publishers

Lyra-Musikhaus "Am Kiepenkerl"
Am Spiekerhof 2, Postfach 892. Tel: 4 30 77.

Oberhausen/Rhld.

Dealers

Kayser, Eugen
Bergstrasse 28. Tel: 6 17 27.
Music, instruments, records.

Möller, W.
Ramgestrasse 7, Postfach 69. Tel: 6 02 07.
Music, instruments, records, repairs.

Opitz & Sohn
Helmholtzstrasse 60. Tel: 2 12 93.
Music, instruments, records, repairs.

Offenbach/Main

Dealers

André, Johann, OHG
Frankfurter Strasse 28, Postfach 141. Tel: 8 35 39.
Music, instruments, records.

Osnabrück

Dealers

Musikhaus Hermann, Bössmann
Neuer Graben 22. Tel: 2 19 38.
Books, music, instruments, repairs.

Musikhaus Rohlfink
Grosse Shasse 24.

Rawie, H.
Grosse Strasse 89. Tel: 2 12 68.
Music, instruments, records, repairs, manufacturing.

Passau

Instrument Makers

Sperrhake
Klavierbaumstrasse Stein W 14. Tel: 33406.
Harpsichord makers.

Recklinghausen

Dealers

Iris GmbH, Inh. August Mallmann
Herner Strasse 64 u. 64a. Tel: 2 21 90.
Music, publishing (wholesale).

Haus der Musik, August Mallmann
Herner Strasse 5, Postfach 740. Tel: 2 21 90.
Music.

Wiesmann, Musikhaus, Inh. Herbert Gade
Schaumburgstrasse 15–17, Postfach 1647. Tel: 2 32 94.
Books, music, instruments, repairs.

Publishers

Iris GmbH
Herner Strasse 64 u. 64a. Tel: 2 21 90.

Regensburg

Dealers

Boesseneckers, J. G., Musikalienhandlung Franz Feuchtinger
Haidplatz 1. Tel: 2 32 92.
Music, instruments, records, publishing (wholesale).

Feuchtinger & Gleichauf, Inh. Oskar Borck
Schwarze Bärenstrasse 5, Postfach 220. Tel: 2 34 70.
Affiliate: Regensburg 16 64.
Music, instrument, records, publishing.

Musik-Weidlich
Wahlenstr. 24.
Music, instruments.

Musikhaus Reisser
Haidplatz 7.
Music, instruments.

Pianohaus Lang
Neuhausstr. 4.
Music, instruments.

Winkelhöfer-Musik
Wahlenstr. 5.
Music.

Instrument Maker

Laudi
Haidplatz 7.
Violin maker

Publishers

Boesseneckers, J. G., Musikalienhandlung Franz Feuchtinger
Haidplatz 1. Tel: 2 32 92.

Feuchtinger & Gleichauf
Schwarze Bärenstrasse 5, Postfach 220. Tel: 2 34 70.

Regensburg

Publishers

Gustav-Bosse-Verlag
Von der Tann-Str. 38. Tel: 55455.

Remscheid

Dealers

Pelzer, Kurt
Remscheid-Rath, Nr. 6. Tel: 4 62 81.
Music, instruments.

Schmitz, R.
Wetterauer Strasse 6, Postfach 38. Tel: 6 12 55.
Books, music.

Saarbrücken

Dealers

Carl, Robert
Rentrischer Strasse 3. Tel: 6 62 00.
Music, publishing.

Franz Hörlh, Inh. Günther Merckens
Futterstrasse 6. Tel: 2 69 29.
Music, instruments, repairs.

Publishers

Carl, Robert
Rentrischer Strasse 3. Tel: 6 62 00.

Solingen

Dealers

Palenschat, Hans, KG
Am Neumarkt 25. Tel: 2 19 69.
Music, instruments, records, repairs.

Suppan, Franz
Casinostrasse 3. Tel: 2 43 83.
Music, instruments, repairs, publishing, records.

Wolf, Fritz, OHG
Keldersstrasse 5, Postfach 426. Tel: 1 51 01.
Books, music, instruments, records.

Publishers

Suppan, Franz
Casinostrasse 3. Tel: 2 43 83.

Tübingen

Dealers

Musikhaus Kreul
Pfleghofstrasse 74.

Wilhelmshaven

Dealers

Freese
Marktstrasse 68. Tel: 2 10 23.
Records.

Heinrichshofen's Verlag
Liebigstrasse 4, Postfach 620. Tel: 2 65 55.
Music, publishing.

Tiemann
Marktstrasse 52, Postfach 1249. Tel: 2 51 46–1 47.
Affiliates: Posener Strasse 66, Oldenburg i. O., Achternstrasse 9.
Records.

Publishers

Heinrichshofen's Verlag
Liebigstrasse 4, Postfach 620. Tel: 2 65 55.

Wuppertal

Dealers

Becker, Edith, Inh. Edith Landsiedel
Höhne-Ecke Concordienstrasse. Tel: 59 21 57.
Music, instruments, records, repairs.

Bongardt, Günter
Gewerbeschulstrasse 117a. Tel: 55 26 22.
Books, music, instruments, repairs, records.

Ibach GmbH
Robertstrasse 3. Tel: 44 38 42/43.
Affiliate: Barmen, Lindenstrasse 1.
Instruments, records, repairs.

Jugenddienst Verlag e V.
Erichstrasse 4, Postfach 217. Tel: 55 77 12.
Books, records.

Kothen, Karl von
Schuchardstrasse 3. Tel: 5 39 18/19.
Affiliates: Elberfeld, Schwanenstrasse 21; Oberhausen, Langemarckstrasse; (Europahaus), Duisburg, Münzstrasse.
Instruments, records.

Kremer, Hans
Karlstr. 10, 56 Wuppertal 1. Tel: 44 09 60.
Books, music, instruments, records, repairs.

Mewes, Ferdinand
Schlossbleiche 32. Tel: 44 60 63.
Music, instruments, records, publishing.

Poyda, Walter
Kleiner Werth 1. Tel: 59 21 90.
Music, instruments, repairs.

Schwiebert Rundfunk Kom.-Ges.
Werth 67–69. Tel: 55 09 33.
Affiliates: -Elberfeld, Schwanenstrasse 27.
Records.

Instrument Maker

Mitsching, L. & Co.
Zollstr. 1, 56 Wuppertal 1.

Publishers

Mewes, Ferdinand
Schlossbleiche 32. Tel: 44 60 63.

Index